THE EUROPEAN UNION SERIES

General Editors: Neill Nugent, William E. Paterson

The European Union series provides an authoritative library on the European Union, ranging from general introductory texts to definitive assessments of key institutions and actors, issues, policies and policy processes, and the role of member states.

Books in the series are written by leading scholars in their fields and reflect the most up-to-date research and debate. Particular attention is paid to accessibility and clear presentation for a wide audience of students, practitioners and interested general readers.

The series editors are Neill Nugent, Professor of Politics and Jean Monnet Professor of European Integration, Manchester Metropolitan University, and William E. Paterson, Honourary Professor in German and European Studies, University of Aston. Their co-editor until his death in July 1999, Vincent Wright, was a Fellow of Nuffield College, Oxford University.

Feedback on the series and book proposals are always welcome and should be sent to Steven Kennedy, Palgrave Macmillan, Houndmills, Basingstoke, Hampshire RG21 6XS, UK, or by e-mail to s.kennedy@palgrave.com

---

General textbooks

Published

Desmond Dinan **Encyclopedia of the European Union**
[Rights: Europe only]
Desmond Dinan **Europe Recast: A History of European Union**
[Rights: Europe only]
Desmond Dinan **Ever Closer Union: An Introduction to European Integration** (3rd edn)
[Rights: Europe only]
Mette Eilstrup Sangiovanni (ed.) **Debates on European Integration: A Reader**
Simon Hix **The Political System of the European Union** (2nd edn)
Paul Magnette **What is the European Union? Nature and Prospects**
John McCormick **Understanding the European Union: A Concise Introduction** (4th edn)
Brent F. Nelsen and Alexander Stubb **The European Union: Readings on the Theory and Practice of European Integration** (3rd edn)
[Rights: Europe only]

Neill Nugent (ed.) **European Union Enlargement**
Neill Nugent **The Government and Politics of the European Union** (6th edn)
[Rights: World excluding USA and dependencies and Canada]
John Peterson and Elizabeth Bomberg **Decision-Making in the European Union**
Ben Rosamond **Theories of European Integration**

Forthcoming

Laurie Buonanno and Neill Nugent **Policies and Policy Processes of the European Union**
David Howarth **The Political Economy of European Integration**
Dirk Leuffen, Berthold Rittberger and Frank Schimmelfennig **Differentiated Integration**
Sabine Saurugger **Theoretical Approaches to European Integration**
Esther Versluis, Mendeltje van Keulen and Paul Stephenson **Analysing the European Union Policy Process**

D0268446

The major institutions and actors

Published

Renaud Dehousse **The European Court of Justice**
Justin Greenwood **Interest Representation in the European Union** (2nd edn)
Fiona Hayes-Renshaw and Helen Wallace **The Council of Ministers** (2nd edn)
Simon Hix and Christopher Lord **Political Parties in the European Union**
David Judge and David Earnshaw **The European Parliament** (2nd edn)
Neill Nugent **The European Commission**
Anne Stevens with Handley Stevens **Brussels Bureaucrats? The Administration of the European Union**

Forthcoming

Wolfgang Wessels **The European Council**

The main areas of policy

Published

Michelle Chang **Monetary Integration in the European Union**
Michelle Cini and Lee McGowan **Competition Policy in the European Union** (2nd edn)
Wyn Grant **The Common Agricultural Policy**
Martin Holland **The European Union and the Third World**
Jolyon Howorth **Security and Defence Policy in the European Union**
Stephan Keukeleire and Jennifer MacNaughtan **The Foreign Policy of the European Union**
Brigid Laffan **The Finances of the European Union**
Malcolm Levitt and Christopher Lord **The Political Economy of Monetary Union**
Janne Haaland Matláry **Energy Policy in the European Union**
John McCormick **Environmental Policy in the European Union**
John Peterson and Margaret Sharp **Technology Policy in the European Union**
Handley Stevens **Transport Policy in the European Union**

Forthcoming

Karen Anderson **Social Policy in the European Union**
Hans Bruyninckx and Tom Delreux **Environmental Policy and Politics in the European Union**
Johanna Kantola **Gender and the European Union**

Bart Kerremans, David Allen and Geoffrey Edwards **The External Economic Relations of the European Union**
Jörg Monar **Justice and Home Affairs in the European Union**
John Vogler, Richard Whitman and Charlotte Bretherton **The External Policies of the European Union**

Also planned

Political Union
Social Policy in the European Union

The member states and the Union

Published

Carlos Closa and Paul Heywood **Spain and the European Union**
Alain Guyomarch, Howard Machin and Ella Ritchie **France in the European Union**
Brigid Laffan and Jane O'Mahoney **Ireland and the European Union**

Forthcoming

Federiga Bindi **Italy and the European Union**
Simon Bulmer and William E. Paterson **Germany and the European Union**
Phil Daniels and Ella Ritchie **Britain and the European Union**
Brigid Laffan **The European Union and its Member States**
Baldur Thórhallsson **Small States in the European Union**

Issues

Published

Derek Beach **The Dynamics of European Integration: Why and When EU Institutions Matter**
Thomas Christiansen and Christine Reh **Constitutionalizing the European Union**
Robert Ladrech **Europeanization and National Politics**
Steven McGuire and Michael Smith **The European Union and the United States**

Forthcoming

Christine Boswell and Andrew Geddes **Migration and Mobility in the European Union**
Cécile Leconte **Understanding Euroscepticism**
Wyn Rees **EU/US Security Relations**

Europeanization and National Politics

Robert Ladrech

palgrave
macmillan

First published 2010 by
PALGRAVE MACMILLAN

Palgrave Macmillan in the UK is an imprint of Macmillan Publishers Limited, registered in England, company number 785998, of Houndmills, Basingstoke, Hampshire RG21 6XS.

Palgrave Macmillan in the US is a division of St Martin's Press LLC, 175 Fifth Avenue, New York, NY 10010.

Palgrave Macmillan is the global academic imprint of the above companies and has companies and representatives throughout the world.

Palgrave® and Macmillan® are registered trademarks in the United States, the United Kingdom, Europe and other countries

ISBN 978–1–4039–1874–1 hardback
ISBN 978–1–4039–1875–8 paperback

This book is printed on paper suitable for recycling and made from fully managed and sustained forest sources. Logging, pulping and manufacturing processes are expected to conform to the environmental regulations of the country of origin.

A catalogue record for this book is available from the British Library.

A catalog record for this book is available from the Library of Congress.

10   9   8   7   6   5   4   3   2   1
19   18   17   16   15   14   13   12   11   10

Printed and bound in China

For Charlie and Olwen

Contents

Acknowledgements

This book has had a long gestation period. The Europeanization concept to which I contributed in 1994 slowly developed over the rest of the 1990s and become a fixture of EU studies in the early years of the new century. I began to teach a class on Europeanization and EU member states at the College of Europe around 2003; this was an excellent exercise in 'packaging' the concept and supplying examples appropriate for MA students. So, my thanks for their continuing interest in the subject over the years and allowing me to 'road-test' a comprehensive approach. My involvement in a research project on Europeanization and political parties from 2003 to 2006 also allowed me to 'test' the concept in the field, so to speak. I thank all my colleagues who were involved in this endeavour. There are numerous colleagues who, over the years, have refined different aspects of 'europeanization' and I hope I have cited them accordingly. I want to particularly thank Steven Kennedy from Palgrave Macmillan for his dogged support over the years, and also to Professor Willie Paterson for his support.

ROBERT LADRECH

Introduction

Since the beginning of the European integration process in the 1950s, scholars have debated the causes and future development of such institutional innovations as the relative autonomy of the European Commission, the development of the European Parliament, and the evolution of EU law through the actions of the European Court of Justice (ECJ). Certain key events or milestones contributed to the focus on European-level developments, from the 1966 'empty chair' political crisis, to the re-launch of the integration process in 1986 with the Single European Act (SEA), to the dramatic halt to institutional 'deepening' as a result of the French and Dutch referendums on the EU Constitutional Treaty in 2005. Throughout most of this period, scholarly, professional and even public attention, whatever the motivation, sought to explain as well as react to the emergence of this unprecedented level of *supranational* governance. However, from the mid-1990s, attention slowly began to focus on an as yet unexplored dimension of European integration, namely the member states themselves. Political events such as the Danish 'no' and French '*petit oui*' results of the Maastricht Treaty referendum in 1992 suggested that domestic public opinion could become a 'wild card' in what had been essentially an elite process of European integration. The Single European Act (SEA) and the Maastricht Treaty (TEU) put into motion steps leading to the launch of the euro by the end of the 1990s and ushered in significant institutional and policy changes increasing the stature and profile of the EU. The more recent perspective, however, is based on an appreciation of how the EU's enhanced influence in policy-making has impacted the *domestic* politics and institutions of the member states. In other words, the consequences of continual empowerment of the EU have begun to be visible within domestic political systems, illustrated by changes to institutions, policies and politics. This process of domestic adaptation to the impact of the EU within member states has been labelled Europeanization.

The purpose of this book is to provide a theoretically informed account of the Europeanization of member states, exploring this process of change in three dimensions: polity (i.e. institutions), politics and policies. The idea that external factors may be the source of domestic change is not new, as the number of studies published under the rubric of globalization since the 1980s demonstrates. The European integration process itself, some claim, may be understood as a regional response to global changes since the end of the Second World War in the military balance of power, the liberalization of the global capitalist economy, or both. What distinguishes the argument concerning Europeanization of national political systems from the globalization thesis is the ability to trace specific domestic changes to developments emanating from the policy-making output and/or decision-making style of the European Union. The issue in this book is therefore not whether there is in fact a link between globalization (or Americanization) and Europeanization, because it is understood that policy developments may have domestic or international origins; the issue rather is how, once the EU policy-making process has produced an output – whether in the form of a directive, regulation, or more far-reaching initiative – this legislation, and more importantly its continuous transposition into member states, engenders some form of adaptational change. Europeanization is then understood as the change within a member state whose motivating logic is tied to a EU policy or decision-making process. The prime concern of any Europeanization research agenda is therefore establishing the causal link, thereby validating the impact of the EU on domestic change.

Europeanization of member states: what significance?

There are a number of reasons why Europeanization and domestic change is an important area for study as well as being a matter of normative concern. First, while the focus of integration studies has traditionally been oriented to the development of supranational structures and their policy competence, what one might term a 'bottom-up' view involving member states' motivations and actions, the medium- to long-term effect of integration upon member states reveals another dimension of the integration process, that is, the connection between supranational and national dynamics of change. Second, by 'un-packing' a member state into the three dimensions of polity, policy and politics, one may acquire a more insightful understanding of issues related to policy compliance and the success or failure of an intended EU policy. This is because the integration process itself may have contributed to the reshaping of various administrative organs of a member state, with potential consequences for policy implementation, a strategic consideration for policy makers as well as policy analysts. Third, as we shall discuss below, the impact of the EU on its member states, a 'top-down' perspective characterizing the direction of causality, is also intimately bound up with the 'bottom-up' dynamic of member state actions and strategies in EU decision- and policy-making. This leads to the conclusion that in order to understand the means and motives of particular actors in the European integration process itself, having a more in-depth account of this reflexive or interactive relationship between the EU policy and its member states is crucial. Fourth, understanding how domestic change may be brought about as a consequence of EU policy output develops a further insight into the evolution of the European nation-state, explains the variation in response to EU influence, and, as a sub-set of this perspective, how post-communist state development is influenced by the EU. Lastly, normative concerns are raised by the Europeanization phenomenon, namely in the area of democratic accountability as well as the uncertainty of continuing elite control of the integration process due to political mobilization around EU issues or the EU itself.

This book investigates the impact of these concerns as it presents evidence of Europeanization in the three dimensions presented above: polity, policy and politics. In the institutional dimension, national executives, national parliaments, national courts and centre–regional relations are investigated and evidence of change traceable to a EU source is discussed. The effectiveness of member state 'uploading' of national preferences in EU policy-making is highlighted in discussion of changes in national executive ministerial coordination; issues of democratic accountability are raised in changes to executive–legislative relations; the role of courts as both national and supranational agents is evaluated in discussing the impact of EU law; and the alleged strengthening or weakening of sub-national actors because of EU Regional Policy is explored. In the policy dimension, different types of EU policy development and output may lead to member state changes, from EU-directed changes in environmental policy that may result in the creation of new domestic instruments to meet new standards, to policy change in which the member states themselves take the lead, and where the EU is purposely employed as a means for disseminating new practices, policy ideas, and so on. A specific focus on how national foreign policy may evolve under the auspices of the Common Foreign and Security Policy (CFSP) demonstrates that even this most inter-governmental and 'sovereignty-charged' area of national state behaviour may respond to a new framework for policy development and action. Finally, in the realm of political change, a discussion of political parties investigates the extent to which the EU may be responsible for changes in programme, organization, patterns of party competition, etc. The degree to which the assumptions under-lying party government have been altered raises issues of account-ability and effective representation. Debates regarding the impact of the EU on de-politicization are also inherent in this discussion. Attention to the role of interest groups and social movements completes the consideration of the politics dimension, and the issue of where effective interest mobilization should be targeted – EU or national arenas – is highlighted, not simply in terms of resource capability but the appropriate site for reacting as well as influencing the connection between national and EU policy concerns. The ques-tion of access to sites of EU decision-making links all domestic actors with regard to the distance between governance and the governed.

Why Europeanization rather than globalization?

The reaction of Western European countries to the major shifts in the wider global environment since the Second World War has been to devise collective responses, manifesting themselves in the creation of supranational institutions with increasing policy scope and influ-ence. This has not been a uniform response, and indeed the dates by which countries have joined the European Community/Union suggest that exogenous pressures are mediated by national circum-stances and structures (as well as by national political perceptions). Two examples that illustrate this national response to international circumstances would be, during their respective periods, the deci-sion by the UK and Sweden to join the EC/EU. For the UK, the deci-sion to join the EC in the 1960s can be attributed, in part, to the international situation with which the UK economy found itself after the decision to stay outside the founding of the EC in 1957 and instead depend on its ties with the Commonwealth. The worsening British economic situation caused political decision-makers to rethink their initial position regarding membership, now weighing the costs of membership in light of the apparent success of early integration projects (Geddes, 2004). Similarly, the Swedish economy did not begin to absorb the shocks of the 1970s until well into the 1980s, and by the end of that decade the relationship between the social democratic government and the trade union confederation, a cornerstone of Swedish economic growth and stability, had begun to fray. Again, the apparent success of the EU, with the additional launch of a plan for monetary union by the end of the 1990s, persuaded centre-left as well as centre-right political party elites of the attractiveness of EU membership (or perhaps more accurately, of the risk of staying outside and dealing with international pressures alone) (Aylott, 1999). In both of these examples, political elites judged their countries' position relative to international trends and the benefits (and costs) of collective or coordinated measures. Thus European integration has been a process developed by national political leaders to *manage* the effects of international inputs/pressures on their domestic economies.

Are there consequences for the member states of the EU deriving from the integration process, and if so, to what extent do they reshape politics, broadly defined? That is, having contributed to the building of a supranational organization without historical precedent, in which national sovereignty is pooled and unique features such as a single currency have been implemented, are there consequences for the manner in which domestic politics operates? The short answer is: yes. In what ways do these consequences reshape domestic politics, for example to what extent does the adjustment of member states' governmental institutions to the EU decision and policy-making regime create subtle yet real constitutional issues? Does the Single Market do more than create a borderless continental-size free market, or does it also engender adjustments by governments, business and interest groups that reshape national systems of interest intermediation, such that new sets of 'winners' and 'losers' emerge? Do citizens of member states simply and passively 'add-on' a European citizenship or identity and accept the profound changes brought about by their political leaders, or is European integration becoming less of an 'elite-driven' process? Finally, is there a cumulative effect of Europeanization changes on national political systems? That is, as the bulk of the changes and developments documented in this book demonstrate, change occurs at an incremental pace, and most often in realms that do not capture the attention of the popular media. Yet it may very well be that over time a form of 'de-politicization' may be taking root, where the transfer of policy competences to 'experts' at the EU level may have an impact on domestic patterns of political participation and mobilization (Mair, 2007). These questions, related to the consequences of 'building Europe', suggest that EU institutions and processes influence national politics, policy and decision-making behaviour so that the concept of Europeanization potentially offers a more accurate sense of, and explanation for, aspects of domestic change than globalization. At the very least, attention to Europeanization opens up the 'black box' of national political systems to a further level of analysis and understanding.

There is no denying the fact that the term Europeanization has become a permanent feature of the European Union studies landscape. Developing since the late 1990s into a body of scholarly research on the effect of the EU on its member states, under the label of Europeanization, studies on the interrelationship of the EU and domestic politics have generated contributions from international relations, comparative politics, policy studies, discourse analysis, and more. Graziano and Vink (2008), in the opening of their book surveying the Europeanization research agenda, comment on the 'contested' nature of the concept 'as to its usefulness for the study of European politics' (3). The specific aim of this book is twofold: first, to introduce the Europeanization concept in an accessible format while highlighting the impact of the EU in the areas of polity, policy and politics; and second, to facilitate the utility of the concept as a research tool by presenting a synthesis of the theories, approaches and a sample of empirical findings. This essentially means moving a further step in the consolidation of the concept, which is employed in ever-increasing analyses of various dimensions of domestic change. Although this attempt may itself be contested, there now exists a substantial body of literature invoking the term such that one can reasonably draw together this material and develop the main outlines of a standard approach. In the end, what one seeks to comprehend is how domestic politics are themselves being shaped by the EU, and at its most basic understanding the concept of Europeanization is an attempt to focus analysis on this multi-level dynamic. The utility of an approach must be judged by its effectiveness in understanding the phenomenon in question, as well as its ability to encompass critical variables in a parsimonious format, as trying to present a framework that can account for every variable is a near impossible task. So the intent set out in this book is to present a synthesis of the Europeanization literature in such a way that the reader can take away an outline of a research framework that can be applied to a wide assortment of political phenomena. This being said, the wider issues presented above, or the big questions that Europeanization conjures up, are also treated in the context of each substantive chapter. The rest of this Introduction presents the intellectual development of the concept of Europeanization, leading the reader through to its present application. The last section details the plan of the book. In the following chapter, the theoretical bases of Europeanization are presented, which then inform the presentation of all subsequent chapters.

Explaining the emergence of the Europeanization concept

Explaining the origins and subsequent development of the European integration process had been the traditional focus of 'European integration studies'. Neo-functionalist and federalist explanations during the 1950s tried to account for the establishment and seeming success of the European Coal and Steel Community (ECSC) and then the European Economic Community (EEC). The dozen or so years after the end of the Second World War witnessed a proliferation of international organizations either in Europe or else with European membership, for example the Council of Europe, the North Atlantic Treaty Organization (NATO), the Organisation for European Economic Cooperation, later to be renamed the Organisation for Economic Co-operation and Development (OECD), and the United Nations. The ECSC and EEC, however, appeared to contain organizational innovations and a qualitatively more significant amount of shared sovereignty, along with an independent supranational institution, that placed these projects in a very different league of their own compared to the other newly founded international organizations. Certain landmark scholarly publications helped to structure the academic study of the phenomenon, most notably Ernst Haas' *The Uniting of Europe* in 1958. The neo-functionalist approach developed in this study and refined over the next decade by others focused on the nature of the shift of authority to supranational institutions and the principles underlying the logic of sectoral integration. Setbacks to the expansion of supranational authority in the latter half of the 1960s, in particular by the French president, Charles De Gaulle during the so-called 'empty chair' crisis, enabled a competing theoretical approach to that of neo-functionalism, inter-governmentalism (derived from an international relations-based realist account of state actions and motivations), to provide an alternative explanation for the integration process, and at the time explain the seeming halt in the pace of integration itself. For the next twenty years, as Börzel and Risse (2006, p.483) portray it, 'the "dependent variable" of these efforts always remained the same: The focus was on explaining the processes and outcomes of European integration itself'.

Further theoretical perspectives on the nature of the integration process were added to the debates between neo-functionalists and inter-governmentalists in the 1980s and 1990s, some borrowing insights from social constructivism, others refining one of the main-line approaches, as in the case of liberal inter-governmentalism. Yet the object of these approaches, as Börzel and Risse remind us, was the process of European integration itself, one that many commentators had taken to label *sui generis*, as the power and influence of the (now renamed) European Union had reached an unprecedented degree of institutional and policy development. While the processes leading to the Single European Act and the Maastricht Treaty on Economic and Monetary Union generated a prodigious amount of research and innovative insights into the re-launched integration process, it nevertheless soon became apparent to a number of scholars that the EU had itself become a dynamic factor within its member states' own politics, polities and policies, broadly defined (Bulmer, 1983).

An interesting point of departure also began to occur at this time, namely the (sub)disciplinary background of those scholars drawn to the study of European integration. Scholars in comparative politics, many of them country or area specialists, turned their attention to the EU and its activity as an explanation for change in their area of research. Two consequences began to emerge from this turn in the nature of EU integration studies. The first was the development of a comparative politics approach to the study of the EU itself, that is, an understanding of the EU less as an international organization, however *sui generis*, and more to its analysis as a newly emergent form of political system (Hix, 1994). The second consequence, more pertinent for the purposes of this book, was the beginning of an approach to understanding or uncovering a linkage between changes in domestic political structures and policies and the decision-making process and policy output of the EU. It is from this 'turn in EU studies' that the Europeanization approach emerged.

What type or types of evidence prompted the search for a 'EU' factor in the domestic political systems of the member states? And why should it have begun to appear in the mid-1990s? Let us consider observed empirical changes in three broad areas of domestic political activity, *politics, political institutions,* and *policies.* When we turn to the realm of *domestic politics* we find the most heterogeneous areas in which to trace the link between the EU and domestic political activity. The term 'politics' is extremely wide and can therefore encompass many forms, formal and informal, from individual to mass-level as well as organizational, but let us define it as the area of activities involving individual and collective actors aimed at expressing, supporting and challenging state-led policies and other actions (we are limiting ourselves to liberal democratic states). There are many formats in which such activities take place, including voting – in elections and referendums; social movement mobilization and protest; interest group lobbying and so on. Public opinion surveys are also employed to chart changes in the public's support for policies and institutions. Political parties may also change, over time, their mix of programmatic positions on public policies. We can therefore ask, what evidence was there of changes in domestic politics that apparently resulted from EU developments? The Maastricht Treaty presented the first occasion when Danish voters rejected the Treaty in a referendum. The Danish government and mainstream party leaders urged voters, in a 'second-chance' referendum, to support the Treaty in order to prevent Denmark from becoming isolated from the rest of Western Europe. This time, the voters did endorse the Treaty, but the first stirrings of public opinion over the nature or direction of the European integration process had been made, and though this had implications for the nature and pace of European integration, it was not widely recognized at the time. Voters again came near to scuttling the Maastricht Treaty when a referendum in France gathered a bare majority, and splinter parties on both the left and right were formed specifically as a result of principled resistance to the direction of the integration process (in both cases invoking a resistance to the perceived dilution of national sovereignty). With the hindsight of several years, these two referendums revealed that the 'permissive consensus' of the prior decades, in which national political leaders and EU elites drove the integration process forward with limited attention to the public impact of their negotiated integration packages, was coming to an end.

No doubt related to voters' reactions against the provisions of the Maastricht Treaty, which after all would usher in the beginning of the end for national currencies in place of the single European currency, researchers began to identify and chart the rise and spread of so-called 'eurosceptic' public opinion. Over the next ten or more years, scholarly efforts aimed at: (a) describing the various intensities of eurosceptic positions – sometimes using terms such as 'hard' and 'soft'; (b) explaining the emergence of these positions – were they related to issues of national identity or reactions against policies?; and (c) ascertaining the impact of these positions for party politics and, indeed, upon inter-governmental bargaining itself, as some national politicians felt obliged to take into account the domestic reaction to new advances in European integration (the case of the UK is a singular case in point).

When we turn to the realm of *domestic political institutions*, we encounter another broad area of investigation, one that encompasses national as well as sub-national institutions and the relations between the two; the central government bureaucracy; executive–legislative relations; and the judiciary. Scholars began to take note of changes that seemed tied to the significance of the EU in terms of both organizing central government in the EU policy and decision-making process, that is, coordination of national policy towards the EU, as well as changes in the very operation of these national governmental institutions. By the mid-1990s, again in response to the speed-up of EU decision-making brought about by the SEA's use of qualified majority voting (qmv) in the Council of Ministers and the subsequent increase in policy output by the EU, changes in national administrations came under the scrutiny of researchers. Changes in central government development of EU policy was observed in the enhancement of inter-agency coordinating bodies (France), the increased involvement of the prime minister (the UK and elsewhere), and the proliferation of EU policy units in line ministries.

Changes in the polity were also noted in terms of constitutional change (required in order to ratify the Maastricht Treaty, for example on citizenship in France or the right of states to be part of the ratification process in Germany), the creation of EU affairs committees in national parliaments, and in some cases, alteration to the nature of relations between central government and sub-national authorities (for example in Spain between the autonomous communities and the central government in Madrid), due in part to the increased spending and accompanying rules of the European Commission and regional development aid.

Finally, in the realm of *domestic policies*, the role or impact of the EU in precipitating change was, if anything, the first to be noticed by scholars. In this particular context – that is, the impact of the EU in domestic policy areas – one must be careful to maintain the distinction between the downloading, so to speak, of EU legislative output that member states are required to transpose to national law to implement what one might term routine EU policy making and the effects on domestic policies from the implementation of such EU policies. In the former case, the implementation of EU policies in the domestic political system, one might for example examine rates of compliance and explain the variation among member states. In the latter case, the effects or consequences for domestic policies, one would search, for example, for evidence of new agencies or structures created to implement the policies; a change in national standards of an existing policy; or possibly an entire new policy dimension not previously part of a member state's domestic policy orientation. Evidence for such change had been accumulating since at least the late 1980s, in connection with the launch of the Single Market programme, originally intended to be completed by January 1992. As noted above, the SEA introduced qualified majority voting in the Council of Ministers for those measures related to the single market, and a result was an increase in legislative output by the EU, a phenomenon that at the very least resulted in some domestic institutional changes among member states' national ministries for purposes of better coordination. But the SEA also transferred to the EU degrees of competence in a variety of policy areas, a list expanded with every subsequent treaty change (e.g. Amsterdam and Nice). This involvement of the EU in policy domains previously monopolized by national governments is the background against which domestic policy change has occurred.

Environmental policy is an area in which the EU was given a significant input early on in the history of the integration process (1960s). However, the EU was given more significant powers beginning with the SEA, and correspondingly changes were soon apparent among member states, though in a decidedly differential manner. An EU environmental policy content is recognized across member states, but administrative change as a result varies according to the country. Centralization in national executives is one such type of change; the introduction of new policy instruments is another. Finally, there is evidence that variation also corresponds to levels of development, that is, southern European member states versus northern; what one scholar has labelled 'leaders' and 'laggards' in terms of implementing environmental directives and regulations. In a few cases, for example the UK, the EU environmental policy orientation is said to have resulted in a broad change in policy style (Jordan, 2006).

Development and (near) consolidation of an approach

If we accept that the Europeanization research concept emerged from a comparative politics approach in general, we then have to explain subsequent theoretical developments by reference to the distinctions within the approach, that is, between comparative policy analysis, comparative institutions (with its rational-institutionalist underpinnings) and domestic politics, which, as mentioned above, is itself one that incorporates attention from a wide assortment of dynamics, including public opinion, political parties and elections, social movement mobilization, interest group lobbying, etc. Thus no unified Europeanization approach can be said to have emerged in the mid-1990s; rather what began to develop was a number of comparative politics analyses invoking the EU as an independent variable to explain changes in national arenas.

This comparative politics turn toward the EU and indeed the use of the term Europeanization date from a cluster of articles published between 1994 and 1999. Ladrech (1994), in a study of the influence of EU in domestic French politics and institutions, gave a definition of Europeanization that would prove to be an early foundation or basis for subsequent studies. He defined Europeanization as, 'an incremental process reorienting the direction and shape of politics to the degree that EC political and economic dynamics become part of the organizational logic of national politics and policy-making' (69). This meaning emphasized the role of domestic factors in shaping the nature of Europeanization effects in each member state, as there would be 'national-specific adaptation to cross national inputs' (84). This early conceptualization of the national adaptation to EU inputs *did not* argue that Europeanization effects would lead to an across-the-board harmonization, convergence or homogenization in member states. This 'differential impact' was further stressed in subsequent studies in the realm of policies (e.g. Héritier *et al.*, 2001). Soon after the publication of Ladrech's article, an edited volume appeared with the specific intent to analyse 'the impact of the European Union on national institutions and policies', and it contained explicit references to Ladrech's definition of the term Europeanization (see Wessels and Rometsch, 1996). Case study chapters – on Britain, Germany and France – stood alongside public policy chapters. A new analytic approach was emerging, and before long attention to ensuring a rigorous framework for analysis was sounded, as the potential for 'concept-stretching' was clear (Radaelli, 2000).

Yet it would by no means be accurate to suggest that the term – more a concept than a theory – did not emerge unchallenged. The term Europeanization is itself laden with different meanings, some preceding the 'refinement process' begun by Ladrech and others in the mid-1990s. Olsen (2002) has suggested five definitions of the term, one of which does indeed overlap with the understanding of the concept employed in this book. First, Europeanization is associated with the external boundaries of the EU, and therefore the process of enlargement is the dynamic in which change in Europe's boundaries incorporating new members is understood. Second, Europeanization may refer to the development of common practices and norms at the European level, suggesting a new form of governance. Third, Europeanization may concern the impact of EU governance on domestic practices, especially seen within the perspective of multi-level governance. Fourth, Europeanization can refer to the export of European norms to the wider international system, whether in the context of international negotiations, or agenda-setting, etc. Lastly, Europeanization may refer to the building up of a distinct European political identity. Featherstone (2003: 5–6), in a survey of usages of the term derived from published articles listed in the Social Sciences Citation Index, identified

> four broad categories: as an historical process; as a matter of cultural diffusion; as a process of institutional adaptation; and as the adaptation of policy and policy processes. The first two are maximalist interpretations and have little direct connection to the impact of the European Union. The other two categories are

minimalist and are more closely linked to the operation of the European Union.

If we narrow somewhat our disciplinary focus, and look to the meaning of the term in the context of European integration studies broadly defined, we see different usages of the term here as well. Quaglia, Neuvonen, Miyakoshi and Cini (2007) summarize the definitions in relation to one's research perspective when employing the concept. The first definition relates to the impact of EU processes on member states. This has become known as the 'top-down' perspective. The second definition combines the 'top-down' focus with a realization that many EU policies that do impact domestic politics have their inception and are moulded by the member states themselves; thus 'bottom-up' has come to label this 'uploading' of national preferences onto the EU policy-making process. This second definition goes further and combines the two directions of causality into a process of feedback, such that member states are adapting to the policies that they themselves have helped shape. The third definition, according to Quaglia *et al.* (2007), de-emphasizes the prominence of EU institutions in place of a process of horizontal diffusion of best practices and policy ideas by member states themselves. This policy emulation does not depend on formal membership in the EU, thus drawing attention to the manner in which policy transfer may occur without the need for compliance with EU directives and regulations in a formal sense. Lastly, Europeanization has been defined as a process of constructing authoritative European-level structures of governance (Risse, Green Cowles and Caporaso, 2001). Although this European level of governance then interacts with national and sub-national levels as well, to produce adaptational pressure in these 'lower' realms, the definition itself is aimed at European-level processes.

Since publication of these early works, the bulk of what we will at this point loosely label 'Europeanization studies' focused primarily on policies and institutions. The Europeanization of policies has represented over the years the single greatest amount of empirical studies, and in a sense this is not too surprising, for under this label one can find attention directed to policy content and policy instruments; policy style and even policy paradigm shift, in which a focus on policy discourses will be of central concern; and administrative structures. What further adds to the quantity of studies is the fact that EU policy competence and the corresponding national responsibility are relatively clear for the researcher to identify, and thereby trace the type of change observed in the domestic sphere to its possible EU input. Additionally, the clearly observed differential impact of EU policies has led to studies explaining how intermediating factors may account for this variation. In the analysis of institutional change, apart from that of a constitutional nature or formal organizational innovation, it may be more difficult to label the EU as the independent variable. This is because the mechanisms of change (see Chapter 2) are more diffuse in this dimension. Finally, with regard to changes in patterns of politics among the actors cited above, it is even more difficult to attribute to the EU a top-down 'pressure', as many of those mentioned have no direct engagement with EU decision or policy-making. In all three cases, as the next chapter will discuss, careful attention must be made to disentangle the EU from other potential factors, such as a purely domestic agenda for change, bi-lateral exchanges, extra-European actors and trends, and so on.

The approach taken in this book, intended to be an aid in directing learning and research in Europeanization processes, is to explicitly situate the Europeanization approach in the 'top-down' perspective in which domestic change is traced back to EU sources. This being said, however, in an influential definition of Europeanization that follows from the second perspective mentioned above, Radaelli (2003: 30) broadens the research focus when he refers to Europeanization as:

> [p]rocesses of (a) construction, (b) diffusion, and (c) institutionalisation of formal and informal rules, procedures, policy paradigms, styles, 'ways of doing things', and shared beliefs and norms which are first defined and consolidated in the making of EU public policy and politics and then incorporated in the logic of domestic discourse, identities, political structures, and public policies.

In this fashion Radaelli is able to invoke a social-constructivist as well as rational-institutionalist methodological approach, leaving it up to the individual researcher to pursue their agenda. The organizing principle for this book will be, for heuristic purposes, the employment of the tripartite distinction of polity, policies and politics as sketched above (see Chapter 2), but Radaelli's definition alerts us to the fact that 'ways of doing things' is a subtle concept and therefore presents the researcher with a host of complicating factors in research design, which will be discussed in the following chapter.

Organization of the book

This Introduction has traced the background and sketched the emergence of the Europeanization concept. The next chapter will explain the framework for analysis that will be employed in the rest of the book. Focusing on the 'top-down' approach, the chapter will address *where* the EU affects its member states, *how* the EU affects its member states, and finally the *nature of the effect* on its member states. This chapter discusses variation among member states' response to the influence of the EU and also discusses the distinction between old (pre-2004 enlargement) and new member states (focusing especially on post-communist states). Finally, a framework for analysis is presented.

The following chapters are grouped around the 'dependent variable' of change: the *where* question of EU impact. In addition, as appropriate, each chapter links its findings to the wider issues briefly discussed at the beginning of this Introduction, for instance. change in the nature of the European nation-state, normative concerns from institutional adaptation,and so on. Beginning with Chapter 3, in the next four chapters the impact on the domestic polity is explored. Chapter 3 deals with the national executive: the institution that appears to have increased its position within the domestic political system *vis-à-vis* other institutions thanks to European integration (one of the so-called winners in the integration process). The chapter investigates internal institutional change and the development of coordinating mechanisms for EU policymaking, providing a comparative politics approach. Chapter 4 discusses national parliaments: the set of national institutions that some have labelled the 'losers' in the integration process. The chapter documents internal institutional changes, presents the differences in functions of different member state parliaments, e.g. scrutiny, law-making, etc., and concludes with a discussion of cross-national patterns in legislative-executive relations. Chapter 5 addresses the effect of the acknowledged 'supremacy of European law' over national legal systems, and then documents the varying ways in which different national courts have adapted to being part of a multi-level system. Finally, Chapter 6 evaluates the argument that the EU's Regional Policy has acted as a complementary causal factor explaining changes between national central government and sub-national levels of governance. This is explored in relation to both federal and unitary states as well as those that have embarked on a process of 'becoming federal' (e.g. Belgium) and those developing significant regional levels of government (e.g. Spain).

The next two chapters necessarily follow the discussion of state institutions, by addressing Europeanization and domestic politics, dividing the analysis between Chapter 7 on political parties and party systems and Chapter 8 on interest groups and social movements. The focus of these two chapters is therefore explicitly actor-centred. In the attempt to provide a concise operational definition of usage of the Europeanization concept, the issue of the EU in domestic politics is not directly addressed, although certainly when discussing the impact of the EU on the political parties issue, salience will be discussed. Nevertheless, in these two chapters organization, strategies and programmatic change are the primary concerns. In each of these chapters, specific attention is also given to the nature of the evidence of Europeanization in post-communist member states, the attempt being to determine whether the same mechanisms of change are apparent as well as domestic outcomes, or if there is a singular Europeanization effect for this set of member states.

The final two chapters are grouped around the policy impact of the EU. Eschewing an approach in which a number of policies are discussed (see Graziano and Vink, 2008 for an example of such an approach), this book instead opts for understanding the different types of policy impact. Therefore, we distinguish between EU policies that may be described as 'hard', that is, compulsory directives and regulations, and 'soft' proposals in which the Commission extols the virtues of best practice, etc., for example the Open Method of Coordination (OMC). Chapter 8 discusses the effect of EU hard policies and uses as a case study the EU's Competition Policy, as well as addressing soft EU policies, using as a case study the European Employment Strategy. Finally, Chapter 9 has as its focus Foreign Policy, that is, national foreign policy developments in the context of their interaction at the European level. This is not a focus on the EU Common Foreign and Security Policy or European Security and Defence Policy *per se*, rather an evaluation of how national foreign policies evolve in the context of a complementary EU field of action.

The Conclusion summarizes the preceding chapters by reflecting on the nature of the EU–member state relationship. Many of the changes described in the book are imperceptible by the public at large, and though eurosceptic opinion in varying degrees appears to be part of the domestic political firmament in many member states, in most cases public mobilization is not directed at the various institutional or policy adaptations that have taken place over the years. Nevertheless, a brief consideration of the cumulative effect of Europeanization on the political foundations of the EU member state is provided.

Chapter 1

Europeanization: Conceptual Developments and a Framework for Analysis

As the Introduction made clear, the concept of Europeanization has established itself in the firmament of European Union studies. This chapter presents the main conceptual developments and analytical tool-kit as it has evolved up to the present. These concerns are necessary to address in order to more effectively understand the evidence of Europeanization that is investigated in each of the subsequent chapters. In this regard, each of these chapters refers back to the main contours of the theoretical framework that is discussed in this chapter.

What is the meaning of 'member state'?

The underlying premise of this book is that in order to fully understand domestic political change in most of the states in Europe today, our understanding of the term 'member state' of the European Union must be given a more considered meaning. Although it is not the intention of this chapter to engage in a theoretical argument for a revised notion of sovereignty – there is a long-standing debate on the meaning of this politically charged concept – it is nevertheless useful to present at the outset of any discussion of the relationship between the EU and its members exactly what is implied by the casually mentioned term 'member state'. As part of any type of voluntary membership, there are rules and responsibilities that bind the member to the organization. Most states in Europe today belong to several international organizations, ranging from military alliances such as NATO, to international economic bodies such as the International Monetary Fund (IMF) or the OECD, and of course the United Nations. There are two main differences between membership in the

European Union and these other international organizations. First, the degree of intensity of interaction, and second, an expectation to download and implement agreed policies that has gone so far as to make the judicial systems of the countries involved co-enforcers with the EU. The degree of intensity of interaction has grown in parallel with that of the EU's own competences. One simple indicator of this interaction would be the percentage of legislation that member state parliaments vote upon which has sole or partial origin in EU-level policy and decision-making (e.g. a rough estimate is that at least 60 percent of legislation can be traced back to the EU). In some policy areas, such as environment, the EU legislative origin may be greater than in others. Another mark of the intensity of interaction is the frequency of meetings between national and EU actors, whether formal or informal. The era of two European Council meetings a year among heads of government has ended, with quarterly meetings now the norm. On a much less exalted level, the opportunities to influence EU policy development – in particular through the Commission – has made Brussels one of the world's most intensive sites for lobbying, by governmental as well as non-governmental actors. As for the expectation to abide by the output of EU decision-making, the important point to bear in mind is that although the basis of the *acquis communautaire* is grounded in treaties, namely the Treaties of Rome and subsequent amendments, a jurisprudence of a highly advanced nature has developed, defining the establishment of these relations to the extent that we speak of the 'supremacy of European law' over national law. Compliance with EU directives is expected, and cases of non-compliance and delay in implementation are considered the exception, not the rule.

Thus the status of a 'member state' of the EU reflects a level of participation – vertically with EU supranational institutions and horizontally with other member states, through EU institutions or on a bi- or multilateral basis – such that we could conceptualize the nature of the EU 'member state' as a condition of embedded interaction in which boundaries are permeable depending upon the specific linkage that is in question. The permeability of modern states is itself not a new understanding of modern politics and international relations, of which the globalization thesis alluded to in the previous chapter is an example. Indeed, as noted earlier, European integration has unfolded during a period of rapid global change, especially in the international economic realm (the liberalization of various sectors) and in the European state system itself (the so-called hollowing-out of the state; the assertion of regional identities; and so on). Although the causes of these changes cannot all be placed at the doorstep of the European Union, it may be the case that domestic adaptation and the shape of these changes have been, to some extent, mediated through the European integration and governance process. This again highlights the meaning of 'member state', because the manner in which a state experiences and responds to exogenous and even endogenous dynamics is very often conditioned by EU rules and processes. For example, measures related to the Single Market and Monetary Union will have had some effect upon how a national economy and government experienced and responded to global economic trends or crises, such as the so-called 'credit crunch' of 2008 and recession of 2009, though the impact itself may be variable, depending on the member state. At the very least then, we should comprehend 'member state' of the EU as a term laden with multiple consequences and meanings.

Providing an analytical framework for developments that arise from the impact of the EU on its members is the aim of this chapter. The term Europeanization encapsulates this process, and although there is no single accepted definition of Europeanization *per se*, this chapter offers a synthesis of the conceptual advances to date, presented in an accessible framework that sets the general parameters of investigation, but allows for specific case study 'fine tuning'. This follows Bulmer and Lequesne's (2005) advice that 'a broad aspiration in the development of Europeanization as a concept should be to ensure precision of use, while not pre-empting empirical findings' (12). To this end, this chapter will proceed as follows. First, as this book is aimed at understanding and documenting domestic change in which the EU is implicated, the 'top-down' direction of Europeanization is employed. Consequently, it is necessary to specify where the EU affects its member states; in what ways this occurs; and finally to understand what the actual effects are. After considering these and other important factors, we can then proceed to present a framework, one that will direct the discussion in each of the subsequent chapters.

The direction of influence: 'top-down'

We are interested in determining how the impact of the EU generates change in domestic policies, politics and institutions. As

Europeanization research developed, it soon became clear that in terms of drawing a causal arrow in a straight downward direction to define 'top-down' Europeanization, that is, from the supranational EU level down to the individual member state, a complex host of domestic factors rendered this image problematic, if not simplistic. The problem, on the one hand, is that domestic actors, ranging from interest groups to national executives, may have had a role to play in influencing the very EU legislation that is to be transposed into national law. This is part of the routine EU policy and decision-making process. On the other hand, a national government (or governments) may have in fact desired the specific policy in question, and had 'uploaded' this preference to the EU level in order to aid in its implementation in its (their) domestic system. In some cases, the motivation to follow this course of action is based on a consideration of the domestic political costs to the national government. If the costs are too high – for example a certain electoral setback – the policy aim may be deflected away from domestic scrutiny via the EU policy-making process, where the same or similar policy initiative could be implemented as an EU directive (and therefore obscured from routine domestic public scrutiny). What this implies is that to view a 'top-down' approach in isolation from domestic political dynamics is to miss the empirical reality in any attempt to generalize. Nevertheless, it can be argued that a 'consensus has grown around the need to understand this as a two-way relationship, but one that has been modelled primarily in terms of the downward flow of effects' (Bache, 2007: 11–12). In this book we are not discounting the domestic political dynamics that may have fed into the EU policy-making process; what we are concerned to isolate is the actual impact – if any – of specific EU-level influences in the domestic arena. What led to the development of the directive or regulation is itself not part of our analysis; what happens afterward is our concern. In this application, we are employing the recommendation of Börzel and Risse (2007) to 'use the term Europeanization as focusing on the dimensions, mechanisms, and outcomes by which European processes and institutions affect domestic-level processes and institutions' (485). Let us now turn to mapping out in more detail the substance of three fundamental questions of Europeanization research: where Europe 'hits' the member state (dimensions), how this occurs (mechanisms), and what type of change actually occurs (outcomes).

Dimensions of domestic change: where does the EU affect its member states?

The discussion concerning the attributes of being a member state of the EU should lead us to the next logical step in understanding EU-influenced domestic change. It would be highly unlikely, with the panoply of contact points between the EU and domestic actors that has developed over the past two decades, that is, especially since the SEA, as well as the expansion of EU competence in a number of policy areas that directly impinge on domestic legislation, that some degree of change – from low to high – would not occur. This is not an argument about inevitability or a deterministic perspective, as (a) the type or direction of change is not specified, and (b) the possibility of resistance to pressure to change is to be expected. This is a practical expectation that interaction between organizational actors, especially where one increases its scope and jurisdictional influence, will result in the *possibility* of changes in the relationship. Indeed, as we will see in the discussion of the mechanisms of domestic change, although the relationship may produce pressure for change in one dimension or area, the specific domestic array of institutions and attendant political dynamics mediate between pressure and outcomes.

In the Introduction three broad areas were specified in which we could organize our investigation of domestic change. These were politics, institutions (the polity), and policies. Asking where the EU impacts its member states is to isolate the dependent variable in our analysis. In this section a more systematic presentation of each of these three areas is provided, as they will structure the following chapters.

Politics

As we noted in the Introduction, 'Politics' is a very wide area in which to apply a particular framework for analysis. As a dimension of change, what is being defined is the field of action and actors therein who are engaged with domestic governance. In the conventional sense, for example, we would turn our attention to political parties and organized interests, as well as the electoral process. Recognizing that there are unconventional forms of political action, we would also evaluate protest and pressure groups operating outside the conventional format of parliamentary government. Europeanization research has begun to analyse the organization and repertoire of activities of these actors, although in comparison with the dimensions of polity and policies, the actors referred to here are, in most cases, different in one very fundamental sense: they have very little to no formal or direct contact with the EU. The influence of the EU in the realm of politics is therefore indirect.

Political parties

Parties are one of the domestic actors that have little to no direct contact with the institutions or policy-making process of the EU. This is demonstrated by the fact that the EU has no direct, legal jurisdiction over party activities or organization, nor is there any direct transfer of financial resources from the EU to national party treasuries that would motivate national parties to invest time and organizational resources redirecting their attention to the EU level. We can also consider the fact that EU policy- and decision-making does not involve national parties in any routine manner. In our Europeanization analysis concerning national parties, we are speaking strictly about the organization, not individuals such as party elites in government. Parties as collective actors are of course involved in campaigns to the European Parliament and the elected Members (MEPs) are also members of their respective national party. This being said, parties' primary operating arenas are in the national executive (single party or in coalition), in parliament (government or opposition), and have an organization connecting membership and elected officials as well as auxiliary organizations. If the EU were to have an impact on political parties, it would necessarily be found in the pursuit of their objectives, that is, electoral campaigns to win office and/or influence policy. Consequently, we can narrow our focus on party change related to the EU – Europeanization – by asking if there is evidence in: (a) party programmes; (b) party organization; and (c) other aspects such as party symbols or affiliations with EU actors. Political parties do change their statutes from time to time, as well as amending programmes and election manifestos, so care must be taken to distinguish when apparent change is related to EU influences or to some other purely domestic factor.

Interest groups

Whether we classify the interest intermediation style of an EU member state as pluralist, neo-corporatist or statist, or some combination of the three, in all member states we find organized interests for whom EU policy output may have an impact, for instance in terms of new regulatory conditions that may place higher costs on a producer. As opposed to national parties, occupying government is not one of the objectives or means of attaining core goals for interest groups, although supporting a particular party that serves their interest is common. Also unlike parties, for whom the national political system represents their exclusive operating environment, interest groups *may* find that the EU presents an appropriate political opportunity structure for the pursuit of their goals, but *alongside* the national arena. This is due to the fact that the European Commission explicitly invites various domestic interests to contribute to its policy development by offering information and perspectives on proposed legislation (or put more bluntly, the Commission and its different working groups welcomes lobbying). The key issue for domestic organized interests – as well as protest groups, whatever their degree of organization – is whether making the effort to influence the EU policy-making process 'pays off' (i.e. engaging in a cost–benefit analysis) compared to their focus on national government institutions and selected actors. Therefore, interest group Europeanization would impact organization – defining an explicitly EU expertise in new personnel or functions, and behaviour – the direction or level of activity, that is, presence and activity in Brussels or changes in domestic strategies.

Polity (institutions)

Institutional change induced by the influence of the EU has a formal and an informal manifestation. Formal institutional change would include constitutional revision, for example making certain amendments to a national constitution in order to ratify an EU treaty. Informally, and here the bulk of Europeanization institutional analyses are to be found, we find changes that represent more of an adaptation of domestic institutions which interact with the Commission or other bodies to better influence the EU policy-making process (a more efficient 'uploading' of national preferences that can be characterized as vertical in direction) as well as changes in relations among domestic actors and institutions, a horizontal direction that can include, among others, the relationship between national and sub-national institutions. The institutions and relationships that can be indicative of institutional change include national executives, subnational (or regional) government, national courts, national parliaments, including executive-legislative relations, and so on. Apart from the example of constitutional change, the other examples of institutional Europeanization are based on an indirect influence of the EU (here is a case in point of 'member state' status discussed in the opening of this chapter). Our focus in this book will be upon four institutions/relationships that provide the basis of member states' institutional framework, namely executives, parliaments, courts, and regional relations (that is, between national and subnational levels of government).

National executives

As the main point of formal institutional interaction with EU actors and institutions, national executives could perhaps be considered *the* most likely candidate for institutional change generated by the influence of the EU. Indeed, one of the most commonly asserted findings in Europeanization research to date is that national executives have been strengthened in relation to other domestic institutions by their 'privileged' position as the prime interlocutor with the EU. The national executive can be disaggregated into a core and periphery, bearing in mind that it is particular government ministries that have the actual connection or relationship with the EU through shared policy competence. Institutional change could be expected to operate on an incremental basis, taking into concern the need to both develop domestic policy as a result of EU directives and regulations as well as to better organize the executive to defend and promote national preferences in the various sites of EU decision-making. As EU policy competence has grown over the years, not just in regard to the scope of policy involvement but also in terms of decision-making, that is from unanimity to qualified majority voting (qmv) in the Council of Ministers, national executives may find that a change in tactic is demanded in inter-governmental bargaining. The nature of particular policies may cut across national government ministries, for example environmental policy, where an EU directive could potentially involve two or more national ministries, e.g. environment, transport and industry, and thus a premium is put upon inter-ministerial coordination. In some member states the EU has itself become a politicized issue, and consequently the formal basis of 'leading' on a member state's EU policy may highlight political management considerations, a coordinating ability perhaps better exercised from a prime minister's office rather than a foreign ministry. All of these points raised so far are potential aspects of institutional change that the national executive may experience, and Europeanization research has indeed investigated evidence of such change and its variation among member states.

National parliaments

If national executives have been portrayed as the relative 'winners' in terms of the impact on domestic institutions, then national parliaments have earned the label of 'losers'. This label has less to do with actual institutional changes within national parliaments, and more to do with the relative position of national parliaments in the domestic legislative process. If we begin with the likelihood of institutional change related to the EU, we can assume the same type of dynamic which all organizations may experience when the amount of information and tasks are altered or expanded, namely revising working methods and/or creating new agencies responsible for managing the increase or change. We noted this same organizational principle for national executives. For national parliaments, this would find expression in the committee system, the means by which policy areas are divided and given some level of expert scrutiny and subsequent recommendation to the full parliament. The increase in scope of EU policy competence that national parliaments are expected to vote upon suggests that they would create a committee or sub-committee to consider EU-generated legislation and make recommendations on the voting. This would be a case of formal change/Europeanization. Informally, in an effort to own or lead on an issue, competition among standing committees would suggest an internalization of EU policies into their specific portfolios, such as transport, energy, etc., had occurred. If we now consider the potentially wider impact of the EU on the position of national parliaments within their own political systems, the discrepancy between the role that national executives play in EU decision-making (through Permanent Representatives Committee (COREPER), Council of Ministers, etc.) and the virtual exclusion of parliaments from this process, only to be brought into it at the final legislative step, explains the evaluation that in relative terms they have 'lost out' in the multi-level policy and decision-making process which now characterizes a vast amount of legislation eventually appearing on national statute books. Europeanization research thus addresses these changes by way of empirical as well as normative analysis.

National courts

In one sense, there is no question that the EU has a direct influence in member states' legal framework. Through the development of EU case law, the legal and constitutional basis of the relationship between the European Court of Justice (ECJ) and national courts now rests on 'direct effect' and supremacy of EU law. Both of these aspects of the relationship are significant in principle, but dependent to a certain extent on the national courts choosing to interpret European law upon national law (this would be a direct impact of the EU upon a national legal situation). However, the indirect effect of European law on national legal systems is perhaps the more probable area in which to observe how the EU influences domestic practices. It is debatable whether an actual hierarchy exists between the ECJ and national courts, namely that there is a clear dominance by the ECJ, but it is undeniable that national courts play a role in European law. It is the consequences of this interaction that interests the student of judicial Europeanization, and here the 'top-down' approach in Europeanization research requires some degree of flexibility, as evidence suggests that concerning some issues, it is national – and particularly lower – courts which become active in sending cases up to the ECJ. Therefore a research focus would be aimed at explaining changes in the operation of national courts, what types of EU law/issues motivate judicial activism, and, perhaps more tellingly for a Europeanization research agenda, how the relations between lower courts and their supreme court have altered.

Regional relations

Whether the term is devolution, federalization, regionalization, and so on, many member states have experienced over the past twenty to thirty years profound changes in the relationship between the central government and sub-national authorities. The cause or causes of this dynamic process is/are not being attributed to the existence of the EU. Rather, the nature of these relations, from the manner in which they construct their constitutional framework to the resource allocation from central to regional government, may be influenced by one of the European Union's major policy initiatives of the past twenty years, the Regional Policy (and in particular the influence of the Structural Funds). Through the partnership, programming and additionality principles of the Regional Policy, the EU engages in a relationship with sub-national in addition to national government actors. The Europeanization research focus would seek to determine if these funds and the relationship between Brussels and sub-national authorities have any effect on the relationship between national central government and its sub-national units. Bourne (2003) has suggested that there is contradictory evidence, ranging from an EU effect that undermines regional power, to empowering regional power, to no effect on regional power. Because of the different constitutional bases of territorial relations, one would expect that variation in this dynamic would be the norm, and comparative research is particularly well suited to this Europeanization research area. More specifically, Europeanization research would focus on the role regions may play in the implementation of EU policies and in the possible creation of coordination mechanisms for the uploading of agreed national preferences to the EU.

Policy

The European Union's legislative output relates to a large extent to Single Market concerns and goals. Consequently, its policy orientation is primarily economic and regulatory in character, rather than social and re-distributive. The means by which the EU – here we are speaking of the Commission – achieves its goals has been supplemented over the past ten years or so with attention directed to 'soft' methods. The so-called 'Open Method of Coordination' is an example of the attempt by member states themselves to provide the means to attain Single Market goals, with the Commission more of an interested and helpful advisor than a director wielding compulsory edicts. Of course there are some areas, such as foreign policy, in which the Commission is only an onlooker, as inter-governmental decision-making remains the norm. The traditional method employed by the Commission would then be labelled 'hard', that is, member states are obliged to implement agreed policies through directives and regulations. Europeanization research must take notice of this distinction, for as it will be demonstrated in the following section on the mechanisms of change, the role of the EU's institutions and policy type can be a crucial variable in the process of domestic change. What must be kept uppermost in the mind of the researcher is the distinction between member state implementation of EU policies – which can be measured by rates of compliance, for instance – and the consequences of this process, which may be reflected in the development or creation of new policy instruments, standards, shifts in policy direction, and so on.

Direct or 'hard' EU policy

The vast majority of EU policy that it implemented by member states falls under what we may call positive integration. In this manner, the EU constructs a policy template derived from intergovernmental negotiation and the involvement of the Commission and the European Parliament. From this template member states are obliged to implement resulting legislation; environmental policy is an example of this type. The downloading of the policy through directives and/or regulations is the key factor distinguishing positive integration from negative integration, in which the removal of barriers is the means to the desired goal. As Bulmer and Radaelli (2005) suggest, the EU's Competition Policy is a good example of negative integration, as removing constraints on economic and firm competition is the desired output.

Indirect or 'soft' EU policy

Whether referred to as 'policy coordination' (Wallace, 2005) or facilitated coordination (Bulmer and Radaelli, 2005), the leading and authoritative role employed by the Commission is replaced by key players from the member states, the Council acts as a venue, and the Commission's role is closer to a facilitator and promoter of ideas, networks, etc. The output of such initiatives are not legally binding, and depend on the member states to refine proposals and implement them, although the Commission may be asked to monitor the actual output. The Open Method of Coordination best exemplifies this approach, and employment policy is a good case of a particular policy that rests on actions such as sharing of experiences, reviews on progress, and so on.

Related to soft policy – that is, member states' control of the process of decision and implementation – are a few other specific policy areas that are different in the degree to which specially constructed cooperative frameworks have been developed, using the EU but not subject to the level of interaction as we see in the examples given above. We are speaking primarily of justice and home affairs and foreign and security policy. Whether it is hard or soft policy, Europeanization research aims at understanding the impact of the EU, and research to date suggests there is evidence in terms of the creation of new policy standards and instruments, though in some cases wider changes in policy style may have been generated; and a differential impact of the EU in policy change among policies and between member states.

Mechanisms of domestic change: how does the EU impact its member states?

This chapter began with a brief discussion of the meaning of the term 'member state' of the European Union. Without attempting to be too restrictive or narrow in the definition, attention was brought to the unique character of the condition of membership, in which the obligatory transposition and implementation of EU policies – covering a broad range of domestic rules and regulations – results in a degree of permeability of state boundaries that should lead one to pause in any reflection of contemporary state sovereignty. Approaching this situation from a multi-level governance or regionalist perspective, there is an unprecedented level of interaction between the EU and domestic actors and institutions that goes well beyond examples of such penetration by wider globalization dynamics. This is our starting point for a discussion of how the EU impacts its member states, namely the background intensity of the relationship.

Before turning to an evaluation of formal theories to explain the causal mechanisms of Europeanization, we need to consider what has become in the literature the single most identified proposition regarding the 'trigger' for domestic change: *misfit*. The term misfit follows from the argument presented by Risse, Green Cowles and Caporaso (2001) in which they argue that the casual mechanism for domestic change is a process labelled 'goodness of fit'. It is a straightforward proposition, in that 'pressure' on domestic actors and/or institutions from EU sources – legislation as well as processes of decision-making – engenders an adaptational response. They write: 'degree of adaptational pressure generated by Europeanization depends on the "fit" or "misfit" between European institutions and domestic structures. The lower the compatibility (fit) between European institutions, on the one hand, and national institutions, on the other, the higher the adaptational pressures' (7). From this early proposition stating that the degree of misfit generates pressure that in turn causes domestic change, has arisen a vigorous debate and multiple research agendas. The notion that pressure will arise between EU output and decision-making structures on one hand and domestic policies and institutions on the other follows from our discussion of the degree of intensity which is a singular condition of EU membership; what the misfit argument presents is an initial refinement of this general finding. Börzel and Risse have further specified the misfit concept, suggesting first, that there are two types of misfit: policy and institutional, and second, that misfit is 'only the necessary condition for domestic change' (2003: 63).

A situation of policy misfit between EU rules, regulations and directives, and domestic policies would be expected in all cases where compliance is an issue, but matters are not so simple and straightforward. The challenge or pressure that EU policies may generate for domestic policies and their style of decision-making and implementation, ranging from standards to instruments, does not automatically result in adaptation. A simple 'action' and 'reaction' does not take into account the complexity and points of influence that domestic actors can activate in attempts to possibly reduce adaptational pressures, for example in uploading their preferences during the EU policy development phase to reduce costs of change. High rates of compliance itself may mask adaptational change, as a national regulatory regime may have to adopt new instruments or even create a new agency to implement a particular EU regulation that departs from the domestic norm. One also has to take into consideration the fact that forces for change can be set into motion, thus necessitating the analysis of a case study in Europeanization over time. It may well be the case that a particular EU policy fits well with domestic regulations, and there is at first sight a good 'fit'. However, as Héritier *et al.* (2001) claim, it is quite possible that an initial 'fit' may put into play changes within the domestic constellation of actors that strengthen 'the strategic position of domestic actor coalitions which oppose European policy objectives and promote a distinctive domestic approach' (29). This 'negative' internal change is also evidence of Europeanization, in which domestic patterns are altered after the inception of apparent policy agreement. Policy misfit is therefore the condition that produces adaptational pressure or costs for domestic actors. A variable response is based upon the degree of pressure, political choices, and potential barriers to change (an important factor we will discuss shortly).

Institutional misfit derives from different causes. First, the differences that arise from domestic actors' relationship with EU institutions and the policy-making process may generate pressure for change. For example, the crosscutting nature of an EU policy may put pressure on the national executive to better coordinate inter-ministerial relations for a better response to EU initiatives. Additionally, EU policies may increase the significance of a ministerial portfolio, stimulating inter-departmental competition for influence and resources. Second, the increased scope – if not pervasiveness – of EU policies increases the need for specialist information and advice, which challenges the traditional leadership role of the foreign ministry and prompts the desire for EU advisors in many different line ministries, parliamentary committees, and so on. Finally, the privileged position of the national executive in the EU decision-making process may produce imbalances between national institutions, for example between the executive and parliament, or between the national executive and sub-national institutions. Each of these pressures arises in an indirect and incremental manner rather than in rapid transformational change.

Policy misfit and institutional misfit present the conditions in which specific changes may take place. As argued above, there is no automatic response to such pressures. As a result, Europeanization research must explain the variation that occurs. The fact that there is a differential response also confirms the finding that Europeanization does not lead to convergence or harmonization. If different types of pressure are indeed created out of the EU–domestic relationship, what intervening factor or factors explain(s) when change occurs?

Intervening factors

The fact that Europeanization has not led to a convergence of national administrative structures, or to a uniform strengthening or weakening in centre and sub-national relations, or to a harmonization of policy instruments across EU member states, highlights the variability of the pressures generated by EU influences on domestic arenas. In fact, attempting to explain the differential impact of Europe has been and continues to be a significant methodological issue in Europeanization research, with an increasing range of case studies, in both the older Western European and newer post-communist member states, further reinforcing an early and authoritative finding, namely, that domestic institutions and politics matter.

The presence or absence of domestic mediating factors helps to explain why EU regulations may stimulate domestic change in one member state and not another. The different state structures, policy styles and political cultures all combine to reinforce the key position that intervening factors play in determining whether Europeanization pressures result in actual change. In their presentation of the goodness-of-fit argument, Risse, Green Cowles and Caporaso (2001) identified five meditating factors: multiple veto points (the degree to which power is dispersed); facilitating formal institutions (domestic institutions that enable domestic actors to exploit EU opportunities); political and organizational cultures (e.g. a consensual or confrontational political culture); differential empowerment of actors (redistribution of power); and learning (a reassessment leading to changed goals and preferences). They suggest these factors can be divided between those that affect structure (the first three) and those that affect agency (the latter two). Börzel and Risse (2003) refined the number of factors to four – multiple veto points and formal institutions (structure), and norm entrepreneurs and informal institutions (agency), but in both cases structure and agency are each theorized by a different approach: rational institutionalism for the former, and social constructivism (or sociological institutionalism) for the latter. The rational institutionalist approach focuses on behaviour that is influenced by pressure affecting actors' environments, and assuming these actors are rational, goal-oriented and purposeful (following March and Olsen, 1998, 'a logic of consequentiality'), there is an expectation for them to see opportunities for strategic interaction. The EU can therefore become a political opportunity structure for actors motivated by an instrumental rationality. The social-constructivist approach emphasizes instead a 'logic of appropriateness' in which social learning influences and defines their goals and action repertoires. EU policy style and norms in a situation of misfit then become specific variables influencing change on the part of domestic actors.

Following Börzel and Risse (2003), we can group the factors influencing change as a redistribution of resources (rational institutionalist) and change as a process of socialization and learning (sociological institutionalism). In a specific analysis of goodness-of-fit and adaptation pressures with regard to policy, Mendez *et al.* (2008) suggest that their relevance for prediction may be strengthened if the following are taken into account: 'the significance of the policy area for the member state; member state expectations regarding the new policy; the level of understanding of Commission requirements; the clarity of policy objectives; and the fit with overarching domestic policy priorities' (294). Many of these suggestions have a wider relevance, especially as regards institutional change, where national expectations may determine whether new or increased agency capacity is warranted. A further consideration offered by Bache (2007) to the above list of mediating factors is the addition of 'political or partisan contestation', a 'response to the observation that the political dynamics of Europeanization are often neglected' (16). This helpful addition to mediating factors takes into account the manner in which the EU is politicized in a domestic political system, which may also add a different set of constraints or opportunities for change, either in structure or agency.

To summarize: the mechanisms of change, or how the EU causes change, are varied, but depend on some degree of misfit between the EU and domestic institutions and policies. Whether adaptation/ change occurs in response to pressure that occurs between the two levels is dependent on the presence or absence of mediating factors, factors that vary according to each member state, thus making any sweeping generalizations about convergence or homogenization of member states' domestic structures unfounded. Further, the mechanisms of change involve both 'hard' EU policy inputs as well as 'soft' methods'. We can now turn to the question of the outcome of change, or what type of change actually occurs.

Outcome of domestic change: what is the extent of change?

The consequences of EU membership, as should be clear by now, is the open possibility of having the EU's 'ways of doing things' (Radaelli, 2003) incorporated into various aspects of one's polity, policies, and politics. But how much of a member state's domestic politics – broadly defined – is actually changed in this way? Are we speaking of a fundamental transformation of a policy paradigm, incremental changes in domestic actor goal-seeking strategies, or what? We have already claimed that Europeanization does not mean a convergence among member states in terms of their structural characteristics, and of course the presence of mediating factors helps to explain this fact. This is a question of measurement, that is, how much is Europeanized. Börzel (2005) and Börzel and Risse (2007) distinguish five outcomes of domestic change in response to Europeanization pressures that range from no change (inertia) to substantial change (transformation). In between are retrenchment (resistance to change), absorption (low degree of change), and accommodation (adaptation without changing core or essential features). The first two outcomes, inertia and retrenchment, signal an absence of change, but a closer reading of these definitions suggests that there is indeed adaptational pressure, but simply the mediating factors which would allow change are absent. These are cases that demand a longitudinal research design, as the lack of adaptation may trigger Commission action against non-compliance (if indeed it is pressure arguing for policy change). This formal pressure to comply or adjust may then upset the domestic balance of interests and launch the sequence of actions that does eventually produce change. The other three outcomes are more straightforward in that they describe degrees of actual change, and some analysts, such as Bache (2007) and also Börzel and Risse (2003), are content to categorize domestic responses to the EU in a threefold manner: low (absorption), modest (accommodation) and high (transformation). A basic assumption of the three change-related outcomes is that the degree of pressure roughly equals the degree of domestic change (i.e. low misfit results in low degree of change/absorption, and so on).

Let us consider these outcomes in some depth, as the investigation of Europeanization outcomes is a central concern of this book. A low degree of domestic change (absorption) suggests that member states respond to a low misfit situation with minor modifications to existing policies, administrative styles, or even preferences. This could mean a revised strategy for attaining a certain goal, e.g. domestic producers joining a European-level association to be able to acquire information on EU regulatory directives at an earlier stage. It may mean minor institutional change that involves redesigning how EU-related information may be better prioritized in a legislative process, for example the French National Assembly committee for European affairs streamlining EU directives into only a few categories in order to focus on the most significant issues to make a recommendation. It could mean policy change only in terms of adjusting existing practices, for instance in strengthening the position of advocates of public sector liberalization – such as in the area of postal liberalization – resulting in either a faster or wider implementation. In each of these examples domestic core practices, beliefs and institutional logic are kept intact, and EU policies are then integrated.

A more defined, yet modest, amount of change (accommodation) means that the adaptational pressures have been more pronounced, and depending on the area in question, there is a medium amount of change suggesting empowerment of certain actors or an advocacy coalition, a lower number of veto points, a salient facilitating institution, etc. Examples would include, for institutional change, the strengthening of the prime minister's office because of the need for better, more efficient coordination in EU affairs. New regulatory initiatives by the EU may increase the scope of an environment or agriculture ministry, finding it necessary to adopt new instruments for compliance. Finally, EU directives intended to liberalize a utility sector may cause modest amounts of policy and structural change in a member state already amenable to the economic tenets of liberalization as well as having a pluralist environment, for example Germany and electricity liberalization (Humphreys and Padgett, 2006).

Fundamental change arising from Europeanization pressure is rare, as it would exemplify a type of change in which existing practices, policies or politics are replaced with new ones or core features are substantially altered. The literature points to crisis moments in which the EU inputs into a member state resonate far more substantially than would be the case under normal circumstances, as an example of this degree of change. Crises are by definition a relatively short-term occasion, yet fundamental change could arise over time, such that a member state's policy style may have evolved significant variations, for example the French statist model developing pluralist tendencies in certain policy fields. Börzel and Risse (2007) also suggest that transformative change may occur via the uploading of government preferences onto the EU such that the resulting EU policy template facilitates that government's intent to pursue fundamental change; France and support for Economic and Monetary

Union (EMU) would be an example (Howarth, 2001). The transformation of the political economies of post-communist Eastern European states is a special case in point, and will be discussed in the next section.

The difference between absorption and accommodation, the most typical change in terms of degree, is not precise. Comparing cases across member states contributes to further refinement of the mechanisms of domestic change, but it would be arbitrary to wield a precise notion of measurement in order to say one example of change has crossed a certain threshold and is thus 'further up the ladder of intensity' by 'x' degree. Better to suggest that the range of domestic change is manifest in clusters of intensity. An historical institutionalist analysis, therefore, becomes indispensable for the Europeanization research agenda, because its use helps to explain how the differences or changes over time build up into adaptational responses to the EU.

Europeanization and the post-communist experience

The Europeanization research agenda developed with an initial focus on the older or pre-2004 enlargement member states. For this reason, the components of the Europeanization research model – misfit, the mechanisms of change as described and the range of outcomes of domestic change – do not appear readily transferable to the case of post-communist member states. First, it is clear that post-communist states' transition to pluralist political systems and market economies was transformative in character, and the direction or goal to which most of these countries aimed was that of EU membership. So the downloading of the *acquis communautaire* has an altogether more significant role in their transformation than for older, established states in the West. Second, and again a glaring difference with the West, was that much of the domestic change (or perhaps restructuring) occurred *before* actual membership, so we are, strictly speaking, discussing Europeanization during the pre-accession process. Third, and following from the preceding points, these candidate states were, for the most part, only downloaders, that is, they were in no position of influence or power to upload their preferences in a meaningful way, thus eliminating some of the examples of mechanisms of change as practised in the West. Finally, in a singular application, EU conditionality pertained to the enlargement process, and, together with the strong desire of these countries for membership in as short a time as possible, this allowed the EU 'an unprecedented influence on the restructuring of domestic institutions and the entire range of public policies in the CEECs' (Schimmelfennig and Sedelmeier, 2008: 88).

Consequently, the research focus when applying Europeanization to post-communist countries emphasizes EU conditionality over other mechanisms that have been posited for older member states, and secondly, the effectiveness of conditionality in terms of implementation or change. Conditionality relates to the relationship between the EU and prospective member states, and because of the nature of their past regime, the initial thrust of conditionality had been on instilling or strengthening democratic norms and practices. Thus political conditionality could be measured by evaluating these candidate countries' progress in meeting and conducting approved legal and political practices, ranging from minority rights legislation and its legal enforcement to the maintenance of free and fair elections, with both sets of activities monitored in a relatively intrusive manner by the European Commission. After official candidate status had been achieved, the conditionality re-focused on the evaluation of the efforts made by the candidate's government to meet the conditions and rules of the various *acquis communautaire*. Again, the Commission would monitor and release progress reports on the efforts made in chapters under negotiation.

Again departing from the Europeanization agenda as applied to older member states, entry into EU membership reflects a sort of 'official' acknowledgement of success in transformation. The post-accession Europeanization agenda, while still acknowledging the differences between East and West, has turned to new questions as regards effectiveness of conditionality, for example: were the officially acknowledged changes deep or shallow (Börzel, 2006)? This is basically a question of the level of institutionalization of EU 'ways of doing things' in these new member states (Dimitrova, 2006). Bearing in mind that these countries have had to download and adjust comparatively weak administrative systems to the demands of regulatory deregulation, trade competition, territorial re-design, etc., in a relatively short space of time, compliance problems, and thus EU pressure to conform, would not be unlikely, and so a second stage in Europeanization research agendas of post-communist member states would appear to be evolving. The examples of

Europeanization provided in this book taken from post-communist member states will focus, as much as possible, on evidence following accession.

A methodological consideration

Toward the end of the previous chapter, the potential methodological problem of extracting a EU factor from the multitude of domestic, European and global forces that penetrate domestic life was indicated. Indeed, the Europeanization literature is keen to warn of the potential pitfalls that await a research design that has not established as precise a causal linkage between examples of domestic change and a clear EU effect as possible, as well as attributing too much to the EU (Radaelli, 2000). Another important consideration is how the researcher judges the relative importance of the EU effect on the observed change when other non-EU factors may have also made a contribution. The solution, as Radaelli (2003) succinctly puts it, is to provide 'systematic analysis of alternative or complementary explanations. It may be difficult to undertake multi-causal analysis, but this is the best way to be relatively sure that changes observed at the national level are originated by EU dynamics, and not by other forces' (50). To this end, Haverland (2006; 2008) has suggested – in the context of a survey of the literature – a threefold research strategy that attempts to answer the question of whether and to what extent the EU matters when demonstrating the causal effects of EU variables: process tracing, counterfactual reasoning, and the inclusion of non-EU cases for quasi-experimental control.

Process tracing is the most widely adopted research strategy, and one that lends itself most readily to examples of policy change. This research strategy is also the most explicit in terms of establishing, or rather attempting to establish, the causal link between observed changes and developments at the EU level. Applied in the context of case studies, process tracing involves the researcher 'deriving observable implications from the EU-level theory and alternative theories. These implications or predictions can denote what should happen, how it should happen and when it should happen if the theories are valid. These "patterns" of implications will then be compared with the empirical pattern by the case study' (Haverland, 2006: 62).

Counterfactual reasoning consists of questioning whether a

particular outcome would have occurred were it not for the EU/European integration. In other words, by removing the EU from consideration, the researcher is forced to consider alternative reasons or factors for the empirical evidence. There should be, as Haverland suggests, some limits as to the speculation of alternatives scenarios, and 'theoretically substantiated counterfactuals are generally more compelling than a-theoretical accounts (2006: 63).

Finally, the inclusion of non-EU cases, as part of a research design, is much more limited in possible application. Choosing a set of countries where the EU factor is absent and then comparing with a set with the EU factor, the researcher can conclude that the EU is not the decisive explanatory factor. Here the challenge is to compare countries that, for the most part, are comparable in general, that is, comparing like with like (minus the EU for one set). It is certainly the case that liberalizing common sectors, for example agriculture, in advanced industrial countries as agreed in a multilateral trade round would present such an opportunity, but these are few in number.

However one approaches a Europeanization research design, the case study method, deriving from comparative analysis, remains the most likely to be employed. Large-N studies are difficult to operationalize, though not impossible, due to the nature of the Europeanization outcomes and the lower numbers involved. Still, in any attempt to account for an EU effect in domestic change, and to develop as precise a research design as possible, one, or a combination, of the three approaches briefly mentioned allows for a theoretically informed starting point. This being said, undertaking Europeanization research from the top-down perspective ideally requires a detailed grasp of the particular situation – policy and institutional – both before and after the EU activity. This adds depth for the comparability across member states, as well as potentially uncovering case-specific factors that may account for differential outcomes. Finally, Mendez *et al.* (2008) also note an added complicating factor that makes process tracing and comparison partial if one is not attentive to possible variation in the motivation of the EU for particular policy outputs; a factor also contributing to differential outcomes. They claim that their research on Competition Policy and Regional Aid 'identifies another source of variation which has so far received little attention ... that the independent variable itself (the EU pressure) may also vary across member states (independently of the degree of fit with member state policies and institutions), thus rejecting the uniformity-of-pressure assumption in much of the top-down literature' (294–5). Again, any case study must have as full a picture of the exact situation as possible, including, if feasible, EU intentions. Establishing a causal link between the EU and domestic change can vary in terms of level of difficulty, and though the undertaking is not impossible, the researcher is well advised to compare initial findings with comparable case studies as a further test of validity, aware of the fact that superficial common-alities may mask potential national-specific factors. In the end, awareness of research design issues such as inferring causal sources, and mechanisms, is crucial, and although Europeanization research to date has generally pursued a trade-off between 'effects of causes' approach rather than a 'cause of effects' (Exadaktylos and Radaelli, 2009), a top-down approach combining attention to bottom-up issues represents the current state of Europeanization research.

From the discussion above, a model of Europeanization and domestic change can be presented, bearing in mind the aforemen-tioned caveats. EU effects, traced to their source – that is, directives and regulations, and decision-making processes, create varying pressures of intensity on particular domestic policy areas, actors, and/or institutions. Mediated by domestic factors, for example multiple veto points, or facilitating institutions, some level of adap-ational change occurs: absorption; accommodation; transforma-tion. As Bache suggests (2007), there is some limitation in this model in that its clearly 'top-down' feature does not account for any 'dynamic or circular process'. This is indeed true in its schematic form, but the advice as regards research approaches, especially process tracing, takes into account the background dynamics which may include domestic uploading in the policy development phase of EU legislation. In other words, I am suggesting that EU effects, in the research design of a case study, have taken into account a prior domestic input, but since what interests us in the end is explaining domestic responses, we need concern ourselves only if the interac-tion has a direct bearing on explaining the subsequent change.

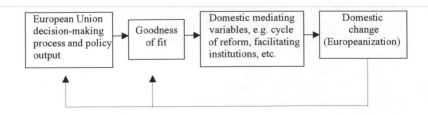

The application of this model in the following chapters is as follows. Each chapter will focus on individual examples from our three dimensions of change, for example national executives in institutional change, foreign policy in policy change, and political parties in political change. As the utility of this book is hoped to provide a template for learning and research, a common chapter structure will be employed. Each chapter begins with a discussion of how EU effects impact the particular actor, institution or policy area. This is followed by a brief summary of the findings in the literature for the subject in question. A case study is then presented in order to illustrate in further detail mechanisms and outcomes of change. Chapter conclusions cover key problems and recent commentary on the topic.

Chapter 2

National Executives

Europeanization and institutional change, particularly of the national executive, has potentially several ramifications for the relationship between the EU and its member states. First, national executives are the constitutional 'gate-keeper' between the EU and domestic policy implementation. Any changes in the operation of the national executive have potential consequences for the uploading of national preferences as well as the implementation of EU legislation, whether measured according to rates of compliance or to other criteria. Second, change inside the national executive may alter the relations between it and other national governmental institutions. Third, adaptation by the national executive to the logic of EU policy-making may have an impact on democratic procedures of accountability and representation. With these concerns in mind, this chapter applies the Europeanization research approach to the polity dimension, assessing the extent to which changes in the national executive can be traced to the EU.

EU decision-making and national executives

For the average citizen of an EU member state, the national executive represents the epicentre of national political life. Political leadership, the stakes upon which general elections turn, policy-making initiatives, etc., all focus attention on this singular component of national government institutions. At the same time, for the average citizen, the manner in which the national executive, in particular the prime minister, interacts with the EU barely registers on the political radar. Apart from some specific interest groups, such as farmers, who are directly affected by EU policy developments, in this case the Common Agricultural Policy (CAP), most individuals have no direct engagement with the EU, and when it does register in domestic politics involving the national executive, it is usually during an extraordinary event, such as a summit. Yet behind the scenes, the national executive has had to devote an increasing amount of time and effort to EU affairs, and although this does not necessarily mean the prime minister or other cabinet ministers are obliged to explicitly divide their schedules into domestic and EU business, it does mean that EU policy matters now infiltrate what had been more traditional and routine domestic decision-making. How the national executive has adjusted to this quantitative and qualitative change in its operation is the subject of this chapter. Although one could say that the Six founding member states have been in continuous interaction with European institutions since the late 1950s, most of the changes that this chapter investigates date from the 1980s onwards, that is, in line with the expansion of the EU's own capacities and policy scope beginning with the SEA. Further, as Chapter 1 explained, Europeanization research has a methodological challenge in isolating the EU effect from a possible myriad other variables. In the case of the national executive, one of the findings most mentioned in the Europeanization literature is a strengthening of the executive as a whole, and the office of the prime minister in particular. Yet, political scientists have documented a shift from parliament to executive since before the re-launch of European integration in the mid-1980s. There are a variety of reasons that have been proffered to explain this trend, and it may be that the 'EU factor' simply reinforces such trends. The concluding section of this chapter therefore attempts to situate the changes that we will trace back to the EU in a wider analytical context.

The formal connection between EU decision-making and member states' input and eventual implementation necessarily focuses our attention on the role of national executives. Whether we conceptualize their role as a 'gatekeeper' between domestic actors and EU institutions, or as a promoter of national preferences in the EU policy- and decision-making process, the national executive is the most significant part of a national government in terms of its direct influence in EU developments and their domestic consequences. Membership has obligations; it generates demands, and also presents opportunities for domestic actors, no more so than for national executives because of their formal insertion both in EU institutions and as the legitimate representative of the domestic political system. Much more so than national parliaments or courts, when Europeanization research invoking institutional change is presented, it is the national executive – the core executive as well as other government ministries – that represents the bulk of empirical evidence of indirect EU effects. This chapter explores the Europeanization of national executives, and in so doing, presents evidence of how member states governments adapt to the influence of the EU in their routine operations as well as the changes made in organizational format considered necessary for more efficient promotion of national interests in Brussels. A possible consequence of EU membership for national political systems, short of transformation, is an alteration in the equilibrium between domestic actors and institutions. In this regard, the chapter discusses the consequences for the domestic institutional balance of power, in particular executive–legislative relations and the role of prime ministers. The chapter begins with a brief discussion of the 'intensity of the EU-member state relationship' presented at the beginning of Chapter 1. This describes the environment within which the executive operates, supranational as well as national. Understanding the nature of the pressures and accompanying dynamics then allows us to evaluate the *misfit* argument in relation to the national executive. The chapter then reviews examples of change, presenting a comparative case in order to provide a temporal dimension to institutional change. The advantage of such an example is that it allows us to more closely analyse specific mechanisms of change over time and thereby gain a better understanding of the Europeanization processes at work.

A privileged position?

Moravcsik (1994) argued that the national executive, because of its privileged position as an intermediary between societal interests and the EU decision-making process, becomes strengthened in its role *vis-à-vis* other domestic institutions and interests. Although his liberal inter-governmentalist approach focused on the process of national preference formation, attention was drawn to a particular consequence of national government interaction with the EU. The greater access to information (through COREPER, for example); the positions taken and bargains struck during inter-governmental negotiations; the ability to contribute to occasional grand initiatives through European Council summits; initiatives launched during rotating presidencies; all of these actions are conducted by national executives very much to the exclusion of other government institutions, such as national parliaments. This position of authoritative *procedural* influence at both the European and national levels, coupled with *political* influence at both levels, makes the national executive the key nodal point of EU–domestic relations. As such, it means the executive incurs costs of adjustment to a more influential EU as well as exploiting the opportunities that may arise to pursue or protect national interests. What exactly are the demands of EU membership for the national executive? Put another way, in what types of engagement, formal and informal, in both low and high politics, does the executive act in and adjust to the EU networked system of governance?

Let us begin with the challenges the EU presents to domestic actors wishing or obliged to navigate its institutional, policy and political currents. As a point of departure, Kassim (2003; 2005) has suggested at least five challenges of membership that the EU presents for national executives, some of which are also applicable for other domestic actors. First, the EU itself is in a constant state of flux or evolution, from enlargement pressures, reform pressures (as evidenced in periodic European-level initiatives and the effect of Constitution-making), the complexity that arises from a formal structure of different 'pillars', centres (capitals) of decision-making, a Community method and an inter-governmental decision-making style. Second, the EU has a policy process that is not only very open – in terms of welcoming as many interested parties as necessary – but as a consequence involves multiple levels as well as large numbers of actors, each emanating from different domestic policy styles of interest intermediation. Third, there is the complexity of the EU decision-making process itself, evolving over time, especially in regard to the legislative process and the Council of Ministers and the European Parliament, namely, from consultation to co-decision, and the different strategies these changes instigate among national governments, the European Commission, EP committees, and so on. Fourth, a high degree of institutional fragmentation characterizes the major EU institutions, from the different Councils of Ministers, with varying power and influence over broad areas of policy, such as the Economic and Financial Affairs Committee (ECOFIN) (and within this group the sub-set which is eurozone members), the committee composition of the EP which represent party group coalitions (and beyond the main party groups voting discipline weakens) with at times competing national delegation interests, etc. As for the Commission, beyond the structural division between the college of

Commissioners and the directorates, the operating style here has shifted with each incoming president, and the additional number of Commissioners after the 2004 and 2007 enlargements has meant more hierarchical division among the Commission portfolios. Fifth and lastly, EU policy competence, although having increased over the past twenty years, continues to vary from sector to sector, 'with each policy sector exhibiting a particular logic and conflict potential' (Kassim, 2005: 290). Not only does each policy sector operate with its own internal constellation of priorities, sources of information and recipients of its output, but there are also wider distinctions, as for example among policies where the EU ultimately develops a template to be employed by domestic actors and those policy areas in which national governments hold an upper hand (e.g. agriculture) or where national governments formally take the lead, as in treaty reform and foreign policy. Overlapping with Kassim's analysis are those that point to the different types of governance which have developed over time, such as 'regulation, common policies, complementary policies, benchmarking and coordination in different policy areas' (Laffan, 2008: 129). This brief description of the EU as an organization but also as an operating environment certainly suggests a challenge for any domestic actor desiring to pursue or defend its interests, and especially highlights the fact that no single member state can hope to control the process to its complete satisfaction. The often-labelled consensual and compromise-oriented nature of EU policy-making rests upon the fact that demands of membership include the recognition of a continual engagement in negotiations, and as Laffan suggests, this 'does not require a one-off adaptation and adjustment' (290).

Let us focus attention more precisely on national executive interaction with the EU. A national executive is obliged (as the formal representative of a member state) to be involved in the EU policy-making process. As the EU has expanded the scope of its policy competence into more areas, national governments must develop the expertise with which to influence the policy development phase. This expertise will be located in the ministry concerned, whether it means interpreting the impact on existing policy or interacting with the European-level counterpart in the working groups of the Commission and Council. Since a particular policy proposal by the Commission can potentially impact more than one domestic policy area – and consequently involve more than one government ministry in evaluating the implications – there is considerable urgency on the part of a national executive to deliver a coordinated response. For example, a proposed Commission regulation on hazardous waste disposal could involve ministries such environment, transport, and industry. Implications for business could generate lobbying directed at all these ministries. The need for a coordinated response may not be left up to the potential ministries involved, as the EU policy and legislation process has its own timetable. Inter-ministerial coordination is then required that can as quickly as possible develop a national response, to either promote or oppose the proposed legislation. The negotiating phase demands constant scrutiny, and member states' permanent representatives (COREPER) are, among other duties, required to be their government's 'early warning system' in Brussels, and so are necessarily integrated into the executive ministries in the member state as an information relay. Again, coordination is required, because a permanent representative cannot negotiate with all potential domestic ministers. Depending on the nature of the specific proposal – that is, whether or not it is amenable to simply technical expertise – resolution over a domestic position may require political intervention, in which case the minister must intervene.

After the Commission formally proposes legislation to the Council of Ministers and the European Parliament (EP), national governments are again obliged to formulate their position for the Council vote or bargaining dynamic (again a matter for the permanent representative to advise), and in particular cases of an especially nationally sensitive issue, they may assert pressure on their national delegations' position in the EP. In some member states the national legislature may have some input, at most usually of an advisory nature, into the national position, so the executive must take account of this domestic inter-institutional relationship. Interaction with the Council involves much more than the relevant minister showing up in Brussels for a vote, for behind the scenes is a large number of working groups of the Council that require national representation. On top of this are the extra demands of holding the six-month rotating Presidency, which means chairing all the various Council meetings. As these occasions offer an opportunity for the member state holding the Presidency to highlight specific national interests on the EU agenda, attention to prior development of policies and negotiating positions during the Presidency requires expert skills. If we turn attention to the European Council rather than the Council of Ministers, even though it meets less frequently (although the days of one summit every six months is long over), preparation is still required, and if particular policy initiatives are planned, then cabinet-level ministers and even the prime minister may become involved.

Finally, after the adoption of legislation, the national executive is obliged to implement EU policies, whether they are regulations or directives, that require transposition into specific national contours. As pointed out above, there are differences as to the political weight given to various policy areas, and some member state executives may have more profound differences if not opposition to some legislation than others at any one point in time (which may be reflected later in terms of compliance). Nevertheless, their obligation to comply with EU legislation is a legal requirement, and as such, EU law takes precedence over national law. The national executive has not only the Commission keeping a careful eye on the implementation of its policy, but the national legal system may also have a role in enforcement of EU law (see Chapter 4). How does the executive ensure that EU policy is transposed into national law and implemented? To a certain extent, the answer is through the usual domestic legislative process and implemented as national policy output. More precisely, though, national civil servants must have some expertise as to the nature of the EU regulations or directives. So as there was a need for expertise during the policy development phase at the European level, so too must there be the capability for national civil servants to take EU directives and shape them to the specificities of a particular domestic setting.

The executive is intimately involved in each of these three stages – policy development, decision-making, and implementation – and must therefore avail itself of the resources – personnel and organizational – in order to maximize its interests, whether this is the promotion or defence of its interests. But the complexity of the EU has grown considerably since the mid-1980s, sometimes at the instigation of national governments. The process just presented is what one might label the *direct* process of EU and national interaction, resulting in EU policy output becoming part of the domestic fabric of law and policy. However, the use of the so-called Open Method of Coordination (OMC) and government-to-government initiatives point to other arenas of European-level policy initiatives that do not follow the route of the traditional Community method. There are, consequently, multiple channels in which the national executive engages as a part of its membership in the Union. This is an important point, because it emphasizes the enormous attention that the national executive must expend in relation to EU policy-making. The mentality that understands a member state's relationship with the EU as confined to 'foreign policy' misses completely the nature of what it means to be a member state in the twenty-first century. Indeed, what the picture sketched above should convey to the reader are the multiple pressures under which national executives operate in regard to the EU.

From pressures of membership to misfit

The Europeanization argument would suggest that the pressures on national executives sketched above, especially in terms of meeting obligations to engage the EU in areas where their own preferences may be at stake – uploading – and implementing EU policy output – downloading, will influence institutional change. More specifically, a rational institutionalist perspective would expect national executives to better protect their interests by influencing the EU arena in order to minimize the costs of policy implementation (Börzel, 2002). The constraints on national governmental policy manoeuvrability and the demands of EU engagement should lead 'rational, goal-oriented and purposeful' actors to adjust behaviour and organizational format in order to pursue and/or preserve resources. Other adaptive change in relation to the implementation of EU policies may result as a product of 'differential empowerment', and is more unpredictable. The 'goodness-of-fit' argument, or misfit, in this case of institutional change, rests on the assumption that national executives will implement change to the extent it brings efficiency gains in their pursuit of domestic goals at the EU level. The Europeanization literature on national executives does indeed produce evidence of change, in particular in the effort to put into place among the ministries coordination mechanisms in which EU policy competence is exercised. Coordination is vitally important in two respects. First, it produces a more integrated domestic voice in various EU forums, the better to argue a unified position and thereby negotiate inter-governmental compromises. Second, conscious effort at coordination reduces the likelihood of inter-ministerial rivalry over the 'ownership' of a particular policy, in light of the fact that many EU policies may cut across domestic policy domains. Apart from the actual coordination mechanisms themselves, there may be secondary effects, such as a change in the power or position of certain key actors, for example in the relationship between foreign ministers and prime ministers. The other major area of executive institutional change is related to the implementation of EU policies. In some cases, existing structures may be inadequate and new ones are created. Below is a more detailed investigation of these two areas of executive change.

Before tackling the issue of how national executives adjust to the demands of EU membership through their management of EU affairs, some definitions and comparative perspective are in order. Evaluating change in the 'core executive' allows us to bring some focus into the unit of analysis, so our definition of core executive refers to 'all those organisations, structures and roles that served to integrate the work of government in relation to Europe' (Laffan, 2003b: 5). This definition emphasizes political actors, such as prime ministers, as well as structures. One can further refine the focus by speaking of an inner and outer core, with the distinction resting upon the degree of Europeanization, that is, the extent to which EU policy competences characterize the work of ministries. Thus the different efforts through which core executives manage EU affairs, from the high politics of an EU Presidency or bargaining during an inter-governmental conference (IGC), to the low politics of coordinating policy areas through various government ministries, constitute the first part of our study. Second, we must bear in mind that national executives vary in terms of their constitutional status among EU member states. We speak for example of semi-presidential (France and Finland) and parliamentary types of executive systems. Within the parliamentary designation, we can also divide executives between those of majoritarian (e.g. the UK) and consensual (Belgium) systems. For our purposes, the differences between these types of executive systems is important because varying responses to the influence of the EU can be explained, among other factors, by different national institutions and structures. Degrees of centralization of the executive may impact on adaptive responses, as this could explain differences in the manner in which coordination among ministries is pursued. An executive usually governed by a single party as opposed to a coalition of parties may also feature in the analysis. In the case of coalition government, ministerial portfolios are held by politicians from different parties, each of whom defends their 'turf' from possible change. Finally, the territorial division of power – unitary, federal or quasi-federal (regionalized) – will also have a potential impact, especially in terms of vertical coordination. In this case, where sub-national actors have a policy responsibility that is also a EU competence, the national executive will have to bring on board the sub-national governments in order to construct a 'national' position. All of these features may influence the Europeanization process.

National coordination of EU affairs

Interacting with the EU in a manner that promotes national interests is the responsibility of the national executive. Kassim (2003; 2005) and Laffan (2003b), among others, have provided key comparative insights into executive adaptation in terms of coordination systems. What emerges from these studies is: (a) an increase in the attention given to EU affairs by prime ministers; (b) a challenge to foreign ministers' prerogatives in the area of EU affairs; (c) the creation of explicit inter-ministerial coordination mechanisms, and in some cases already-existing systems have gone through successive stages of evolution; (d) EU expertise according to policy area is now routine inside line ministries; (e) the linkages between permanent representatives and domestic executive functions have been strengthened; and (f) the creation of coordination mechanisms with sub-national actors in non-unitary states.

Prime ministers and EU activity

In many EU member states, prime ministers have become more engaged with EU affairs for at least two reasons, external and domestic. First, regarding the external context, the European Council, to which the prime minister acts as the government's representative, has become much more active since the early 1990s. Although formally the frequency of meetings has doubled, from only two to four, it is the workload that has increased in significance – in terms of both content and political impact. Lewis (2007) notes the accumulation of responsibilities of the European Council in 'such key subjects as institutional reform, the budget, enlargement, and foreign, security, and defence policy' (158). The European Council also becomes the scene at which politically sensitive issues are thrashed out between government leaders, for example reforms of budgetary contributions, constitutional design (the

EU Constitutional Treaty) and its re-design (Lisbon Treaty), and crisis management (after the French and Dutch referendum rejections of the Constitutional Treaty in 2005 and Irish 'No' to the Lisbon Treaty in 2008). The six-month rotating Presidency of the Council has also increased in its workload, a task that informally commences 18 months prior to the start date. Apart from the formal requirement to chair all COREPER and ministerial meetings, the Presidency also offers 'an important source of leadership in the EU, and member states see their turn at the helm as a chance to leave their imprint on the integration process' (Lewis, 2007: 160). Since the Presidency speaks on behalf of the EU on foreign policy matters, international crises can also test the diplomatic skills of a prime minister and foreign ministry. The first post-Communist member state to hold the Presidency, Slovenia in 2008, had a set of high expectations as not only a small state but the first of the new post-communist member states to hold a leadership position. The Slovenian Presidency was put under further pressure when, because of its EU foreign policy role, it had to respond to the events in Serbia regarding the unilateral assertion of sovereignty by Kosovo. The fact that this event happened in the territory of the former Yugoslavia, of which Slovenia was also a part, was not lost upon those with expectations of a suitable EU response (see Chapter 9 on Foreign Policy). The increased significance of EU summit decision-making also confers authority on the prime minister, and a 'knock-on effect of the growing authority of chief executives in coordination is a shift in resources toward the offices of the prime ministers, regardless of whether they are structurally weak or strong by tradition and constitutional design' (Johansson and Tallberg, 2008: 27).

The second, and domestic, reason for prime ministers to become more engaged with EU affairs is the rising political saliency of the EU in domestic politics. Whether it is the rise of eurosceptic public opinion or support for eurosceptic political parties, the EU has, in some member states, become an issue necessitating more considered political management. For this reason, it is plausible to assume that a prime minister, or his or her office, would want to assert more direct control over the public profile of their country's EU affairs, at the very least for electoral considerations (we will return to this development in the context of political parties in Chapter 6. Evidence of a trend to consolidate or take a leading role for EU affairs near to the prime minister – where this was not the case at first – is abundant. In France, the growth of EU influence over an ever-widening array of policy issues broadened the role of the prime minister in EU affairs rather than that of the president (further accentuated during periods of co-habitation). The president still takes the lead on foreign and security matters, but the prime minister is now much more involved in coordinating the vast amount of French involvement with EU decision-making than was the case before the SEA. In the UK, the prime minister's office, No 10 Downing Street, has since 1997 further strengthened its control over most aspects of EU affairs (to the detriment of the Foreign and Commonwealth Office), where the European Secretariat of the Cabinet Office has augmented its staff and resources, and its head given the 'position of Permanent Secretary, and the title of Prime Minister's Advisor on Europe and an office in No 10' (Bulmer and Burch, 2006: 43). In some cases an explicit shift of coordination of EU affairs from foreign ministries to prime ministers' offices occurred, for example in Sweden (Larue, 2006). There is also the case of Germany where an attempt by Chancellor Schröder in 2002 to expand the chancellor's role in EU coordination – already shared with the Economics and Finance ministries – at the expense of the Foreign Ministry (itself upgraded since only 1998) was made but rebuffed by the foreign minister, Mr Fischer (who as leader of the junior government coalition party, the Greens, was in a position to resist the attempt at centralization). In the post-communist member states, the immense effort to download the *acquis communautaire* as well as the politically high stakes of ensuring membership was attained, necessarily focused leadership on the prime minister's office, very often with the creation of a ministry for European affairs to explicitly coordinate efforts at meeting Commission targets. In all of these cases, the domestic political salience of EU matters determined the need for more politically sensitive calculations on the part of governments, perhaps an indirect acknowledgement that the EU was more than simply foreign policy and the potentially high stakes for national interests (especially for post-communist states).

The role of foreign ministers

The growing prominence of prime ministers in EU affairs, together with the emphasis on the coordination of ministerial responsibility, has come at the expense of the traditional role and influence of foreign ministries. Although it is not the case that there has been a wholesale transfer of responsibility out of the hands of the foreign minister, it is true that more coordination across ministries means less initiative by any one, including the foreign ministry. Apart from Hungary, all the post-communist member states opted to have prime minister-led coordination systems, but 'even in countries with Foreign Ministry led systems, the role of the Prime Minister in European affairs has increased' (Laffan, 2003b: 9). According to Kassim (2003), the role of the foreign minister in EU affairs has been eroded for a number of other reasons. One, the spread of EU competences in more policy areas brings additional ministries into the coordination system, thus reducing the prominence of the foreign ministry. Second, the increased number of EU-influenced policy areas means the need for better coordination among a greater number of line ministries, a capability that puts a foreign ministry at a disadvantage (and adds to the accretion of influence to the centre, that is, the prime minister's office). Third, officials from sub-national authorities are increasingly involved as well, for example in agricultural or development policies (more on Europeanization and sub-national actors in Chapter 5). Fourth, there is the spread and impact of 'new technology – fax machines and email – which puts domestic ministries into direct contact with their interlocutors in Brussels' (Kassim, 2003: 90).

Foreign ministers continue to be prominent actors in the coordination of a member state's EU policy, but the ability to project domestic preferences has become more complex due to the widespread intrusion of EU policy competence throughout central government. Specialization of foreign ministries to engage with EU responsibilities has occurred in foreign ministry-led member states, and very often where a minister for European Affairs exists it is placed in the foreign ministry. However, at the same time that the EU has become more involved in domestic policy, there has been a slow and incremental expansion of European foreign and security policy-making. So at the same time when there is a greater need to coordinate domestic policies that are intertwined with EU competences, member states are also, primarily through their foreign minister, obliged to engage at the European level on traditional issues of diplomacy and security in the context of CFSP. It may be more accurate to see member state foreign ministers having diminished responsibility for coordinating their overall EU responses and instead adapting to the EU architecture involving matters for which they traditionally were responsible.

Inter-ministerial coordination

A challenge for national governments seeking to promote their interests in EU policy-making is to ensure they 'get it right back home' in terms of putting forth their best response to EU policy initiatives or else in uploading their own preferences (Kassim *et al.*, 2000). Because the EU legislative timetable does not exactly match that of each member state, and further because the nature of many EU policies cuts across ministerial responsibility – environment being one of the most noted in this regard – there is a premium put upon coordination among national ministries in order that the government speaks with 'one integrated voice' in Brussels. The danger is that more powerful ministries will attempt to exert their own departmental preferences over those of others, and in the process a suboptimal position may be put forward. The challenge is therefore to put into place an inter-ministerial coordination system that aims to achieve the best national response over potential inter-ministerial rivalry. Bearing in mind that multi-party coalition government is common across EU member states, the need for an authoritative coordination system is all the more desirable if not urgent. For this reason, it is not surprising that in most cases the prime minister's office is the central site for these systems.

Inter-ministerial systems include Cabinet officials, committees set up to coordinate among ministries, special committees dealing with specifically cross-sectoral issues, etc. In post-communist member states, the great need to manage EU accession prompted the creation of inter-ministerial committees on European issues. Unlike the older member states, these countries' ambition to enter the EU as soon as possible put enormous pressure on the coordinating capacity of government ministries in order to download the *acquis communautaire* in as speedy and rational a manner as possible. In some older member states, pre-existing coordinating structures were given a new mission, as with the French SGCI (General Secretariat of the Interministerial Committee for European Economic Cooperation Affairs), originally set up to coordinate Marshall Plan resources in 1948 and then re-focusing on European integration issues with the signing of the Treaty of Rome in 1957. In some cases, such as in the UK, a progressive strengthening of the coordination structure has taken place in which the Cabinet Office European Secretary has become an integral part of the Prime Minister's advisory team. Both France and the UK point to the centralization of coordination under their respective prime ministers. In Germany, however, the original set-up did not include the prime minister (chancellor), and progressive reforms to coordination capacity, in which some actors changed, namely from the Economics to Finance ministry, the general logic remained the same. It has already been pointed out above that Chancellor Schröder attempted to bring coordination more firmly into the chancellery but failed. Inter-ministerial coordination, then, is widespread, but convergence as to the structure is absent, though the intent is manifest.

EU expertise inside line ministries

We began this section delineating a distinction between inner- and outer-core ministries. Inner-core ministries are those whose policy area is heavily intertwined with EU competence, for example Agriculture, Environment, Finance (especially for eurozone member states), Trade, and so on. Ministries with marginal EU involvement form the outer core, for instance Education. Special EU policy units, or at least an individual acting as the 'EU coordinator', inside line ministries have been created in order to interpret domestic responsibility for downloading EU policy but also in the drafting of the specific sectoral position. In addition, interaction with a ministry's sector clients requires knowledge of EU points of reference, and again the expertise in the ministry will rest with these EU policy experts.

Compliance with EU directives and regulations implies, among other things, the effective transposition of EU legislation in the first place. In most cases, existing national ministries and bureaucracies take responsibility. However, in some cases, EU policy will cause substantial changes, such as where an EU policy has no domestic counterpart. In these cases, new agencies within a ministry will have to be created. In other cases, the liberalization of a sector, for example energy, may mean a fundamental change in the nature of the mission that civil servants in the ministry or department concerned operate. In both of these cases, it is not simply the addition of EU policy experts that is needed, but a change in the administrative style that was previously the norm.

Permanent representatives

Permanent representatives of the member states play a crucial role in their respective government's attempts to coordinate national interaction with the EU at the supranational level. A basic and important factor backing up this claim is the location of the permanent representatives in the Council in Brussels. Holding the rank of Ambassador, all of the permanent representatives together constitute the body known by its French acronym COREPER. COREPER itself is part of the Council of Ministers routine operation, in which it prepares the agenda for Council meetings. The proximity to decision-making has a number of advantages, especially for those member states geographically distant from Brussels. First, it allows face-to-face interaction with EU officials as well as other national representatives. Second, the continual interpersonal interaction allows for informal methods of working alongside formal duties and procedures. Third, following from the previous point, permanence allows informal networks to develop that may be useful in the information-gathering duties of the representatives (Hayes-Renshaw and Wallace, 2006). These attributes are necessary for the function the permanent representatives play in the national coordination of EU policy. Kassim (2003) suggests that the permanent representatives have, in general, two functions: an 'upstream' function which is to act as the agent of the national executive in Brussels, and in which the aforementioned attributes are crucial, and a 'downstream' function which is to provide information and advice to the national executive that is used in its inter-governmental negotiation and policy development activities.

Although permanent representatives play a critical role in national EU coordination, there are marked differences among them, with many differences reflecting the policy styles of their respective member state executives. We have already distinguished between prime minister-led and foreign ministry-led coordination systems and an inner and outer core of EU policy-influenced ministries. Deriving from how the national coordination system operates, the permanent representatives themselves fit into this pattern. Following the distinction between upstream and downstream functions, Kassim (2003) maps these differences as follows: regarding *upstream* functions, some permanent representatives are actively involved in lobbying and attempting to influence EU institutions and policy agenda, whereas other are not, whether due to fewer resources to expend in this area and/or a different conception of the mission. Additionally, many permanent representatives are participants in the Brussels universe of private interest activities, allowing themselves to be contacted as part of the lobbying tactics of domestic actors. Finally, a minority of permanent representatives are involved in inter-sectoral coordination. In these upstream functions, resources, which in this case necessarily include personnel, are crucial in presenting a credible presence in Brussels, and together with a concerted focus on influencing the EU policy agenda, the UK permanent representation is regarded as the most intensive of the national delegations in Brussels. The UK permanent representative, which holds the rank of ambassador, is also firmly integrated within policy-making in London, with the opportunity 'to participate in EU policy making meetings within both the FCO [Foreign and Commonwealth Office] and Cabinet Office – an opportunity resented by some home-based officials and envied by some other ambassadors' (Allen and Oliver, 2006: 60). As for *downstream* functions, Kassim draws a distinction between 'centralized and department-led coordination systems' (2003: 101). In the former, permanent representatives are intimately involved in the inter-ministerial coordination system (whether prime minister- or foreign minister-led), including communication with line ministries and also to ensure nationally agreed positions are upheld by other national actors operating in Brussels. In the latter, permanent representatives are more directly the agents of the line ministries, with reduced status in relation to the central coordinators.

The overall picture, then, is of permanent representatives performing a key function in national EU coordination systems, but their part in this process varies from member state to member state. In the case of the post-communist member states, regardless of the type of coordination structure, the first few years of membership have demonstrated that their impact on EU agenda-setting is marginal, due to lack of resources and the time needed to 'learn the rules' of informal Brussels personal interaction. To this extent, they have been bystanders more than active participants in upstream functions, but this may change over time.

Coordination between national and sub-national actors

In federal or quasi-federal (regionalized) member states such as Germany or Spain there is an additional coordination process, that of aligning national policy positions with those actors at a sub-national level which also have some input, if not outright responsibility for certain policy areas. This relationship will vary according to constitutional frameworks, and it is also the case that relations may evolve over time and thereby impact the relative position (responsibility/power) of one or the other actor over policy development (see Chapter 5 for discussion of national–regional relations). National executives may be obliged to reach an agreement with sub-national actors, for example in agricultural policy, where the latter hold implementation influence or even jurisdiction. Thus, prior to national executive action at the EU level, an intra-governmental 'horizontal' coordination is necessary. Special central government–regional government coordination committees may be created (Spain), and in some cases sub-national actors even attend Council of Ministers meetings in Brussels alongside the national minister responsible for the policy that directly affects sub-national authority (Germany).

Institutional adjustment to EU policy output

Organizing the national executive in order to 'manage Europe from home' (Fink-Hafner and Lajh, 2003; Laffan, 2003b) is one indication of Europeanization or institutional change. Increasing the efficiency of decision-making, seeking to reconcile competing national ministries over policy jurisdiction, projecting national interests to appropriate actors in Brussels, etc., are all efforts that may occasion institutional change as a result of EU membership. To the extent changes are made, this reflects how a goal-based actor (the national executive) may adjust to the imperatives of its environment. The example of the resistance by the German foreign ministry to a change in its position in the national coordination system demonstrates that this adjustment is susceptible to veto players and other types of resistance, for example coalition partners, policy styles, etc. In general though, how national executives have managed their responsibility to project the national interest in the EU policy-making process is but one side of the coin in terms of Europeanization and national executives. Changes may also be brought about as a *consequence of complying* with Brussels, and it is to this phenomenon that we now turn.

A powerful incentive for national executives to arrange their coordination systems in order that a maximum effort is made to influence EU policy-making is the reduction of implementation costs. As EU competence has spread to more policy areas, and coupled with an expansion of qualified majority voting (QMV), member states may find that they are increasingly asked to implement directives and/or regulations for which there is no existing or a substantially different equivalent policy. Policy studies have captured the sometime disjuncture between an EU policy output and a member state's ability to implement it or the shift required in a domestic policy orientation. Examples of EU policy initiatives for which a domestic equivalent may not have existed previously is environmental policy, whether in the level of standards expected or even the nature of the specified area, e.g. habitat preservation. A EU policy initiative in which a member state's pre-existing policy domain requires a shift in the basic tenets of its operation, if not *raison d'être*, is Competition Policy, especially where it challenges the notion of so-called national industrial champions. In both policy areas, a national executive is expected to expend resources in (a) constructing the means by which to meet EU directives or regulations, or (b) revising the mission in which a policy actor has been invested over time, or both. Let us take these two examples and examine them in more detail, because it tells us much about the manner in which national executives institute change in their domestic operation, an obligation from which only non-compliance (itself generating a different set of costs) may temporarily deflect implementation.

Most of the EU policy output is regulatory in nature. As an example of positive integration – where after long negotiation a policy template is approved and then intended for national transposition and implementation – EU directives and regulations have an impact on domestic policy development and operation. But this impact varies the further away from the EU policy goal a member state's political economy is structured. For example, the development of a major EU responsibility in the area of environmental protection, especially since the mid-1980s (Lenschow, 2005), coincided with the preferences of a number of especially northern European member states. In fact, many of these same member states argued for and supported the expansion of EU competence in this policy area as a means of complementing their own policy goals. For other member states, though, environmental protection may have had a much lower priority for domestic public policy aims, yet these member states will be obliged to put into legislation and practice the measures aimed at reaching the goal set out in EU directives and regulations. In regard to institutional change, it has been the case that in order for certain member states to comply with the main thrust of EU environmental policy, it was necessary to first create an environment agency or ministry (as was the case in Spain). Even where such an authority existed, EU regulations may have caused these 'laggards' to build up their regulatory structures to meet new EU legislation, in a sense 'catching up' with environmental leaders. Nevertheless, administrative change traced back to EU inputs can affect all member states. A comparative study of ten EU member states' environmental policy by Jordan and Liefferink (2004) suggested that meeting EU goals 'helped to further centralize policy-making responsibilities in the hands of central government departments (e.g. the UK) and technical agencies (e.g. Sweden) at the expense of sub-national pollution control bodies and local or regional government (e.g. Germany)' (228). It may also be the case that a national policy is substantially altered in terms of its operating assumptions by engagement with EU policy norms and legislation, as the case of British environmental policy demonstrates. According to Jordan (2006), the UK, an early instigator of environmental policies – but premised on different operating bases than either the EU Commission and continental member states – gradually altered its policy focus and methods such that having 'once been a reluctant "taker" of policy determined in Brussels, the deep and politically painful Europeanization of national policy (Jordan, 2002: 2003) has gradually forced Britain (and in particular the Department of Environment) to invest more time and resources to positively "shape" EU policy in its own image' (246).

The impact of EU environmental policy on national environmental policies, and more importantly, the responsible central ministry or agency charged with meeting EU obligations, is but one example of how institutional change may arise as a reaction to the obligation to implement EU policy. Other examples could include the creation of national competition authorities to monitor aspects of mergers, a consequence of EU Competition Policy. The capability necessary to implement EU directives and regulations also has an effect on administrative structures. Although the EU has not been charged with creating an EU 'administrative space', and as there is no legal mandate for the EU to harmonize member states' public administration, nevertheless the obligation to fulfil EU legislative outputs does impact national administrative structures (Knill, 2001), for instance where they are weak (to increase the pressure for more resources) or where the inter-governmental relationship does not allow an agency the independence to carry out EU mandates. All of these are examples where the EU has, indirectly, impacted various dimensions of national executives through the obligation to implement EU policies.

Let us turn to the second EU policy area that distinguishes insti-tutional change, that of Competition Policy. Competition Policy falls more clearly into the category of negative integration, in that its purpose is to ensure that barriers to trade and other aspects of the Single Market which could be distorted due to national practices are reduced if not eliminated. Consequently, the aim of the Competition Policy is to ensure as level a playing field as possible for economic actors to freely compete. Scrutiny over mergers of a certain size, the legality of state aid, surveillance over certain types of monopolies, and so on, are all are activities in which the EU's Competition Policy has direct competence. As a consequence, national executives in some member states, where the political economy may reflect princi-ples somewhat removed from the EU model of free competition, find themselves in a position of having to redefine the mission of their economic intervention. A case in point is that of France, for which a policy of national champions meant that certain companies, reflect-ing a state investment preference, were given state aid in order to raise their competitiveness on a European or global scale. To the extent these payments could be considered as unfair to other domes-tic or European economic actors, such policies were required to be revised. The same can be said for state-owned monopolies, often seen in the area of public utilities such as water, gas, electricity, and so on. Long-standing national concepts of a social contract have maintained a public service requirement on the part of such compa-nies, and in countries such as France this has been manifested in monopolies (that is, competition in these areas was considered to be a threat to the public service tenet of universality). In another exam-ple, Germany, not only are national principles and practices of economic activity challenged, but also relations between national and sub-national actors and between sub-national actors and the Commission. In the former case, since the mid-1990s the Commission, backed by the ECJ, has criticized the operation of German *Landesbanken*. These banks provide cheap credit to German small and medium-sized industries, and have done so for decades, contributing in part to the German post-Second World War economic miracle. These banks are supported by state guarantees, and have been the target of the Commission and private banks that consider their position to be unfair. Although German authorities have sought to protect the role of *Landesbanken*, from 2005 their state guarantees have been stripped and the Commission has contin-ued to insist on their restructuring. On the other hand, the German states, or *Länder*, have sought to protect their prerogatives through influencing German national government negotiations at the EU level and so maintain subsidies for social protection where they have responsibility. Competition Policy has employed, as a method of increasing competitiveness in certain sectors, a liberalization process. Essentially the opening up of an economic sector of activity to competition, it may lead to privatization of state monopolies and/or deregulation, the intent being to open a sector to previously excluded competitors, national and international.

How does this impact the national executive? Certainly the *role* that a national executive plays in regulating economic activity is changed. In a member state with a large public sector this means redefining the role and responsibility of the national executive, essentially introducing a more pluralist operating environment. Where, for example, liberalization in railways has proceeded, the relationship between a transport ministry and the public railway agency will change in fundamental ways, as the nature of direction and autonomy is altered. Héritier and Knill (2001) suggest the variance of such changes depends on three factors: (1) the prevailing stage of liberalization (quite often we see the UK and France at either ends of the spectrum in this regard); (2) the dominant belief system; and (3) the reform capacity of a country. Whatever the specific constellation of these factors in a member state, it is the national executive that will be in the front line of absorbing the pressures for conformity if EU inputs are particularly pronounced. Executive ministries or agencies will find their mission redefined – this may mean the scaling back of interventionist activities, and a further consequence will be their relative position within the overall executive in terms of resources and political influence. Another area outside of market considerations in which executive functions may be redefined is in the policy domain of justice and home affairs, especially with regard to immigration issues such as asylum. Although the development of EU directives regarding asylum have been long in the making, the national ministries involved have been obliged to develop new discourses and adjust to the new legal norms that have been introduced. Guiraudon (2004) characterizes the influence of the EU in national immigration actions as one that favours 'soft norms and informal and technical co-operation. Consequently, the impact of EU decision-making on national policies cannot simply be measured in terms of the transposition of EU laws. EU policies influence the way in which immigration and asylum are perceived and discussed in the member states, and legitimize a restrictive approach to migrant and refugee flows' (179). For some member states whose pre-existing approach to migrants may have been different from the post-9/11 emphasis, their relevant ministry will have had to import new operating assumptions.

Strengthening of the national executive vis-à-vis national legislatures

Let us return to the argument advanced by Moravscik that the national executive has been strengthened by the process of European integration relative to other domestic actors and institutions. The argument turns on the privileged position of the executive, which is part of the EU decision-making process as well as the main interlocutor between the EU and the domestic polity as a whole. We have already mentioned that the changes influenced by the EU within the executive may alter the relations or balance of power among ministries, with the prime minister's office seeing the greatest accrual of influence, for example *vis-à-vis* the foreign ministry. Analyses of the impact of the EU on domestic inter-institutional relations, especially between the executive and the legislature, have generally concluded that executives are the 'winners' while legislatures have become the 'losers' in this process of adaptation. In this particular case, it would be more accurate to speak of a *relative* strengthening. Although the impact of the EU on national legislatures is explored in more depth in the following chapter, the basis of the argument concerning winners and losers, at least in executive–legislative relations, is based upon proximity to decision-making, control of information, and institutional versus partisan prerogatives.

What the preceding discussion has made clear is that above all other domestic actors – government institutions as well as private actors – the national executive is embedded in many of the most crucial decision-making pathways of European governance at the supranational level. This unparalleled proximity to decision-making, which allows advance warning of *other* member state initiatives, is something that continues to place the national executive at the centre of domestic pressure for policy-related change. Because of its inclusion in key parts of EU decision-making, the national executive remains the best avenue, instrumentally speaking, for private domestic actors to transmit their demands as well as a site for pressuring the EU, that is, via the national executive as a member of the Council of Ministers and the European Council. With regard to a national parliament, the stated need to have 'room for negotiation' in inter-governmental bargaining is a major reason why national executives find themselves free of *ex ante* controls from their respective parliamentary EU affairs committee. Further reinforcing this point is the national executive's control of information. It is not just the proximity to EU decision-making, but it is also control over information inside the Brussels policy-making process that allows the executive a dominant position *vis-à-vis* the parliament. This is not to say a national parliament is completely bereft of the means with which to monitor developments in Brussels. At the very least, members of the European Parliament are representatives of national political parties, most of whom are found in national parliamentary parties, so a liaison function can exist. Still, as will be discussed in Chapter 3, national parliaments have a domestic priority and details of European policy-making occupy a minor part of their daily work. Even more, the process of voting on EU legislation, that is, its transposition into national law, involves responding to executive preparation of EU directives and regulations, so that the dependent relationship is part of the national legislative process. National executives send information on the details of EU legislation to their respective parliaments, but the amount and timing of this is usually, in most cases, such that only a portion of the mass of information can be processed by the parliament or its committees. Finally, we can note that the national executive is reinforced in its position *vis-à-vis* a national parliament by partisan politics, that is, government–opposition dynamics, which in most cases means that the majority in a parliament will not use their institutional basis to undermine their party (or parties) in government. These three factors, therefore, act to strengthen the national executive *vis-à-vis* the parliament. An unintended consequence no doubt; but pressure to change the status quo in favour of more substantial parliamentary control has not been forthcoming.

The national executive in the post-communist context

In a sense, the same dynamics that have resulted in the strengthening of national executives in the older member states have been present in the post-communist states as well, though in what one might term a 'hyper-intense' form and occurring before the actual date of entry into membership. The difference is explained by the pressure to ensure a successful coordination of the accession negotiations, and made all the more intense because of the desire of the post-communist political elites to complete the various chapters in the negotiation process as quickly as possible. Sedelmeier (2006) notes that a 'novelty in the context of eastern enlargement is that the EU has undertaken considerable efforts to influence administrative practices in candidates, including civil service reforms, or anti-corruption' (15–16). Lippert *et al.* (2001: 1004) and others high-light the impact of the pre-accession period on post-communist executives, and although arguing against convergence across these states, underline the centrality of the role of the 'core executive':

> membership negotiations are the 'hour of the executive', and central executives have intensive interactions with the EU institu-tions, especially the Commission and Council at political and, even more intensively, expert levels. In the context of the membership negotiations, an EU-related 'core executive' is emerging within the national arenas ... including national cabi-nets, officials from the Foreign Ministries, the national European integration bodies and other high-ranking civil servants from the ministries involved.

Pre-existing structures, however fluid in this period of new regime institutionalization, together with national traditions also explain the variation of the special ministries or agencies set up in most post-communist states to coordinate EU affairs, in particular negotia-tions over the various chapters of the *acquis*. In particular, Dimitrova and Toshkov (2007) argue that 'institutional change in the context of domestic politics offers the most useful way forward' (982) to explain not only the diversity of such arrangements, but also the 'lack of "stickiness" of the EU coordination structures in the new member states' (982), many of which have changed since accession in terms of organization and respective influence within the executive. Overall, the strengthening of the post-communist executive can be explained partly by the historic nature of the efforts to join the EU, encompassing a significant focus on inter-ministerial coordination, a mobilization having consequences for the develop-ment of executive–legislative relations as well.

Conclusion: explaining national variation in executive change

The discussion of national executive adaptation to EU influence has remained at a fairly general level in this chapter. Certainly there are structural differences between national executives across member states, and these differences may indicate the ease or resistance with which change takes place. We have already drawn attention to the fact that prime ministers may have the desire to centralize 'high' EU affairs in their hands or offices, but this may be resisted by foreign ministers and others, especially when they are representatives of another political party (in this sense their political position may characterize them as a 'veto player'). Division of an executive between a prime minister and a president, especially where the president wields more than ceremonial duties, for example in France or Poland, may also call into question the line of responsibility for EU affairs in areas of foreign and security policies. The territorial division of authority and administration is another factor, as federal systems' dispersion of competences may act as a brake on national executive centralizing tendencies, even on the issue of representing national interests in EU forums. National executives are also situated on top of national public bureaucracies, and these too represent different national traditions: the Anglo-American, the Napoleonic and the Germanic. Such structural and political differences filter external pressures and explain why there is not a convergence around one style of national executive behaviour. This said, however, there appears to be an exception: post-communist national executives. The literature points quite strongly in the direction of a strengthening of national executives precisely because of the enormous challenge to make entry into the EU a speedy success (and not to be left behind other such states). In the process of taking charge of pre-accession negotiations, these national executives had to ensure the successful legislative transposition and implementation of the entire *acquis communautaire*, all the while aware they were scrutinized by the Commission to an unprecedented degree. With such high stakes, national executives, in a period of institutional transition from the previous regime, were able to assert their authority and therefore reinforce their resource base much more than other governmental institutions. The Europeanization of post-communist national executives was consequently a much more highly visible and rapid process than in the West.

Finally, it is appropriate to discuss some of the methodological issues involved in analysing Europeanization and national executives. As discussed in Chapter 1 isolating the EU effect is crucial, as there may be simultaneous competing influences, both internal and external to the actor or institution in question. With regard to national executives, other pressures may have been occurring simultaneously, or are even endemic to the institution. First, we have put a great store in coordination pressures upon national executives, particularly the core executive, that may result in strengthening some ministries or departments over others. Yet coordination pressures, between core ministries and those agencies or departments that have specialized clients, have been a major problem in governing for quite some time. Second, changes experienced in terms of the so-called New Public Management reforms of the past couple of decades, affecting public bureaucracies, are motivated less by international obligations than by the spread of ideas about efficiency and market-competitive dynamics. As for alternative explanations of change related to international forces other than the EU, it could be said that although the development of the EU since the mid-1980s has been important, a case could be made that successive multilateral trade rounds and the authority of the World Trade Organization (WTO) has been critical. Coupled with the liberalization and internationalization of financial markets, national executives have had no choice but to be sensitive towards international economic conditions, to the extent that late twentieth- and early twenty-first-century globalization arguments claim to be witnessing a change to the very nature of western states. Nevertheless, this chapter demonstrates that at the very least, the EU has had a profound impact on national executives and their relationship to other domestic institutions through the added role and responsibilities they play in the context of European governance. Indirectly, national executives' involvement in EU decision-making also contributes to a distancing of elected and non-elected national officials from citizens and their representatives in national parliaments.

Chapter 3

National Parliaments

Europeanization and institutional change regarding national parliaments very quickly bring into centre stage the issue of how the EU may impact the quality of democracy – or at least the efficacy of national parliamentary procedures in relation to representation and accountability. The degree to which executive–legislative relations have altered was briefly treated in the previous chapter. This present chapter takes a much more direct focus and investigates institutional and behavioural change by national parliaments in order to maintain some part of national government input in EU policy-making; put another way, this chapter evaluates the steps taken by parliaments to keep themselves 'in the loop' as regards EU matters. Such efforts may be linked with normative concerns about representation, especially when one considers that elections to national parliaments have virtually no 'EU' content, and yet it is the national parliament that votes on legislation in which the national executive may have been involved in fashioning.

National parliaments: 'losers' in the integration process?

Any discussion of how domestic politics may have been impacted by the European Union could follow several paths. One line of debate could focus on institutional change, as was the case in the preceding chapter on national executives. A second strand of inquiry might analyse the terms of partisan competition, as, after all, the member states of the EU are all parliamentary democracies in which competitive elections allow the choice of government. Yet another angle on the question over how domestic politics, or rather the *practice of democratic* politics, to be more precise, may have altered due to the influence of the EU, would be to evaluate issues of representation and accountability. The national parliament is the institution that brings all three of these lines of analysis together in a discussion of Europeanization and national politics. As with all national governmental institutions in EU member states, there will of course be variation on the precise role this institution plays in relation to the national executive, the details of the legislative process, and the attraction it holds for organized interests. From the relative marginality of the French legislature (the Assemblée Nationale) to the centrality of the German parliament (the Bundestag) in national political life and decision-making, parliaments remain the institution from which executives emerge (or in the case of France, must share a portion of power in *co-habitation* episodes) and thereby structure the critical political 'moment' in any parliamentary democracy's political cycle. How the EU might affect the operation and role of this national institution is therefore a vital question in relation to the issue of Europeanization and parliamentary democracy. This chapter explores the argument that national parliaments have become the 'victims' of or 'losers' from the European integration process. The basic point made in this charge is that the process of EU decision-making has added to a broader 'de-parliamentarization' in which 'the development of European integration has led to an erosion of parliamentary control over executive office-holders' (O'Brennan and Raunio, 2007a: 2). Chapter 3 touched briefly on this phenomenon from the position of executive enhancement *vis-à-vis* other domestic governmental institutions. In this chapter, the 'loser' thesis is explored more fully, as well as any evidence of adaptive change. This will then allow a discussion of the misfit hypothesis in order to characterize any Europeanization dynamics. As in the previous chapter, isolating the EU effect is a paramount task in Europeanization research, and consequently the de-parliamentarization thesis must be analysed in this light. The chapter will conclude with a discussion of the normative consequences of the alleged loss of status by national parliaments, usually framed in a discussion labelled the 'democratic deficit' and focused on executive–legislative relations.

The national executive has been the prime interlocutor between domestic interests and policy-making and the EU (see Chapter 2). Where do national parliaments fit into this relationship? This is a critical question, because if a case is to be made concerning the Europeanization of national parliaments, whether a direct or indirect impact, we must know the lines of interaction in order to be able to trace and isolate the EU effect from competing pressures. The simple answer is that national parliaments engage EU decision-making through their relationship with their respective national executives, not directly with EU institutions. This is not to say that there is a complete absence of contact between national parliaments and EU institutions; for instance, through a committee known as COSAC (Conference of Community and European Affairs Committees of Parliaments of the European Union), member state national parliament and European Parliament representatives meet to discuss mutual issues affecting relations between themselves. Put simply, national parliaments are not directly involved in the routine decision-making process at the EU level. Their primary role in the process of European governance is at the end of the legislative process, that is, to ratify EU legislation that has been put before them by the national executive. We will see that there are national variations, as would be expected with different traditions of parliamentary democracy. But the general characteristic of all EU member state parliaments in regard to European policy-making is their marginality. With this being the historical context, if change occurs in the internal operation of parliaments or in their relation to the executive, identifying a EU causal link, or more precisely the EU-related mechanism of change, may require an additional approach to a strictly institutionalist one, including a constructivist understanding. Likewise, identifying 'veto players' or institutional rules that affect institutional change will be important. All of these factors are considered below, but first a general description of the role of national parliaments is presented, and particularly where EU legislation is concerned.

Role and responsibilities of national parliaments in EU affairs

Historically, national executives were responsible for the early development of the European integration process, as befits what was primarily an inter-governmental organization with an innovative supranational actor. Although the role of the Commission as a key player from the 1980s onwards is recognized, the absence of a politicized public opinion – the so-called 'permissive consensus' – enabled national executives to negotiate among themselves without having to take into account any domestic constraints; in other words, during the first few decades of European integration, national executives did not play a two-level game involving their domestic publics (but differing conceptions of European integration among the founding members and later entry conditions for post-communist candidates could be construed to be a type of constraint, though externally generated). The permissive consensus extended to most mainstream political parties as well, and European integration was therefore not an issue in national elections at least until the late 1990s. The few exceptions prove the rule – Denmark and the United Kingdom being the only two member states in which eurosceptic attitudes in major parties and public opinion were found. The absence of a role for national parliaments in the European integration process was therefore not contested – internally the main parliamentary groups did not push the issue in the context of government-opposition dynamics and externally national parliaments did not challenge the prerogatives of national executives in EU negotiations. Their role in most cases, apart from the occasional ratification of a new treaty, was to vote on the legislation that had made its way from the EU to the national level. National parliaments, removed from the process of uploading and negotiating domestic interests at the EU level, and uninvolved in most executive shaping of EU directives in which some national input is allowed during transposition into national law (that is, framework directives), have been passive actors playing a bit part at the end of the legislative process. This state of affairs characterized the situation in most member states (Denmark being an exception, which will be discussed below). That this set of circumstances did not arouse any concerted calls for change by national parliaments can be explained, at least until the mid-1980s, by the fact that a good portion of European-level legislation was (a) of a non-controversial nature, (b) did not amount to very much in terms of its impact on domestic policies (apart from policies such as agriculture), and (c) the EU itself (or EC) had a very low profile in member states' national politics, the integration process itself bearing depictions such as 'euro-sclerosis', etc. All told, attention to the role of national parliaments in the European policy and decision-making process was minimal because there was no perceptible need for them to alter their relationship with the national executive.

Before turning to the question of Europeanization and national parliaments directly, it is necessary to keep in mind the variation that exists among national parliaments. Although Chapter 3 discussed national executive relations with the EU in general terms, this is justified not only by the fact that they are constitutionally responsible for the position taken by a member state in regard to EU legislation, but also by the fact that in relation to other domestic actors and institutions, one can also acknowledge a common orientation. This is despite slight variations in terms of federal vs. unitary states, pluralist v. neo-corporatist interest intermediation systems, and executive–legislative relations. However, on this last point, characterized as the dominance by the executive of member state policy and decision-making *vis-à-vis* the EU, from the reverse perspective there is very much an institutional variation among national parliaments in regard to their relationship to the executive. Put succinctly, national parliaments differ in terms of responsibility within their respective legislative processes, and we should consider this fact before proceeding to discuss their role in EU affairs and matters of institutional change. The first point to consider is the role of parliaments in lawmaking, and this can be divided into types of governments – majoritarian or consensual – and their role regarding oversight of the executive, and this is a matter of degree. In the first case, lawmaking in majoritarian systems, the executive has a predominance over the legislative process. In consensual systems, usually a strong system of committees allows the parliament to have a considerable role in the development of legislation, from amendments to control over the agenda. In both of these cases there is of course a degree of variation, but majoritarian systems in general – for instance UK, Ireland and Greece – the parliament does not play a decisive role in the domestic legislative process, while in consensual systems – Germany, the Netherlands and Austria, for example – the executive must take into account positions of parliamentary parties in order to successfully promote its agenda. The other role of parliaments, in addition to lawmaking, is to scrutinize the legislation promoted by the executive. The most widely employed and most effective means to do so is through the use of committees to monitor government departments. These 'select' committees, as well as others such as standing committees, focus on scrutinizing legislation and investigating matters of concern. Their influence may depend on several factors, such as expertise, administrative support, and size (small is better).

In both roles, however, a key intermediating factor explaining the nature of the institutional relationship between the parliament and executive is the role and influence of parties, whether in single-party or coalition government. The degree to which a parliament – as an institution – interacts with the government, is conditioned by the central fact that the internal operation of parliaments is controlled by political parties organized into parliamentary party groups. The most common mode of parliamentary–government relations is the inter-party mode, that is, a relationship characterized by government-opposition dynamics (Andeweg and Nijzink, 1995; and Holzhacker, 2008). The least common type of interaction is the non-party mode in which parliament acts as a whole body. The effect of this reality is that the party in government is also a prime actor within the parliament, even more so in a majoritarian system. Even in consensual systems, parties in the government coalition have an incentive to work together to pass 'their' legislation. There may of course be other factors that slightly mitigate the influence of parties, such as the particular political culture or constitutional or other institutional rules, but the central fact that even committee work is influenced by party calculations brings the power of parliaments into some context for a discussion of how they may be affected by the development of the EU. In other words, if change were to occur that could be traced to the influence of the EU in some manner, then the mechanisms of change and potential veto or facilitating actors would have to include political parties.

Institutional change: multiple causes?

From the picture sketched so far as to the role of national parliaments in the business of EU policy and decision-making, Europeanization-related dynamics of pressure or 'misfit' might seem inappropriate in this institutional case. Yet, as this section will demonstrate, there has indeed been, interestingly, a common type of institutional change across all member state parliaments. If the picture sketched so far of parliamentary detachment from EU affairs is correct, how can we speak of pressure from the EU producing any adaptive change? If, as suggested, there is indeed evidence of change, can we trace the source back to the EU, or are there other competing or even complementary factors? The focus of this discussion will be directed to examples from parliaments of the pre-2004 member states, while the case of post-communist states are treated in a separate sub-section below, as the impact of the EU on parliaments in the process of institutionalizing or consolidating political pluralism is fundamentally different from that of already established parliaments in the pre-2004 member states.

EU affairs committees

Institutional change among all national parliaments relating directly to EU concerns took place primarily during the 1980s and early 1990s, that is, the creation of EU affairs committees (EACs). Variously known as the EU Scrutiny Committee (UK), Delegation for the European Union (France), Special Committee for EC Affairs (Italy), and so on, these committees were created mostly in the mid-to-late 1980s. They are similar in their general purpose, that is, to coordinate parliamentary scrutiny of the government in EU affairs and legislation. O'Brennan and Raunio (2007b) state that 'the exact roles and legal powers of these committees do vary, but this should not hide the plain fact that the EACs perform broadly similar functions throughout the Union' (274). These committees represent a refinement of the parliamentary scrutiny of EU legislation that was in place beforehand, either in standing committees or as part of the remit of a foreign affairs committee. The states which acceded in 1973 set up EACs, but these varied widely in their actual influence, from almost nil (Ireland) to the most powerful in all EU member states (Denmark). The membership of these committees varies, from MPs to a combination of MPs and MEPs (the case for instance in Belgium). In almost all cases, the EACs play an advisory role, evaluating EU legislation and producing a position that the executive may or may not follow. The exception to this relationship is found in only a few member states, such as Denmark, in which ministers are required to spell out their general negotiating positions, and Austria and Germany, where proposed legislation that may have an effect on federal–*Länder* relations are given more direct scrutiny.

In line with the Europeanization assumption that prior institutional arrangements explain not only whether or not adaptational change occurs, but also the degree and nature of the change, so too with national parliament's creation of EACs one can detect how prior executive–legislative relations influence the nature of the EAC role. Auel and Rittberger (2006) have argued that, as a 'comparative analysis of domestic parliaments' responses revealed, the strategic adjustment of national parliaments to European integration depends to a large degree on the respective institutional context' (137). They note both a formal or institutional Europeanization, and an informal, 'strategic' Europeanization, what we might also term institutional and behavioural. In the first example, the institutional response has resulted in the right for parliament to receive information from their respective governments on EU affairs, and to process and coordinate a parliamentary response through the creation of an EAC, giving them a scrutiny function. Auel and Rittberger recognize the inherent weakness in a parliament's position *vis-à-vis* the executive, and how this institutional response does not, in itself, establish any co-institutional equivalence between the two in national–EU decision-making. They point to the centrality of party politics and the continued dependence of the parliament upon the executive for information. Nevertheless, they suggest that in practice, there is a variety of strategic actions that help to mitigate the institutional weakness. The ability of a parliament to expand its potential in EU affairs does, however, depend on its structural position in a political system. Consequently, there is a range of possible strategies that can emerge, but success is not guaranteed. From parliaments most dominated by the executive, for example the House of Commons in the United Kingdom, where the EAC position may be ignored by the executive, a strategy of public debate and scrutiny, even 'public embarrassment', is endorsed in order to have the government at least explain its position. The other end of the spectrum is represented by Denmark's EAC in the Folketing, where through internal cooperation with the executive, and a primary interest in the strategic interests of Denmark rather than an adversarial position invoking the withholding of a mandate, the government takes seriously its obligation to keep the parliament informed of its negotiating positions in the Council of Ministers (Jensen, 2007). These two examples also represent another type of party-political dynamic in parliament, the Westminster or confrontational government-opposition setting (the UK) and the consensual, multi-party (and minority government) model. This political-cultural aspect of legislative–government relations also goes some way toward explaining the differential Europeanization response by national parliaments.

Finally, EACs do in fact have a European-level dimension, a relationship of sorts with the European Parliament (EP). The institutional linkage between national parliaments and the EP is the Conference of EC Affairs Committees of the National Parliaments and the European Parliament, known by its French acronym COSAC. COSAC was established in 1989 after a meeting of presidents of the parliaments of member states agreed in May 1989 to reinforce the role of their respective parliaments in the EU process by bringing together their EACs. The first meeting of EACs with representatives of the EP took place in November 1989, and subsequent meetings took place at biannual intervals. These meetings of COSAC afford an opportunity for the EP to brief its national counterparts on developments that have led to its own enhancement since the Single European Act, the Maastricht and Amsterdam Treaties, etc. From the perspective of the EP this dialogue is important because concern has been expressed in some member states at one time or another that the increase in the EP – or any supranational EU institution – would lead to a concomitant weakening of national institutions, a type of zero-sum equation. COSAC has allowed the EP to communicate its position regarding the desire for a general enhancement of national as well as EU-level parliamentary input into the EU process directly to national parliamentary representatives. The formal recognition of this position was recognized in Declaration 13 of the Treaty on European Union (Maastricht), on the role of national parliaments in the European Union. Later, national parliaments were to appear again in an EU treaty, this time in the ill-fated Constitutional Treaty and its successor, the Lisbon Treaty. In the Constitutional Treaty (and carried over into the Lisbon Treaty), two protocols deal with the role of national parliaments: the 'Protocol on the Role of National Parliaments in the European Union' and the 'Protocol on the Application of the Principles of Subsidiarity and Proportionality'. The 'former Protocol is designed to make national MPs better informed about the European decision-making process, while the latter focuses specifically on monitoring the subsidiarity principle' (Raunio, 2007: 83). Inter-parliamentary relations between the EP and national parliaments are part of the protocols, so although only in the form of protocols, national parliaments have a right, as agreed by their national governments, to a limited role in the EU process.

Intra-regime pressure to adapt?

The Europeanization argument emphasizes mechanisms of change such as the 'goodness of fit', in particular for institutional change. This mechanism of domestic change, as suggested above, would seemingly be difficult to attribute to national parliaments, as they have no formal interaction with EU policy and decision-making *per se*. As we have seen, national parliaments come into the picture at the end of the entire process, essentially to ratify decisions taken and policies crafted by EU institutional actors and national executives.

If, as presented in the previous chapter, national executives have undergone institutional change that we can trace back to the EU (among other influences), this is because they are intimately, if not constitutionally, key actors within the EU governance process itself. The pressure, such as it exists, derives from domestic goal-seeking motivations on the part of national executives, wishing to both exploit the EU as an opportunity structure and seek to protect what prerogatives they do maintain by uploading their preferences, for policy-related issues as well as EU institutional matters. National parliaments, on the other hand, do not *act* in Brussels, whether to lobby for a particular policy or for reform of an institution. National parliaments are not, in a *formal* inter-institutional sense, part of the domestic preference-formation process that national executives then promote and/or defend in Brussels. The expansion of the EU's policy scope also has no direct bearing on the function of national parliaments, as some have argued is indirectly the case with national executives, namely, the transfer of certain policy competences from the national to the EU level results in narrower policy manoeuvrability for national governments. In the case of national parliaments, less direct involvement in certain policy areas does not, in itself, 'upset' parliamentary processes, though an argument based on normative standards of parliamentary democracy could be invoked. If the traditional functions of parliaments can be listed as representation, deliberation, legislation, authorization of expenditure, and scrutiny of the executive, the formal increase in the power and influence of the EU does not directly impact any of these except scrutiny of the executive. In this case, the actions of the executive, such as negotiating positions taken before or during Council of Ministers or European Council meetings, that is, *ex ante* and *ex post* accountability to parliament, escape the routine channels of parliamentary scrutiny (this is mitigated slightly in the case of Denmark's EAC). Thus the case can be made that, unlike national executives, the EU has no direct impact upon the domestic operation of national parliamentary action. Can one also make the same claim in relation to indirect influences?

An indirect EU influence on a domestic institutional actor – one that has no formal interaction with the EU – must by definition suggest the introduction of new variables in the wider operating environment of the institution, variables whose source involves the EU. Can the case be made, then, that there is an indirect EU impact on national parliaments? In order to answer this question, one must first discern whether or not there are indeed any 'pressures' on national parliaments' wider environment, and then determine the cause. In this context, we turn to the de-parliamentarization thesis, an argument that the EU has indeed contributed to changes in the wider domestic political system of member states with consequences for parliaments. The de-parliamentarization argument is based on twin dynamics emanating from the EU (O'Brennan and Raunio, 2007a; Goetz and Meyer-Sahling, 2008). The first component of the argument is constitutional; very simply, the formal (constitutional) transfer of policy competence to the EU – either in part or whole – has deprived a national parliament of that proportion of legislative policy oversight that it might ordinarily have. Therefore, so the argument runs, parliaments' involvement in the policy output that they are called upon to ratify has diminished. The second part of the argument concerns political control in the EU policy process. Not only are national parliaments uninvolved at early stages of EU policy development, but also the strengthening of the national executive due to its position or function in supranational decision-making further distances parliaments from intimate knowledge of negotiation at various levels and points in the process. The expansion of qualified majority voting in the Council of Ministers over an ever-widening set of policies further distances the ability of any single member state parliament from influencing EU decision-making. The result of these twin dynamics has been the labelling of national parliaments as the 'losers' (Maurer and Wessels, 2001) of European integration. From another perspective, to be discussed in more depth below, the de-parliamentarization thesis also contributes to the debate concerning a so-called 'democratic deficit' in the EU, especially as it is identified at the national level (complementing the deficit at the European level, which takes into account the relative weakness of the European Parliament *vis-à-vis* other EU institutions).

From the perspective of Europeanization research, where isolating the EU factor is crucial in any attempt to develop a research agenda, one must ask if there are any other plausible alternative explanations to the weakening of national parliaments. In fact, O'Brennan and Raunio (2007a) present an important corrective to this picture of EU-related factors impinging on domestic parliamentary perquisites. They draw attention to the literature of the past twenty to thirty years analysing the growing weakness of parliaments *vis-à-vis* the executive based on factors that generally do not involve the EU (exceptions include, for example, Strøm, Müller and Bergman (2006)). In general, a variety of analyses point to a decline in the power of parliaments relative to their respective executives based on a number of reasons, from the longer duration of coalition governments, presidentialization of executives, of which globalization may be a contributing factor, to the growth in the role of the public bureaucracy. So, to assert that national parliaments have been weakened by virtue of the growth in influence of the EU must be set into a more complex context. The concern in this chapter is whether the de-parliamentarization argument that is affiliated with EU influences should rather be reconstructed into an argument that the EU acts as a contributing factor to a broader dynamic of de-parliamentarization, and what changes, if any, have been instigated by this particular input. In this respect, then, we need to be able to isolate the role of the EU in this more general phenomenon. If there are trends already in play weakening the position of national parliaments, then does the example of EU de-parliamentarization add to this state of affairs, or have no impact at all? Have parliaments sought to correct for their decline, in particular in relation to EU influences? Investigating these questions demands a careful focus, and as changes in the role of a parliament can be of a constitutional or behavioural nature within the domestic political system, or both, attention must be directed to both institutional and non-institutional types of evidence.

If we accept a *general* de-parliamentarization thesis, it is then more accurate to state that within this broader phenomenon the relationship between EU decision-making and national executive behaviour has added to the growing marginality of national parliaments. As national parliaments are not directly engaged at the supranational level, the diminution of their role lies within their respective political systems, and, more exactly, in their relationship with the executive. Here one must note that not all legislative–executive relations are alike. In other words, some are more influential in their political systems than others, with the main differences manifested in their ability to influence domestic legislation and hold the executive accountable. Bearing in mind that that the inter-party mode is predominant, for a parliament to act in such a manner that the executive must make an effort in maintaining support, there is usually an institutional explanation: the rules defining roles, which are often fairly well rooted in a political system, and often underpinned by the political culture. Lawmaking and scrutiny are functions constitutionally regulated in national political systems. The means by which this is carried out – and strengthened where possible – is through the use of committees. The power among parliaments in their ability to influence legislation and hold executives accountable varies, with a rough distinction in effectiveness among parliaments with a few large-member committees, those with smaller and more numerous committees, and those of a majoritarian or consensual political culture. For example, countries such as Germany and Denmark have effective scrutiny committees and a consensual political culture. France and Greece have weak committee systems and are majoritarian. In majoritarian countries the government dominates the parliament, and, bearing in mind the role that parties perform, the opposition parties in such political systems have an extremely limited capacity to influence legislation or to affect government activities. In consensual systems, the effort on acting as politically inclusively as possible allows committees a more integrated role in the legislative process. As for committee scrutiny powers, where they are smaller and more numerous, even in consensual systems, government-opposition dynamics mark the limitations of these committees in their ability to press the government on certain issues.

With these distinctions between parliaments in terms of their relationship to the executive in mind, how might the EU intrude upon this relationship? The 'EU de-parliamentarization' argument posits that national executives are increasingly able to escape scrutiny by their parliaments and also that parliaments are only involved in the legislative process towards the final stages, when the opportunity for amendment is practically non-existent. Indirectly, then, both the more direct change between national executives and the EU and the indirect change on the part of executive–legislative relations do highlight the influence of the EU in domestic parliamentary fortunes. Even so, the EU as an environmental factor does not directly change – in formal or legal terms – the executive–legislative relationship. Furthermore, the internal operation of national parliaments is not disturbed, and in fact the supranational connection to EU policy-making – that is, national executive participation in EU policy and decision-making in Brussels – remains, for members of national parliaments, unknown or unimportant to the practice of politics in the domestic parliamentary arena (Poguntke *et al.*, 2007). Despite the fact that opportunities do exist for national parliamentarians to acquaint themselves with greater detail of EU policy and legislative matters, especially through the activities of their respective party members in the European Parliament, this has not made any fundamental difference to the operation of executive–legislative relations. The simple reason for this is that the goals of individual members of national parliaments as well as intra-parliamentary politics as practised by parliamentary party groups are unaffected by the dilution of parliamentary influence in those policy areas transferred to the EU, or to the greater executive control of information in policy development. Although national parliamentarians may recognize the gradual marginalization of their institution in the context of growing EU influence, concerted action to protest against this state of affairs does not arise because their interests are not threatened (certainly not in any fashion which communicates a sense of urgency). Therefore, although a political analyst and, when questioned, a parliamentarian may agree that the EU has indirectly and partially contributed to a marginalizing of national parliaments, there does not appear to be a form of 'pressure' from the EU – directly or indirectly – that prompts an adaptive change on the part of national parliaments.

Despite this conclusion, however, as discussed above, there is incontrovertible evidence that in fact institutional change in national parliaments has occurred, and this change has been roughly uniform in all member state parliaments, that is, the creation of European affairs committees. The significance of these committees, the parliamentary response to the influence of the EU, and in particular to the manner in which national executives have increasingly been able to 'cut slack' (Moravscik, 1994) in relation to legislatures, is explored below. But the mechanism of change, the process that can account for their creation, is not immediately apparent, at least in terms of a rational institutionalist perspective. It is certainly the case that the workload of national parliaments increased, simply due to the added volume of legislative output from the EU. Yet, as most commentators have concluded, the EU impact is not in itself enough to cause a shift in domestic executive–legislative relations, the key political dynamic from which one could hypothesize a change in parliamentary structure and/or practice. Raunio and Hix (2000) attempt to explain the creation of EACs by highlighting the information gap that had arisen between parliaments and executives. Focusing on intra-parliamentary partisan politics, they argue that 'realising that an information gap has been emerging in the area of EU affairs, opposition parties were eager to use EACs to gain access to European documents at early stages in the EU policy process and also to force ministers and bureaucrats to explain their actions in the European arena' (162). The subsequent information could be turned into an asset 'in the process of domestic party competition – in the preparation of party policy positions on European issues in party manifestos and other policy documents' (162–3). Hussain (2005) suggests that the expansion of the EU's powers under the SEA, and the run-up to the Maastricht Treaty, stimulated calls for greater parliamentary involvement (299). This view follows on from that of Norton (1996), who argued that it was national parliaments' 'awareness' of how much influence – indeed a quite noticeable leap in influence – the SEA would transfer to the EU that prompted a reaction or adaptation. Just as national executives were required to adapt to the increase in EU policy competence, '[s]o too did most of the national parliaments. There was a realisation not only that the policy competence of the EC was being extended but that a shift in the decision-making process was also taking place' (Norton, 1996: 178). This 'realisation' translated into action: 'For national parliaments, there was the problem of how to respond to the changed conditions. It was at this stage that we witness the institutional change taking place that we hypothesised would occur [greater specialisation, greater activity, integration of MEPs]' (Norton, 1996: 179).

In the Raunio and Hix account (2000), government-opposition dynamics within parliaments explain the decision to create a new committee exercising scrutiny over the executive. In the view of Hussain (2005) and Norton (1996) there was an apparent widespread realization that a fundamental imbalance in the domestic executive–legislative relationship was to take place, and something needed to be done to keep parliaments 'in the loop', so to speak. The common denominator in both sets of account, though, was a *perception* among some parliamentarians of a challenge to the constitutive principles of their institution, and in the years between the SEA and the Maastricht Treaty, attention to the newly coined term 'democratic deficit' highlighted the deteriorating situation of national parliaments (as well as serving as an argument employed by the EP to justify the enhancement of its position *vis-à-vis* the Council). The resulting two declarations in the Maastricht Treaty regarding the involvement of national parliaments in the activities of the EU and also with the European Parliament certainly demonstrate a concern expressed among political elites; however, the issue

managed to find itself placed in negotiations during the inter-
governmental conference. The Europeanization thesis argues that a
social-constructivist approach may better explain change when
'incompatibilities of norms and meaning structures between Europe
and the domestic level' occur (Börzel and Risse, 2006: 493). The
evidence of a discursive mobilization during the late 1980s and early
1990s suggests that a 'misfit' was apparent and growing, but here
one must also return to the actual institutional processes and power
relations embedded in parliamentary politics. The first and most
significant point to bear in mind is that we should not speak of a
parliament acting as an autonomous institution; rather, we should
recognize the centrality of party dynamics. The 'reason why the
"governments versus parliaments" framework is not particularly
fruitful for analyzing European parliaments is that both of these
institutions, like nearly every other aspect of political life, are dominated by political parties, and these parties are powerful and generally well disciplined' (Gallagher, Laver and Mair, 2006: 58). It
follows, then, that any institutional change that occurs within a
parliament – short of an historic nature – will no doubt be something agreed among the main parliamentary party groups. Further,
as these same parliamentary party groups are also supportive of a
government – whether single party or coalition – there are no incentives to undermine the ability of the executive to promote national –
or even partisan – interests at the European level. Consequently, as
the description of EACs above has demonstrated, although they do
provide an extra veneer of legitimacy to national decision-making in
regard to EU legislation, they are not a fundamental change to the
system. The creation of these committees follows – in principle – the
parliamentary function of scrutiny of the executive. In practice,
however, power relations have been maintained, as the key veto
player – party leaderships – consented to the provision of a formal
but mostly symbolic increase in parliamentary oversight, thereby
protecting their prerogatives in government and flexibility in EU-
level bargaining.

The European Parliament and certain member states committed
to its enhancement, for example Belgium and Germany, also played
a role in highlighting the issue of parliamentary democracy in the
EU – at both the European and national levels (Ladrech, 1993).
Though some member states such as France may have been reluctant to cede more influence to the EP, the proposal – later protocol
– to at least consider the role of national parliaments brought such

governments on board to approve the Treaty language and countenance the creation of EACs. As for the Hix and Raunio argument (2000), creating EACs could be seen as a ploy to defuse and/or channel opposition parties' and even government parties' dissent from undermining government participation in EU decision-making. Thus 'realization' that national parliaments were liable to become marginalized in an environment in which the EU was looming ever larger was certainly widespread, at least among MPs and MEPs, but for the reasons listed above, the 'pressure' that elicited an institutional response was manifest in a campaign to rescue parliamentary democracy, not to formally insert national parliaments into the EU decision-making process (such calls for another EU chamber or institution made of national MPs, as suggested by France, have never garnered much support). A social-constructivist approach toward understanding the creation of EACs is consequently a more fruitful line of analysis than one grounded in a rational-institutionalist argument.

European Union influence on post-communist parliaments

As could be expected due to their vastly different political history and previous regime experience, parliaments in post-communist member states exhibit different reactions to European integration than their counterparts in the West, or more precisely to the EU enlargement process. Two features stand out, though, for any discussion of Europeanization and post-communist parliaments. The first is that the engagement of these countries in their initial formal relationship with the EU – the run-up to candidate status – greatly impacted the institutionalization of the entire political system. As institutions, parliaments were weak, and exacerbating this was the weakness of parliamentary parties, where for many 'party discipline' was in short supply. Once candidate status was endowed, in 2000, as much of the literature on the EU and post-communist states attests, it was the executive that emerged strengthened, in a manner that seems magnified in speed and capacity compared to the West. This is because the critical significance of downloading the *acquis communautaire* fell solely upon the executive, and to facilitate this task, most parliaments agreed to remove EU-related issues from normal partisan debate and competition.

Consequently, although the various chapters of the *acquis* were subject to legislative ratification, the details were 'fast-tracked' to the institutional benefit of the executive. Since 'domestic innovation on issues related to the adoption and implementation of the *acquis* was very limited, parliaments lost a substantial degree of sovereignty' (Chiva, 2007: 196). Thus in a relatively short amount of time, while these political institutions were still in the process of domestic legitimation, the constitutional balance between executive and legislature was impacted by the EU. The second feature is the resemblance that post-communist parliaments, in particular the EACs that were rapidly set up, have with their western counterparts. As argued above, even where some parliaments do have the potential to wield more influence *vis-à-vis* their executive over EU affairs, they do not exercise this option. Findings of the behaviour of EACs in the newer member states' parliaments (e.g., O'Brennan and Raunio, 2007b) reveal a similar reluctance to exercise the full range of their influence, whether because of a lack of expertise or the inaccessibility of documentation or the behaviour of MPs, etc. The experience of the pre-accession process may have initiated an institutional path-dependent relationship that would be difficult to alter, especially as parties and party systems slowly become institutionalized. Still, according to Kopecký (2007), although these parliaments during their second post-communist decade have increased their institutional capacity, 'the institutional reforms of core executives, as well as the EU enlargement process, have also reduced parliaments' independent input into the policy-making process' (160).

Conclusion

This chapter has argued, in a narrow sense, that the institutional change which has occurred in national parliaments – the creation of EACs and the right to information – has occurred because MPs, MEPs and certain national governments have recognized that growing EU influence could result in further marginalization of national parliaments. Indirectly, the EU has created constraints on the operation of domestic parliamentary functions by removing them from direct involvement over those policy areas transferred to the EU. This 'distancing' affects their relationship with the executive. However, from a Europeanization perspective, the nature of the response suggests less an effort to close the gap in executive–legislative relations – a resource dependency argument (or rational institutionalist) – but a *partial* adjustment to the overall legitimacy of executive–legislative relations; it is debatable whether EACs and the right to information have actually amounted to much more than a fig-leaf in this respect. The degree of correction that the institutional change has brought about has not in reality altered the relationship in favour of parliamentary control – that is, neither in terms of effective *ex ante* or *ex post* accountability over the executive. The key factor that explains this situation – a state of affairs found in all member states – is the nature of party control of executive–legislative relations. Parliamentary party support for the government – a majority party or coalition of parties – is not inclined to put added pressure on a government in its involvement in the EU policy- and decision-making process; party elites are charged with making this so as part of their routine responsibilities. Government-opposition dynamics act in such a way as to neutralize any possible politicization of an EU policy or issue, in both *ex ante* (setting a mandate) and *ex post* (scrutiny) parliamentary actions. At the same time, at the level of inter-institutional relations, national executives have warned parliaments of the potential weakening of national bargaining at the inter-governmental level by heavy-handed *ex ante* mandates, and, coupled with a tradition of deference to the executive in foreign policy matters, this danger also contributes to the near absence of parliamentary motivation – government supporting or opposition – to 'tie ministers' hands' in Council meetings.

The increased yet modest involvement of national parliaments in their governments' EU activities has also had, according to some analysts, a contradictory effect. If the increased role of parliaments in EU affairs through the establishment of EACs and a right to information has not amounted to a real and effective improvement of parliaments, it has, however, had the effect of further reducing parliamentary autonomy in executive–legislative relations – in an institutional as well as normative democratic sense. Auel and Benz (2007) and Börzel and Sprungk (2007) argue that most parliaments have chosen to concentrate on an *ex ante* relationship with their executive rather than trying to hold the government accountable after voting in Council meetings. The result of becoming closer to the executive, even in the Danish system, has not meant any flexing of parliamentary muscle in terms of imposing mandates; rather, the more intimate relationship regarding government policy positions to be negotiated in Council meetings has shifted the focus on advice for the minister in question, rather than attempting to impose the parliament's (or EAC's) position. In the case of Denmark, Auel and Benz note that despite the influence a strong parliament could have on a Danish minority government, 'neither the governing nor the opposition parties exploit this power, because they are well aware of its negative impact on Denmark's strategic position in the Council's negotiations. Instead, they cooperate with the government, provide it with flexible guidelines, and monitor the negotiations in Brussels' (2007: 70). Another strong parliament, especially in the relationship between its committee system *vis-à-vis* the executive, the German Bundestag, also avoids exploiting the potential to explicitly mandate its position, preferring an informal relationship with ministers. In sum,

> the Bundestag does not explicitly insist on a consideration of its own position by the government. Even in the follow-up of resolutions, the Bundestag does not request a regular report by the ministers in times of heavy workloads. Thus, to have an impact in EU policy-making, the Bundestag relies on and intensifies its contacts with the Federal Government instead of actively using its relatively powerful opportunities vis-à-vis the executive branch of government for regaining autonomy. (Börzel and Sprungk, 2007: 127)

The result, both sets of authors conclude, is actually a fusion (Börzel and Sprungk) with the executive, or less autonomy (Auel and Benz). The attempt to increase parliamentary influence in EU affairs has actually decreased national parliamentary autonomy.

This leads to the conclusion, again from a social-constructivist perspective, that members of national parliaments, even when presented with the facts of the situation, are not inclined to raise the issue to one of political principle, that is, to transcend party politics. There are two reasons that explain this state of affairs. First, EU affairs are of a second order to the pattern of politics that animates political life for MPs and the business of parliament, no matter the extent to which a parliament may assert both an *ex ante* and *ex post* influence with regard to the executive. Second, and related to the 'business as usual' focus of MPs, is the fact that EU affairs, as presented to MPs in the EAC or in policy-specific standing committees, have no political resonance outside parliament that may affect their (re)selection (this of course exempts eurosceptic parties, but many of these either have no parliamentary seats, e.g. UKIP in the UK, or are so marginal in national parliaments as to be unable to influence the rest, who by and large are neutral or pro-EU). The lack of politicization over Europe inside parties, a condition monitored by party elites, provides little incentive for individual MPs to upset the status quo. As Andeweg concludes, '[f]uture institutional engineers are well advised to search for reforms that increase the European content of political representation, that emphasize ex post accountability rather than ex ante mandates, and above all, that politicize EU policy-making' (2007: 109). We will return to Europeanization and party politics in Chapter 6.

The Europeanization of national parliaments highlights, then, one of the unintended consequences of the European integration process, a strain on traditional formats of parliamentary democracy. What appears to be clear is that attempts by national parliaments to close the gap between their domestic role and function of scrutiny of legislation and oversight of the executive on the one hand, and some relevance in regard to EU policy-making on the other hand, has produced minimal results. By constructing a specialized and dedicated forum on EU matters, namely an EU affairs committee, national parliaments have simply demonstrated the limitations of traditional parliamentary structures when confronted with the nature of EU membership, namely the volume and pace of EU legislative output. This suggests that either more fundamental institutional innovation is required, or that the content of national parliamentary election campaigns begin to offer European policy choices, thus bringing into these national chambers debate on matters they will eventually be obliged to ratify in due course.

Chapter 4

Centre–Regional Relations

One of the critical issues linked to the debate over the Europeanization phenomenon is the extent to which EU-induced domestic change is reshaping the state (or state structures). Chapters 2 and 3 have considered national governmental institutions, but these institutions also have relations with a sub-national level of government, especially national executives. Although state territorial frameworks differ from member state to member state, if the EU does in fact exercise a particular influence on the relationship between national and sub-national actors, and if there is any discernible pattern to these changes, then a contribution will have been made to the broader issue of European state evolution. The strengthening or weakening of one or the other level, or other qualitative changes in relations, for example the nature of decision-making over resource allocation or input into national positions *vis-à-vis* EU policy, are examples indicative of Europeanization.

The potential for EU-related change in member states is not confined to institutions or relations between institutions (e.g. legislative–executive relations) at the national level. There are, of course, institutions below the national government, from states in federal systems, to de-centralized regions in unitary systems, as well as local levels of governance. In Chapter 2 it was argued that the national executive acts as a 'gatekeeper' between domestic interests and institutions on the one hand and the decision-making process of the EU on the other. As the national executive is responsible – constitutionally – for domestic policy implementation, alone or in partnership with sub-national authorities, it is unlikely that the impact of the EU is confined solely to the national level. Indeed, the development and significance of the EU's Cohesion Policy from the mid-1980s has sparked a debate over the issue of whether or not the EU has had an impact on state structures, in particular the relationship between the national state and sub-national units, or regions. Within the parameters of this debate, there is the further question of whether the result of changing relations strengthens or weakens the region or central (national) state. The phenomenon of changing centre–regional relations is one that also presents certain challenges to the Europeanization research agenda, as political scientists have recognized a shift in these relations before the re-launch of European integration in the mid-1980s, attributable to a number of causes. This chapter considers the background of centre–regional relations in EU member states, presents evidence of EU-influenced change between the central state and regions, and then addresses the possible Europeanization mechanisms of domestic change in this area. The focus of this evaluation is the issue of coordination mechanisms between the national and sub-national levels of governance in relation to uploading preferences to the EU arena and downloading and implementing EU legislation. As mentioned above with regard to the EU Cohesion Policy, or in terms of the costs of implementation, national and sub-national institutional actors may adapt to the opportunity or constraint that the EU may directly or indirectly provide. This chapter also evaluates the impact of the EU on centre–regional relations in post-communist member states. As with many other examples of Europeanization, the experience of Central and Eastern European countries (CEEC) is quite different to that of the West in the case of centre–regional relations, not least because of the absence during the communist period of legitimate levels of decision-making below the centralized national state. In concluding this chapter, a brief summary of the findings of the EU impact on the general relations between central state and sub-national regions is examined. Here evidence of change in the constitutional order, or in the balance of power, is considered, bearing in mind alternative or concurrent dynamics affecting these relations.

The changing nature of territorial relations in Western Europe

The West European nation-state had long been considered a centralized and united (as opposed to unitary) political construct. Whether unitary or federal in constitutional framework and relations, it had been assumed by many to be a developed and stable form of political organization. There have been, in some countries, an identifiable centre and periphery, for example in the UK between the government in Westminster and the 'nations' of Wales and Scotland, but these relations were not overtly politicized. However, beginning in the 1960s and 1970s, this edifice of stability came under pressure, in some cases in a centrifugal manner. The peripheries, in other words, came alive with demands and pressures on the central government. The accommodation of sub-national demands resulted in some cases in a fundamental change in territorial relations, for example in the case of Belgium, where regional pressure from Flemish groups resulted not only in the federalization of the country, but also the division of the party system into two linguistic parts, serving the Flemish and Walloon (French-speaking) communities. In the case of Spain, post-Franco democratization overlapped demands for autonomy (and in the case of Basque separatists, independence) from a number of previously suppressed groups, most notably the Catalans. The responses by national government to regional demands varied, obviously due to pre-existing structures, histories and the exact nature of the demand. In the examples of two unitary states, the UK and France, the British first attempted devolution in the 1970s and finally followed through in the 1990s, granting varying amounts of decision-making to the UK's various nations – Scotland, Wales and Northern Ireland. In France, political views regarding the integrity of the national state meant that similar recognition of ethnic, linguistic or cultural minorities was not feasible, but a process of de-centralization was nevertheless begun in the 1980s leading to elected regional assemblies. The study of centre–periphery relations thus took on a new focus, trying to explain the causes and variation in responses to this widespread phenomenon. In addition to this 'bottom-up' pressure from linguistic, ethnic or cultural minorities, decisions and policy initiatives instigated from the central state, often for economic development purposes, for example programmes aimed at developing poorer regions of a country, were implemented. In 'the 1960s, many European states adopted regional development policies as an extension of schemes of national and sectoral planning' (Keating, 1995: 2). An unintended consequence of this 'top-down' regionalism in some countries was to contribute toward the mobilization of subnational groups, who pressed for more input and control of regional development. By the 1990s, the vibrancy of regional political and economic mobilization, ranging from newly politically empowered regions such as Catalonia in Spain or Flanders in Belgium, or examples of post-industrial economic powerhouses such as Kent in the UK or Baden-Württemberg in Germany or Lombardy in Italy, fed into an apparent enthusiasm for regional representation at the European level itself. The Committee of the Regions, established in the Maastricht Treaty, was considered by some during the 1990s as the beginning of a formal, multi-level organization of European political and economic space.

One of the first comprehensive works in this area, *Centre-Periphery Relations in Western Europe* (Mény and Wright, 1985), attempted to systematize the study of the political changes which had been unfolding over the previous twenty years, followed soon thereafter by a special issue of *West European Politics* (1987) devoted to territorial relations within Western European countries, in which some authors questioned the continued viability of the nation-state. As Bursens (2008) makes clear, different analytical approaches have emerged toward understanding the changes between the central state and regions. All of them view the EU as an important part of territorial politics, but differ in their exact research question. By the end of the 1980s and early 1990s, the study of *regionalism* focused on relations between the central state and regions, encompassing political, economic and administrative dynamics. In this approach to understanding change within the nation-state, the implications of European integration were incorporated into the study of how new relationships were being formed between the central state and the regions, in many cases a triangular relationship when certain policies were highlighted (Jones and Keating, 1995). In the 1990s, another approach emerged toward understanding the relationship between the central state and regions, but explicitly linking these two levels with the expansion of EU competences. This approach became known as *multilevel governance*, and it conceptualized the local, national and European levels as interrelated fields of politics and policy, with the boundaries separating functions and lines of authority portrayed as much more permeable. The multi-level governance approach essentially relativized the position of the central state, seeing it embedded in a growing and interlocked political system incorporating the EU as well as sub-national institutional actors. Although not arguing that the national level would disappear or play simply an intermediary role between the regional and European levels, there was in early works an implication that the strength of regional–EU relations would have a profound impact on the stature of national government (see Marks *et al.*, 1996; Hooghe and Marks, 2001). A more recent application of the multi-governance thesis distinguishes between two types, roughly corresponding to relations between formal territorial levels of government, for example in a federal system, and 'governing arrangements in which the jurisdiction of authority is task-specific, where jurisdictions operate at numerous territorial levels and may be overlapping' (Bache, 2008: 27). In both types, the impact of the EU policies can be seen to have an effect on relations between levels, but not necessarily to the detriment of the central state.

This brings us to the Europeanization approach to centre–regional relations. Both regionalism and multi-level governance acknowledge the significant influence of the EU on centre–regional relations. Where the Europeanization approach distinguishes itself is in the consideration of the mechanisms of change, an explanation for the differential impact, and more broadly how these changes may affect overall state structures. 'Misfit' – in particular institutional misfit – and pre-existing domestic structures mediating the nature and degree of change, are incorporated in the approach but also important is the role of politics, especially as we recall that pressures for change are only a necessary precondition, but in themselves insufficient to generate it. In the next section we turn our attention to the more narrow issue of national coordination followed by a broader discussion of the impact of the EU on centre–regional relations.

National and regional interests in EU policy-making

Member states are the recipients of EU policy outputs that have a very real impact in terms of resources – for example the Common Agricultural Policy (CAP) and Cohesion Policy, policies we may consider redistributive. The implementation of funds from these two policies within the member state, while influencing the EU in the development and allocation of these resources through the uploading of domestic interests, brings national and regional actors together in a specifically EU-triggered activity. The issue at hand, then, is how member states organize themselves in relation to meeting the requirements of these EU policies and also in their pursuit of influencing the Commission decision-making process. In this respect, the EU can be seen as a political opportunity structure, and acquisition of EU resources is explained by a resource-dependency approach (rational institutionalist). The 'pressure' to coordinate actions within member states of course varies according to the internal structure of each member state, namely federal or unitary. In short, the need to coordinate might lead to an assumption of centralization of decision-making in the hands of the national executive because of its prime position between the needs of the sub-national actors – whatever the formal territorial division of power – and the decision-making process in Brussels. The evidence of coordination structures that have been put into place display a variety of relations, but there are at least two main characteristics. The first includes what are labelled member states with constitutionally defined sub-national actors, such as federal states (e.g. Germany) and those of a quasi-federal status such as Spain. The second set of member states includes essentially unitary states. How coordination structures operate and the changes in the degree of power that has arisen in the relationship between regions and the national government vary, though many commentators, for instance Bache (2008), Hooghe (1996), and others, suggest that changes in which sub-national actors are drawn into national coordination should not be conceptualized in a zero-sum manner, that is, a decrease in power for national governments equals an increase for regions, and vice versa. For the purposes of this chapter, it is enough to realize that there have been changes, though we will return to the question of the overall impact on centre–regional relations at the end of this chapter.

In addition to redistributive EU policies such as Cohesion Policy, there are a number of EU policies – shared with member states or not – that increase the pressure on member state governments to coordinate their decision-making with sub-national actors. For example, the EU Competition Policy rules governing state aid can impact national decisions where sub-national authorities, such as a Belgian region or German *land*, share jurisdiction with the national government for development projects. Similarly, where the costs of implementing EU directives or regulations may be shifted to local areas, for example aspects of environmental policy concerned with hazardous waste, again local authorities may react by advocating changes in the cost allocation. These examples point to the fact that implementation of EU policies, even if they do not have regional administrative actors in mind, very often have repercussions for national–regional relations, and this in turn may bring pressure for changes such as the construction of new coordination or cost-sharing structures. Such innovations serve to reduce the friction that may develop within a member state over the costs and potential concentration of decision-making influence in the hands of the national government at the expense of (especially constitutional) regional actors, but also to enhance the process of constructing and subsequently uploading national preferences during the EU policy development phase. Thus we can speak of a general impact of EU policy outputs leading to the potential for national coordination structures, whose administrative contours and internal power relations depend on the nature of national centre–regional relations, and especially the distinction between constitutional and non-constitutional regional levels of government. However, in the specific case of the EU Cohesion Policy, we find an EU policy that directly engages sub-national actors, thereby providing a political opportunity structure – if not supranational advocate – that has contributed in a singular manner to challenging, if not changing, centre–regional relations.

In brief, the Cohesion Policy, as it emerged in 1988, was a substantive increase in funding originally launched in 1972 (the European Structural and Development Funds), that is, it increased funds to the poorer regions of the EU as well as creating governance measures that moved decision-making from an inter-governmental basis to one with a more pronounced supranational dimension. The specific policy innovations that had a key impact on the development of a multi-level relationship – EU, national and regional – were 'the prominence of regional objectives, the partnership principle, and the programming requirement' (Bache, 2008: 152). In terms of obliging national governments to work with regional actors, and therefore to develop coordination mechanisms, these three factors had the following impact: *regional objectives* directed attention to territorial units below the national level, with defined criteria for the allocation of funds, e.g. regions seriously affected by industrial decline; the *partnership principle* required regions and the EU Commission, besides the member state national governments, to have a role in the preparation of programmes and in their assessment and monitoring as they were implemented; the *programming requirement* replaced ad hoc, project-by-project funding with pre-planned, multi-annual programmes, coordinating a range of programmes within individual regions. The overall effect of this EU-promoted policy initiative (vigorously supported by certain member states, in particular Spain) was to enhance the role of regions in member state coordination, development and implementation of these funds (the financial incentive of course is quite straightforward). How regions interacted with both the Commission and their respective national government was left up to each member state, and here pre-existing national structures – e.g. constitutional entities – and histories explain the variation that the examples below illustrate. Regions or sub-national units were certainly given degrees of input into coordination mechanisms, but an accrual of power has not been uniform, as one would expect from the structural differences among member states. Nevertheless, regions became partners not only with the Commission but also with their national governments. Coordination structures, then, developed as a response to the Cohesion Policy, the more general need to coordinate between national and regional levels because of the growing competence of the EU in an increasing number of policy areas, and, in selected cases, due to the evolution of the territorial division of power within certain member states. Below are brief sketches of coordination structures in states with constitutionally defined separate levels of power and jurisdiction (federal, regionalist or compound for a general label) and unitary states (or simple, however decentralized they may have become).

Compound states

Spain

The Spanish Constitution recognizes the autonomy of Spain's 18 regions, though the regions themselves vary in the amount of political power that they wield, for example Catalonia, as an historic region with a distinct language enjoys a level of political significance more than regions designated by administrative functions. This imbalance among Spain's regions has given rise to the label asymmetrical federalism. Further, unlike Germany (see below), the regions have for most of the post-Franco years had a more competitive rather than cooperative relationship with the central state (Börzel, 2002). It is in this context that Spain's regions have adapted to the impact of EU legislation on the Spanish policy-making process. The regions, or Autonomous Communities (*Communidades Autónomas*) have developed, in stages, a form of inter-governmental cooperation with the central state in Madrid in which they can participate in Spanish policy preference formation that is uploaded to the EU as well as in the downloading of EU policies (Structural and Development Funds for example, though in a limited manner). The coordination mechanisms by which the Autonomous Communities interact with Madrid include sectoral conferences (*Conferencias Sectoriales*), which cover a wide range of policy areas, in which the central state must inform the relevant sectoral conference of the measures that it proposes to take to implement an EU directive (a downloading action), while also being the form in which Autonomous Communities arrange a common position on a policy area that is then transmitted to the responsible central government ministry as part of the development of Spanish negotiating strategy in the Council of Ministers (an uploading action). In addition to sectoral conferences, since the mid-1990s an Inter-ministerial Conference on European Affairs (*Conferencia para Asuntos Relacionados con las Communidades Europeas*) has become the mechanism for incorporating the Autonomous Communities in Spain's overall EU participation, by 'developing the framework for an intrastate participation of the [Autonomous Communities] in European policy-making through the sectoral conferences or other instruments of intergovernmental cooperation' (Börzel, 2002: 123). There is also an advisor for Autonomous Communities affairs in the Spanish Permanent Representation in Brussels, created in 1996. Again, as part of the competitive nature of centre–regional relations in Spain, the Autonomous Communities were able to change the designation of this individual from one appointed by the central state to two chosen by the Autonomous Communities.

The sectoral conferences and the conference on European Affairs demonstrate how the Autonomous Communities and the central state negotiate their respective preferences in relation to Spanish EU policy-making and implementation. However, the Autonomous Communities have also been able to develop their own direct relations with EU decision-making bodies, or at least participate with central state ministers in EU decision-making. With regard to the numerous working committees of the European Commission, representatives of the Autonomous Communities participate along with representatives of the central government, though not to determine the final position of the national delegation. Still, involvement gives the Autonomous Communities an insight and information that otherwise would be acquired only through the central state ministries. Since the Autonomous Communities must have a prior arranged position on the policy issue, involvement also serves to enhance coordination among them. In the case of the Council of Ministers, the Autonomous Communities had since 1998 requested participation at ministerial level, at COREPER, and in working groups, but did not succeed in attaining agreement with the central state until the 2004 Agreements covering central state and regional relations. The position of the advisor in the Permanent Representation has already been noted; the Autonomous Communities now have participation in Council working groups, and in particular, within the Spanish delegation they can partici- pate in the following four Council policy areas: Agriculture and Fishing; Environment; Employment, Social Policy, Health and Consumer Affairs; and Education, Youth and Culture. Their influ- ence depends on a coordinated position, and they do not formally determine the final Spanish position; nevertheless their participa- tion marks another milestone in Spanish multi-level coordination processes.

Germany

Unlike Spain, whose system of territorial relations has been evolving quickly since the late 1970s, the Federal Republic of Germany has from the beginning a clear and constitutionally defined federal structure, a system of relations often characterized as 'cooperative federalism'. The regions, or *Länder*, have exclusive policy compe- tence in some areas, and shared competence with the federal govern- ment in others. The nature of German cooperative federalism places the responsibility for policy implementation – federal or otherwise – upon the *Länder*, and the influence of the EU can be seen in two areas of this relationship. The first is the issue of which level bears the costs of implementing EU policies, and second, in the incremen- tal shift of policy responsibility from the *Länder* to the federal government as part of the transfer of policy areas that had been part of *Länder* responsibility to the EU (the federal government then increases its role *vis-à-vis* the *Länder* as part of the need to central- ize national decision-making in the context of the national-EU rela- tionship; see Chapter 2). German federalism in practice has meant that the *Länder* have developed extensive relations with the federal government, and through the upper legislative chamber the *Bundesrat*, they have a considerable role to play in national policy- making. Unlike in Spain, where funds from the EU Cohesion Policy were an added factor in the assertion of regional prerogatives *vis-à-vis* the central state, the relative prosperity of Germany meant that these funds did not act as a major stimulant in federal–*Länder* relations (the unification of the former East Germany after 1989 did then create a new demand for funds, but the decision-making architecture or pattern was already in place).

In the case of *Länder* bearing the costs of implementing EU policies, there is a clear departure from their acquiescence toward previous centralization measures by the federal government affecting *Länder* competencies between the mid-1960s and mid-1970s (Börzel, 2002: 50–1) and the actions taken to redress the potential centralization due to federal involvement in EU decision-making. The intensive cooperative nature of *Länder* participation in policy-making with the federal government led them in the past to transfer selected legislative competences to the federal government in return for participation in the formulation of these policies and federal assumption of the cost. In the case of regional policy transfer linked to the pressure to centralize policy decision-making at the national level in relation to EU policy competence, the *Länder* essentially adopted the same strategy, although with a complementary and confrontational twist. There is a basic difference though, when *Länder* competences are transferred to the federal level and when they are transferred to the EU level. In the former case, as already mentioned, the *Länder* secured participation rights with the federal level. In the latter case, policy competence is transferred outside of the national political system. In this respect, the *Länder* cannot demand participation rights with the EU. Additionally, the flexibility over implementation costs, which had been a hallmark of cooperative German federalism, is severely circumscribed when the issue is implementing EU directives. The response to this situation by the *Länder* has taken place in the following manner. First, the *Länder* accepted the centralizing-driven shift of policy competence to the federal level, but with the proviso of *Länder* participation in the elaboration of national policy positions to be uploaded to the EU level. As regards the burden of funding, although the *Länder* attempted to avoid the cost of implementing EU policies, they have only been partially successful in this endeavour. The federal government has been able to absorb only a portion of the costs that fit into the existing structures of federal–*Länder* policies. With EU-specific policies, this bargain has not been able to be replicated. Instead, a reduction of implementation costs has been reached by 'upgrading German regulations to the European level, on the one hand, and absorbing and watering down of mismatching European policies, on the other hand' (Börzel, 2002: 209).

When we turn more specifically to the participation rights of the *Länder* in national policy-making, two features stand out. The first is their involvement at the federal level; the second is involvement at the EU level. In the former, comprehensive co-decision powers in the formulation and representation of *Länder* interests in German EU policy-making have evolved, especially since the negotiations between the *Länder* and the federal government during the ratification of the Single European Act (SEA). Up until this time, the *Länder* had developed informal methods of participating with federal ministries in policy areas that directly affected them, in both their exclusive and shared competences. Gerstenlauer (1995) notes that 'the inclusion of EC issues in the domestic practice of vertical co-ordination between federal and *Länder* governments gave the latter additional channels of information, participation, and monitoring of EC affairs without the creation of specific new bodies' (195). From the mid-1980s onward, in reaction to the deepening of European integration and the apparent shift of competences to the EU, the *Länder* managed to upgrade their participation in national EU policy-making through a formal presence in the German permanent representation in Brussels (itself a strengthening of what had been until 1988 a Land Observer), and the creation of a new Bundesrat committee on EU affairs staffed by *Länder* executives. The Maastricht Treaty represented another milestone in federal–*Länder* relations over Europe when the *Länder* succeeded in making their role constitutional (Article 23 GG) – through the Bundesrat – to approve of any transfer of *land* and federal competences to the EU. As for their participation beyond the federal system, that is, directly within EU institutions, the *Länder* have the ability to represent themselves in Council meetings where their exclusive competences are debated, for example Culture or Education; the missions of each *Land* based in Brussels (Moore 2006); and finally the participation of *Land* politicians in the Committee of the Regions. Taken together, the German *Länder* have, since the re-launch of the European integration process in the mid-1990s, continued to follow the path of integrating themselves in the style of cooperative federalism that has marked their relationship with the federal government, improving flows of information, and having the ability to voice their concerns. It also has brought an added degree of horizontal coordination between the *Länder*, as a common position reinforces their influence in relation to the federal government in negotiating the national position *vis-à-vis* the EU. The extra-state activities of the *Länder* represent an innovation in their behaviour toward the EU; however, in this respect they are not the exception among other European regions in having a presence in Brussels.

Belgium

Since the 1960s changes in the territorial division of power in Belgium have been dramatic. From its establishment in the early nineteenth century as a unitary state, it has become one of the most de-centralized of federal states in Western Europe, the last major phase of its transformation having taken place in the early-to-mid 1990s. A string of constitutional reforms, culminating with the so-called Saint Michel Accords in 1993, completed the federalization of the country. With inter-communal strife and economic imbalances further aggravated by linguistic-nationalist sentiment, the resultant federal structure of Belgium has a particularly complex nature. When one turns specifically to sub-national governmental actors that have constitutionally defined policy competences that the federal government must involve in the corresponding EU policy area, there are three regions – Brussels-Capital, Flanders, and Wallonia – and three communities – French-speaking, Flemish-speaking, and German-speaking. Horizontal coordination among the appropriate sub-national set – regions or communities – must take place in order to assure vertical coordination. An agreement signed between the federal government and the regions and communities in 1994, based on innovations in the Maastricht Treaty, also allows for a representative of the respective sub-national government to participate on behalf of Belgium in those Councils (of Ministers) that are pertinent to the policy competence of the sub-national actor. In other words, as Belgium undertook a series of constitutional revisions beginning in 1970 that put it on the road which eventually led to a federal state, new mechanisms of coordination were necessary in relation to EU policy-making and for the development of Belgian 'national' preferences that would then be uploaded.

The regions and communities of Belgium are fully involved in the coordination process, reflecting the political power that they wield in the Belgian political system. Two federal ministerial departments are involved in coordinating Belgium's European policy: the Ministry for

Foreign Affairs and the Ministry for Economic Affairs. The committee charged with the upward coordination of Belgian policy is known as P.11 (while the P.12 is charged with downward coordination). Representatives of regions and communities attend P.11 meetings as well as policy-specific representatives from both sub-national entities. The regions and communities themselves have developed expertise on the EU influence in policy areas by use of so-called 'European coordinators' in the respective ministry. There are a number of policy areas that the regions and communities have exclusive competence, for example culture, education, tourism, housing and land planning, and some, such as industry and research, for which they are chiefly responsible (in which the federal government has some input). In these areas any proposed EU directive or regulation is reviewed and negotiated in working committees, formally and informally – until the P.11 committee is able to produce a position, which is then eventually communicated to the level of the Belgian Permanent Representation in order for the Belgian position in the respective Council to be forwarded. However, and this is a sign of the significance of sub-national input into the national position formulated and defended in the Council, the regions and communities have an indirect veto. This can occur if a consensus is not reached, by the refusal of a region or community to support a proposed position. When disagreement occurs, a Concertation committee (*comité de concertation*) is formed, made up of the prime minister and the minister-presidents of the regions and the French-speaking community. If a consensus still cannot be found, 'the Belgian representative has to abstain from voting or from taking a position within the Council of Ministers' (Franck *et al.*, 2003: 78). The ability to withhold support effectively puts a premium on early coordination and highlights the influence of the sub-national level *vis-à-vis* the national government. The regions and communities presence in the coordination process also extends into the Belgian Permanent Representation in Brussels, as they each have an *attaché* placed in it. Finally, these sub-national governments also represent Belgium in the Council of Ministers when it affects their exclusive policy competence, and in those policy areas in which the federal government is chiefly, but not exclusively in charge, an 'assessor-minister' representing the regions and communities assists the federal minister.

This brief sketch of three compound states demonstrates the gradual integration of the regional level of government into the overall European policy-making of EU member states. Although the

Cohesion Policy, and particularly the Structural and Development Funds, may have contributed to the direction of travel among national and sub-national actors in each of these three countries, the more widespread need to adjust and coordinate across many EU-influenced policies and the constitutional position of the regions helps to explain the robustness of the various coordination structures.

Simple states

United Kingdom

The devolution process that began in earnest in the 1990s in the United Kingdom may have redefined the state from unitary to 'asymmetrically devolved' (Armstrong and Bulmer, 2003: 391), but the central state remains in control over the actions of the devolved regional administrations, English regions and local government when the issue is coordinating responses or forming preferences to upload at the EU level. The coordination of EU policy across central ministries in the executive was noted in Chapter 2, but this centralization, especially in financial matters, extends vertically to the subnational levels of government as well. As for the devolved regions, such as Scotland, the change of the Scottish Office to the Scottish Executive and now the Scottish Government – answerable to a Scottish Parliament – has not fundamentally changed the process by which the central state controls the decision-making process related to EU issues (although this is not to say that there is no Scottish input into the development of particular policy positions, especially in policy areas such as agriculture, fishing and the structural funds; see Smith, 2006). The EU Cohesion Policy has been a significant and influential input into the British system and, through its partnership and programming principles, it has stimulated greater regional development and contributed toward the creation of a degree of functional multi-level governance. This was more pronounced in the early phase of the implementation of the Cohesion Policy after the 1988 reforms, and contributed to the 'revival' of English regionalism (Bache, 2008; Burch and Gomez, 2006). Local government has found itself incorporated into the national mechanisms of EU policy-making, again due to the involvement in structural development funding and related projects (Marshall, 2006). However, as Bache concludes, though the British unitary state may have undergone change over the past thirty years, some of it attributable to the impact of EU Cohesion Policy, it would be wrong to conclude that a fundamental shift has occurred: 'while Britain may be understood as a *regionalizing* state – that is, one in which the regions have increasing autonomy, but where the central state remains formally unitary and still expects to exercise power over the periphery – it still has some way to go before it can be genuinely described as *regionalized* in the same sense as Spain' (2008: 158).

France

During the early years of the first Mitterrand Presidency – 1981 to 1988 – the Socialist Government embarked on a series of de-centralization reforms (the *lois Defferre*). Eventually elected regional assemblies were created to represent the 22 regions that now occupy the regional level of government in France (below the national level but above the departmental). However, in relation to EU policy-making, and in particular to the EU Cohesion Policy, it may be said that even less change has transpired in the French central state–regional relationship than has been the case in the United Kingdom. Though a modest amount of *political* power may have accrued over time, the regions have not seen any commensurate increase in *policy* influence, and in the case of EU structural and development funds, they are 'still almost non-existent in European decision-making, their functions being confined to the implementation of EC programmes addressed specially to them' (Szukala, 2003: 230). Through central state control over information, and most importantly the fact that the state involves its own personnel – *préfets* – at the regional level to coordinate and manage funding through contractual plans between the region and central state, French regional enhancement is not comparable to other unitary states. The partnership principle of the Cohesion Policy included representatives of the central state – in a dominant position. Balme and Woll (2005) also suggest that French regions 'failed to exploit all the resources the EU offered them. Due to a lack of administrative and political capacities, in some cases even a lack of political legitimacy, the regions were not able to fully commit themselves to Community initiatives ... or even to maintain a permanent representation in Brussels' (109). Central state control of local development, despite the de-centralization reforms, explains the lack of even incremental regional influence in French EU policy preference formation. Nevertheless, it would be wrong to assert that nothing has evolved. Although regions continue their subservient position relative to the central state, they are now, due to the partnership and programming principles of the Cohesion Policy, legitimate actors with the central state, and, in many cases, local levels of administration, in planning development projects.

Ireland

In contrast to the UK and France, both of which had launched reforms to the unitary nature of the state (though without the intent of fundamentally weakening the centre) and distinct from the consequences of the EU's Cohesion Policy or the general nature of policy coordination with sub-national actors, in the Republic of Ireland a regional level of administration was deliberately created in order to maximize the distribution of EU resources. Following the 1988 EU Cohesion Policy reforms, the Irish government, mindful of the large proportion that EU structural and development funds occupied in national development strategies, responded to the partnership requirement with the establishment of seven regions (Holmes and Reese, 1995). These regions 'were largely an administrative expedient which added a weak regional layer to the implementation of the CSF [Community Support Framework] and thereby satisfied the Commission about the operation of the "partnership principle" in Ireland' (Laffan, 2003a: 259). Although these regional authorities did evolve some small portion of influence, especially after a Local Government Act in 1991 established EU Operational Committees, for each region, which have become a part of the policy-making process, the decreasing share of EU funds to Ireland is expected to result in a diminution of their influence. Another example of the industriousness of the central state to manipulate regional boundaries came about in the creative subdivision of the country into two NUTS II (Nomenclature of Units for Territorial Statistics) regions, ostensibly to maintain a certain level of funding once the Objective 1 entitlement – which had classified the entire country as an Objective 1 region – was predicted to end. Although seen by the EU as a self-interested tactic, it was successful in the short term. The Irish case demonstrates the artificial nature of subnational regions especially when conjured up in reaction to resource distribution. In this particular case, the EU and its Cohesion Policy represented a classic case of a political opportunity structure out of which a regional level was created.

Regional developments in post-communist member states

The impact of the European Union on the domestic politics and institutions of post-communist states has been profound. In the specific area of centre–regional relations, the EU, and in particular the Commission, has acted in a more direct manner compared to the older member states. First, the Commission initially promoted the development of sub-national levels of governance (or so many government officials in these countries believed (see Keating, 2006: 259–61). This effort went beyond the conditions of Cohesion Policy *per se*, that is, the Commission believed that an active sub-national strata would contribute to the consolidation of democracy in the region, especially in light of the weakness of civil society under Communist Party rule. Second, and related to the prior issue, most of the post-communist states had no functioning level of regional government with which to enter into partnership with the Commission, and what may have existed lacked political leadership, prompting the Commission to take a more proactive stance as compared to the older member states. As with the older member states, there were a variety of national differences among the new member states, not only in terms of size and historical development, the presence of ethnic minorities, etc., but also in the very fact that some were relatively new states themselves (for example the Czech Republic from Czechoslovakia and Slovenia from Yugoslavia). Following the argument that different pre-existing conditions play a major role in mediating domestic change in reaction to EU influence, it is not surprising that from the mid-1990s, when these governments demonstrated their desire to join the EU through to their entry into membership in May 2004, the differences in regional development have been many. Finally, the lack of administrative capacity, whether at the regional or central level, also explains the weakness and variety of regionalism, despite a targeted EU mobilization in this area of government reform.

The role of the Commission in the development of regional governance in post-Communist member states changed over the course of time from when the central and east European states first demonstrated an interest in joining the EU and until membership became a matter of simply completing negotiations in the early 2000s. In the earlier period, the Commission and potential partner acted under the mobilizing theme of a 'Europe of the Regions', and the EU attraction and power through the dispersion of Structural Funds was a significant factor in developing regional governance outlines (Keating and Hughes, 2003). However, as Bruszt (2008) explains, '[w]hilst in the 1990s EU incentives were used to encourage power dispersion, as accession approached they were used to push Central and East European (CEE) countries in the direction of re-centralization and a hierarchical mode of governance' (615). The shift on the part of the Commission from promoting a regional level of government to attention to administrative structures and efficiency itself does not fully explain the diversity of outcomes. Historical legacies and domestic transition politics go a long way in supporting the argument that the EU's asymmetrical power relationship with the candidate countries and conditionality was in itself insufficient to provide for a common regionalist development (see Hughes *et al.*, 2004, about the 'myth of conditionality'). We should also differentiate between regional policy-making and regional institution-building, in both of which the EU wielded a significant influence. However, what transpired by the early 2000s was variation in both of these dimensions. In Hungary, decentralization mostly in the form of statistical-planning regions rather than regional identification and development occurred; in Poland and the Czech Republic, by contrast, prior experience with local and regional elected governments managed to establish a form of regional policy-making and institutions. In all cases, the EU's influence was manifested in the Structural Funds, the *acquis communautaire*, and political conditionality. The Annual reports released by the Commission detailing progress by the respective candidate country toward meeting the various chapters in accession negotiations also acted as a stimulant for change. Overall, the EU relationship with post-communist countries in the area of central-state relations with regions and regionalism stands in stark contrast to that of the West. Comparison at this stage of development is therefore not warranted.

Mechanisms of change in central–regional relations

In both eastern and western EU member states, the policies and influence of the EU has, in some cases, been a critical factor in explaining developments since the 1980s. In the post-communist states, the overwhelming desire to join the EU explains the attention given to developing appropriate structures of regional planning, and in some cases, this response intertwined with demands by sub-national political actors. But the starting point, even for a country such as Poland, with a background in regionalist initiatives prior to 1990, is one of a high degree of centralization as compared to the West. In the West, it seems clear that in some cases such as Spain, the EU Cohesion Policy, especially the partnership and programming principles, acted as an added resource for regional mobilization. However, as in the cases of regionalist and federal countries, there is already either a well-established constitutional level of sub-national government (Germany), an unfolding process of sub-national constitutional development (Belgium) or a redefining of central-state relations with historical regions (Spain). In these cases, the EU input has been translated into specific national contours. In the case of Germany, the gradual erosion of *Länder* competences to Berlin and Brussels resulted in a reaction such that the *Länder* have secured a role in uploading national policy preferences in the Council of Ministers in Brussels. In Spain, by contrast, the resources available to the regions, both material and political, strengthened their position *vis-à-vis* their struggle for more constitutional power. In both cases, East and West, the EU has acted as a political opportunity structure, but the ability and means by which to access its resources remains in the hands of central government authorities. This is seen most clearly in the cases of Western European unitary member states such as the United Kingdom or France, for which the EU Cohesion Policy has not, in itself, managed to promote the sub-national level in the same way as federal or compound states. At the very least, and depending on the nature of national–regional relations within a country such as Spain or Italy, the EU has been an ally of aspiring regions.

Conclusion

Does the EU influence the pattern of relations between the central state and regions? The answer seems to be, yes, Europeanization in state and sub-national relations has taken place. Beyond this finding, the outcomes of EU-member state relations in this area remain ambiguous, especially in reaction to the question whether regions are strengthened *vis-à-vis* the central state. If the question is empowerment, then even within a country the results can vary, as Bourne (2003) argues with respect to the Basque Country and its taxation regime. What does not seem to be in doubt is the significance of pre-existing constitutional structures that allow the central state a critical position in how sub-national authorities respond to the opportunities which the EU presents, especially in its Cohesion Policy. In her 1996 book *Cohesion Policy and European Integration: Building Multi-level Governance*, Hooghe asked: 'have diverse territorial relations converged under the pressure of this uniform EU policy [Regional Policy], hence moving towards a systematic involvement of sub-national authorities in all member states? Or are uniform European regulations being bent and stretched so as to uphold existing differences in member states?' (2). In relation to the more narrow issue of central state and sub-national relations in the creation of coordination mechanisms for the uploading of agreed national preferences and downloading of EU policies, it is fair to say that no convergence has been manifested. The impact of the EU, that is, a pressure to coordinate between different levels of competence within a member state – i.e. the 'goodness of fit' factor – is mediated by pre-existing domestic power balances. There is a trend, though, toward a strengthening of the sub-national level, more so for strong regions such as German *länder* and Belgian regions. When we turn to more general domestic central state and sub-national relationships, it is also fair to say that domestic state structures in terms of central–regional relations are affected by the EU, but in a differential manner, due to the different pre-existing characteristics of the national polity. It is also important not to forget the role of political agency in all of the attention given to state structures. In both the United Kingdom and France, devolution and de-centralization reforms were conceived and promulgated by central governments (though in some cases sub-national actors mobilized to place their interests on the national agenda, e.g. Scottish devolution), and the limited changes that the EU Cohesion Policy has inspired in terms of local and regional attempts to secure funding would be even less had these reforms not taken place. In the case of Spain, although the relations between the autonomous communities and Madrid have been conflictual during the course of creating new coordinating structures and the overall balance of constitutional power, it certainly seems an accurate assessment to say that what political party is in power in Madrid can influence the degree to which these relations are constructive. In the case of post-communist countries, the lack of regional political leadership may also explain the re-centralization that occurred in many cases from 2000 onwards. All told, the impact of the EU on centre–regional relations is a phenomenon that has accompanied wider changes in territorial government in some of the older member states (Burgess, 2006) and in the case of post-communist states, has been 'inconsistent and so variously interpreted as to prevent us stipulating any common logic of Europeanization' (Keating, 2006: 266).

Chapter 5

National Courts

National parliaments were found to have experienced an indirect type of pressure from the EU leading to modest internal organizational change and, more importantly, a further justifying factor for the de-parliamentarization thesis. As a national institution of government, parliaments do not formally interact at the EU level in any of the main formats of decision- or policy-making, unlike national executives that are present in the Council of Ministers, and therefore intimately as well as formally involved in EU dynamics. National courts, unlike executives, are not 'present' in EU institutions, but unlike parliaments they are much more intimately linked to EU decision-making dynamics through their relationship with the European Court of Justice. This suggests a further difference in the manner in which national institutions are 'hit' by the EU, and also highlights the probable variation in the potential change experienced by national courts in their respective member state. If indeed this supranational–national relationship between the ECJ and national courts does lead to changes, whether in the internal organization of courts or in wider domestic inter-institutional changes in relationship, or even more profound constitutional re-balancing, then again the nature of European state evolution and normative concerns regarding parliamentary democracy may be brought into relief.

A discussion of Europeanization and national courts is a tentative one, as research in this area is still at an early stage. For example, 'very little is known about the effects of Europeanization upon the internal composition of national courts, their legal procedure and application of EC law' (Nyikos, 2008: 183). Indeed, readily available comparative information is absent, though a national report may be published from time to time. For example, a 2005 report written for the Dutch Raad voor de Rechtspraak (Council for the Judiciary) 'focuses on the consequences of the "Europeanisation" process of in particular, Dutch law for the organisation of the Dutch

114

judiciary' (Prechal *et al.*, 2005: 4). One point that is certain though, is that judges, operating within national courts, have exercised a degree of discretion in their actions despite the embedded nature of their institutions in the process of legal integration involving the European Court of Justice (ECJ) that has unfolded over the past decades. Indeed, if 'such discretion did not exist, constitutionalization [the diffusion of the ECJ's rulings on supremacy, direct effect, and related doctrines within national legal orders] would not have taken place, and the Europeanization of the law would be a preordained, mechanical process rather than the fluid and multidimensional one that we see' (Stone Sweet, 2003: 47). In Chapter 1 concerning the nature of EU membership, the issue of sovereignty was discussed, and the Europeanization theme was referred to as a process in which the boundaries between national and supranational policy- and decision-making was increasingly blurred. In regard to legal integration, the sovereignty issue is at the fore, as legal scholars 'identified how ECJ decisions limited state sovereignty and forged a new supranational legal order' (Conant, 2007: 47). This chapter focuses on how national courts fit into this supranational legal order as well as the indirect effects on their relationship *vis-à-vis* other national government institutions. In other words, we are interested in discovering the direct and indirect effects of EU influence on national courts' relationship to the EU level and its consequences for their place in their respective national political systems. Whereas in previous chapters the European Commission has been the pre-eminent EU institution involved in top-down Europeanization dynamics, the ECJ is the key EU institution involved in transmitting authoritative rules and rulings to the national courts. In order to grasp the relationship between the ECJ and national courts and the consequences of legal integration, it is necessary to provide a brief background to the development of the ECJ's position *vis-à-vis* member states, touching on the concepts of direct effect and supremacy. The issue for legal scholars interested in European integration has been to explain why national courts have entered into the relationship they have and the variations thereof. After addressing the development of the ECJ's position in regard to national courts, the chapter then turns to a comparative presentation of the behaviour of national courts as they engage the ECJ decisions, ranging from resistance to cooperation. The chapter next considers what could be termed a bottom-up Europeanization dynamic that involves lower national courts and private litigants.

Changes in national inter-institutional relations that have derived from the 'empowerment' of national courts are then explored, in particular the relationship between national courts and national parliaments. Finally, the post-communist experience of the influence of the EU on emerging constitutional courts is examined.

Legal integration and mechanisms of change: the development of the ECJ

How do EU institutions affect member state decisions and institutions? In the discussion of national executives, attention was drawn to the fact that as the constitutional representative of the member state, they are obliged, indeed legally bound by treaty obligations, to implement policy regulations and directives as they are legislated by the EU. In this process, the key institutions are the Commission and Council of Ministers. National executives, unlike other national institutions, are part of the Brussels decision-making process. When attention is turned to national courts and changes in their behaviour and internal organization, the EU institution to which a causal link can be made in terms of direct influence is the European Court of Justice (ECJ). However, the manner in which the ECJ wields its influence such that national courts have taken on new or additional duties is different than in the case of the Commission and Council in relation to national executives. The rulings of the ECJ are in themselves not an output that is binding upon national courts. Rather, it is the development of European case law over time – legal integration – that has produced an authoritative position for the ECJ in a multi-level environment in which national courts' own position has been modified. Nyikos (2008: 183–4) makes clear this point about the nature of the national–supranational judicial relationship:

> legal change [at the European level] does not directly affect a national court until a related case is brought before it. Even then, it can ignore European law. It is only when a national court chooses to interpret the effects of EC law upon national law, or to engage in judicial dialogue with the European Court of Justice, that it is directly affected by Europeanization.

And yet, national courts participated in the constitutionalization of the Treaty of Rome. The ECJ, 'in complicity with national judges and private actors, authoritatively revised the normative foundations of the treaty without the consent of member-state governments' (Stone Sweet, 2003: 22). The manner in which national courts engage the ECJ comes about through the preliminary reference process, whereby a national court refers a question of European law to the ECJ for interpretation. It is this process involving litigants (ranging from private individuals, companies and even governments), national courts and the ECJ that actually triggers or engages the Community mandate. How did this come about? There are two sets of actors involved in answering this question: the ECJ and national courts. The easier part of the answer focuses on the actions at the supranational level. From the ECJ side, decisions in two cases were critical in establishing the ECJ's right to involve itself in the national arena. These concepts are *direct effect* and *supremacy*. In *Van Gend en Loos* (1963) the ECJ first asserted the principle that EC law conferred rights on individuals as well as on member states: this established direct effect. In *Costa* v. *ENEL* (1964) the ECJ first asserted the supremacy of EC law over national law, on the basis that if there were to be a single body of EC law throughout the Community, it could not be subject to interpretation in each member state in the light of the individual laws of that state. In essence, the ECJ created a Community mandate for national courts. This Community mandate doctrine consisting of direct effect and supremacy culminated in the *Simmenthal* case of 1978, 'where the court held that every national court must in a case within its jurisdiction apply Community law in its entirety and protect rights which individuals derive from it, and must set aside any provision which may conflict with it, whether prior or subsequent to the Community rule' (Claes, 2006: 108). But as Nyikos stated above, national courts must still participate in an active sense in the logic developed by the ECJ. This brings us to the other part of the answer concerning how national courts became part of the national–supranational judicial matrix. Put simply, why did national courts become involved with the ECJ, especially if one of the 'costs' would be a portion of state sovereignty?

There are multiple answers to this question, that is, a variety of reasons have been advanced without being mutually exclusive. The following items have been presented to explain national courts' acceptance of a Community mandate, placing the ECJ in a potentially dominant position.

- '*Legalist*' *explanations*: due to the status of Treaty obligations and the legal reasoning by the ECJ itself, national courts became convinced of the validity of the supremacy of EC law.
- *Judicial dialogue*: once the preliminary referral process is employed, over time the judicial dialogue between the ECJ and national courts itself strengthens EU case law legitimacy and contributes to the conviction by national courts that the ECJ has a necessary role to play.
- *The empowerment thesis*: engaging with the supranational ECJ provided national courts with enhanced powers, for example judicial review where it had not existed before or was weak, more institutional power especially for lower courts within a national system, and finally the promotion of certain policies for which European law offers a facilitating edge.
- *Inter-court competition*: related to the second factor in the empowerment thesis, bureaucratic competition between different levels of national judiciaries, e.g. lower courts and constitutional courts, means that European law can be invoked by lower courts to advance their interests, usually of a policy nature.
- *National–supranational conflict resolution*: as the amount of transnational trade grows and the scope of EU regulatory competences widens, the more disputes between national and EC law increase, and national courts find resolution of at least some of these conflicts in referral to the ECJ.

Debate in the literature continues as to the explanatory strength of these reasons (Alter, 1998), but it is clear that over time national courts in the older member states did engage with the ECJ and thereby substantiate the Community mandate. For example, in the UK the judiciary asserted a right to review government legislation conformity to EU law beyond the much more limited request of the plaintiff, in this case the Equal Opportunities Commission (EOC) (Craig, 1998: 217). When one turns to the question of Europeanization, attention is focused on the consequences of this new relationship for the national courts themselves, both in terms of their redefined role and their place within their respective national political system. The next section therefore turns to a brief consideration of the changes that have occurred in national courts' role, specifically as institutions accessed by groups/litigants seeking EC law redress as well as their expanded judicial review power based on EC law. After this discussion the following section will more directly address how national courts' relationship with other national government institutions, in particular national parliaments, has fared.

New roles for national courts

By engaging with the ECJ, national courts entered into a relationship that has taken on a life of its own, or put another way, 'Europeanization of the domestic legal system is difficult to halt because of its endogenous nature' (Nyikos, 2008: 188). According to Weiler (1993), 'the willingness of national courts, especially of lower courts, to play their role in the partnership will widen the circle of actors, individuals, corporations, pressure groups and others who may build a stake and gain an interest in the effectiveness of Community norms' (423, quoted in Nyikos, 2008: 189). Before proceeding with a presentation of the consequences of this relationship, it must be noted that the acceptance by national courts of the supremacy of the ECJ did not occur in a uniform manner. Indeed, not only was this process long in the making – for example, the French *Conseil d'État* demonstrated its acceptance in the 1989 *Nicolo* decision only twenty-five years after *Costa* v. *ENEL* – but thereafter patterns of national court resistance to as well as cooperation with ECJ supremacy persists. Although the reasons given above to explain acceptance of EC law supremacy are fairly straightforward, the explanation for variable timing in acceptance has more to do with factors such as national legal traditions, the existence of national constitutional courts, incentives and constraints faced by national courts *vis-à-vis* executives and legislatures, and so on (Mattli and Slaughter, 1998). The persistence of occasional national resistance to a blanket acceptance of supremacy occurs when, for example, a national court does not refer a case to the ECJ. It may also arise in the logic of a judgment, as was the case with the German Federal Constitutional Court (FCC) during the ratification of the Maastricht Treaty. In this case, the FCC, in dismissing a challenge to German ratification of the Treaty, used the opportunity to create a new basis from which EC law affects national decision-making, essentially making 'the primacy of EC law contingent on national constitutional stipulations' (Conant, 2002: 93). As we shall see in the Conclusion of this chapter, the self-perceived role of the German Federal Constitutional Court to protect national democracy can have ramifications beyond a single member state. From its judgment concerning the Maastricht Treaty, whereby the FCC 'preserves to itself the competence to determine the limits of Community jurisdiction (*Kompetenz-Kompetenz*)' Kokott, 1998: 78) to its ruling concerning the Treaty of Lisbon, the FCC sees itself determining how far EU competence may extend until it affects German democracy and the Basic Law or the constitutional order (Koch, 2008). From the Europeanization research perspective, however, exactly how national courts have been altered in terms of their role within their respective national political systems is the main concern. The ECJ imagined the relationship with national courts to be one in which national judges 'become agents of the Community order – they become Community judges – whenever they resolve disputes governed by EC law' (Stone Sweet, 2000: 164). In practice this may be the case, but evidence of resistance suggests that some national courts accept EC law on their own terms, thus rendering the notion of 'agent' too simplistic. Craig (2003) describes four types of cases in which EC law has clashed with national constitutional norms, ranging from an acceptance to modify its constitutional status quo to disagreement over the legitimacy of ECJ competence in a particular area. What does seem to be the case is that national courts have easily incorporated 'direct effect' without major national reactions, but supremacy has been slow and difficult (De Witte, 1999: especially 196–8). Nevertheless, a consequence is that national courts now have the power to evaluate and rule on the EU constitutionality of national law. What have been the consequences of this behaviour? If the mechanisms of change are represented by the various reasons for acceptance of EC judicial supremacy (as displayed in the logic of decisions and preliminary referrals to the ECJ), the dimensions of change that can be observed to date through empirical studies are reflected in the relations between national courts and national law and institutions. This is the subject to which we now turn.

National courts as channels for societal interests

Once national courts entered into a relationship with the ECJ, potential litigants gained another avenue with which to secure their interests, that is, by invoking the principles of EC law on their behalf. To the extent statistical evidence is available, it is clear that domestic actors have used the legal route in addition to other interest group tactics. While knowledge and resources will be a determining factor in explaining what types of litigants have employed this strategy, it is also clear that national political and structural factors also explain the variation, that is, the presence of facilitating institutions. For example, in the United Kingdom, one source of cases referred to the ECJ has come from the area of gender discrimination. According to Alter and Vargas (2000), the fact that the British Equal Opportunities Commission (EOC) was available to help sponsor support made a significant difference in successfully achieving outcomes that invoked EC rights. Conant has suggested that 'participation of (1) actors with the means to finance litigation, such as commercial enterprises, (2) societal interest organizations, or (3) public agencies engaged in enforcement and advocacy contribute to higher rates of references for preliminary rulings' (2002: 89). The increase in volume of litigation seeking to complement traditional strategies of interest satisfaction has resulted in 'altering the way they [litigants and lawyers] approach litigation, and ultimately, domestic court functions and legal procedure' (Nyikos, 2008: 188). Nyikos concludes that the increase in national court engagement with EC law and referrals has, for some countries 'in which individuals had not had the ability to protest the constitutionality of national law, such as in France and Great Britain, such a change in institutional parameters alters the very core of the legal system' (2008: 188). Kelemen (2006) has suggested that by complementing or indeed influencing and/or instigating domestic groups' increasing use of the EC law route, EU lawmakers are producing an adversarial legalism as a by-product of European governance. He states that 'given the EU's limited implementation and enforcement capacity, EU lawmakers have an incentive to empower private parties with justicible rights and rely on adversarial legalism as a means of decentralized enforcement' (102). Although variable across all member states, the domestic 'push from below' by litigants aware of additional avenues to secure their interests by recognizing EU rights through the domestic legal system adds another dynamic aspect to the role and function of national courts.

National courts vis-à-vis other national governmental institutions

In addition to Germany and Italy, which established constitutional courts in their post-Second World War re-design, several other West

European countries initiated the use of constitutional courts, allowing a judicial review of parliamentary legislation, for example France, and with the return of democracy in the mid-1970s, Spain. Stone (1992) has suggested that the influence of the EU in the form of legal integration is a key factor in the development of judicial review in France. More generally though, another change for which the ECJ and the constitutionalization of the EU are significantly responsible is the fact that the power of judicial review has extended down to ordinary courts as well as constitutional courts, 'at least in the context of Community law' (Claes, 2006: 244). From the perspective of the ECJ, the national constitutional division of powers should not prevent lower or ordinary courts from exercising a right to review parliamentary legislation in order to make sure Treaty obligations are met. This has not been so easy to translate into practice, as for example in the United Kingdom with its principle of parliamentary supremacy; nevertheless, it has indeed transpired in many member states. So the place of courts – all courts – within a national constitutional system has been modified.

The empowerment of courts by way of this ECJ-promoted judicial function has a necessary impact on the constitutional order of each member state, and in particular the inter-institutional balance between the judicial, executive and legislative bodies. Prechal (2007) suggests that a 'direct empowerment' of national courts occurs 'in order to fulfil effectively the task assigned to them by the Court of Justice' (447), and though the formal source of law is national, the effects deriving from the changes to the role of national courts arguably affects other national institutions. In the case of those member states that prior to joining the EC/EU had never before enshrined the notion of judicial review with a constitutional court, for example the United Kingdom or Denmark, the ability to do so now must have *some* effect. Whether the changes are a clear strengthening of courts – and by association, the rule of law and its application in a more transparent manner – or the weakening of the position of parliaments, this is the type of change that has occurred indirectly and thus can be labelled an outcome of the Europeanization process. Although explicit national constitutional changes have not been a direct effect of the new judicial functions, from the logic empowering courts, 'there is no doubt that the Legislature is subject to control exercised by all ordinary courts, a fact that diminishes its traditional superiority over them' (Georgopoulos, 2003: 537). Jupille and Caporaso (2009) also suggest that the 'indigenization' of EU law may 'spillover into otherwise purely domestic areas of law' (6) with unforeseen consequences for institutional balance. As stated above, national political traditions, political structures, the ease or difficulty of access by litigants to courts, etc., all combine to explain, for example, the variation in preliminary referral rates (Conant, 2001), yet the control exercise in the narrow context of EC law nevertheless remains. Also added, in a fashion, to this control function is the responsibility of administrative agencies to protect EC rights. Georgopoulos (2003) suggests that this 'obligation of administrative organs to set aside national legislation incompatible with EC law not only contests the place of legislation as the borderline of administrative action but also establishes administrative departments as 'first-instance judges' of national law's compliance with communitarian norms' (539–40; see also Graver, 2002).

The post-communist experience

The return of democratic politics in Eastern Europe, and the corresponding efforts by post-communist governments to gain membership in the EU, has had a singular impact on the role of constitutional courts as well as the relationship between their courts and the ECJ. On the one hand, the weakness of the newly established governmental institutions – executive and parliament – as well as the volatility of election patterns (see Chapter 6) – has contributed to a relatively higher profile and role for courts in these democratizing countries. According to Kühn, 'constitutional courts have been established in all post-communist states. Indeed, judicial review has become even more important given the relative immaturity of parliamentary structures and party organization in the transition countries, which have resulted in poorly developed systems of parliamentary oversight' (2006: 219–20). In several examples, it has been the role of courts to maintain the steady course of a candidate state in terms of corresponding to the EU's political conditionality, especially in regard to Copenhagen political criteria on minorities. On the other hand, much as many constitutional courts in older member states have found it difficult to accept the supremacy of EC law on the terms of the ECJ, so too have constitutional courts in the newer member states also developed national positions for justifying their engagement with EC law. For example, in an analysis of three court cases – Czech, Hungarian and Polish – in which the decision by the respective constitutional court dealt with an issue involving the EU, Sadurski (2008) suggests that the nature of the decisions, although 'not a picture of audacious judicial defiance in the face of Europe ... [was also not] ... a picture of a timid deference towards the ECJ's doctrine of supremacy' (42). A fundamental difference between the sequence of cases that has led older member state courts to 'adjust' to the supremacy of EC law – from the German Constitutional Court's reasoning regarding the Maastricht Treaty ratification to the French *Conseil d'Etat* logic preserving the republican constitutional model – is that these were already established and legitimate governmental systems (despite the interlude of the Second World War in both countries). The part of western national courts in the constitutionalization of the EU has been incremental and has not had overt transformative effects on their political systems. By way of contrast, acceptance by newly established or re-empowered constitutional courts in post-communist countries to the supremacy of EU law has posed certain specific domestic risks. National courts have been sensitive to demands of sovereignty and the need for legitimating national institutions in general, especially pronounced after the years of Soviet domination, and their own institutional position in particular, so too early a demonstration of 'submission' to ECJ could undermine such efforts (Sadurski, 2008). Second, empowering constitutional courts also strengthens their position *vis-à-vis* executives and parliaments, both of which have had weak popular bases of legitimacy in the post-communist transition phase. Outwardly, then, most post-communist constitutional courts seem to have followed the route of their western counterparts, such as the German Constitutional Court, but the stakes have been different.

Another difference between the post-communist constitutional court experience with EC law and those of the older member states is the issue of transferring norms. Engagement with EC law through direct effect allows the transfer of EU norms into national legal and political systems. Again, in the case of older member states, depending upon the member state in question, the discrepancy between EU and national legal norms may not be such that significant changes are produced. In the case of post-communist candidate or member states, twin pressures or international constraints are involved in norm transference. The first, and more direct, was the EU accession conditionality, especially the political conditionality based upon the

Copenhagen criteria. The European Commission practised surveillance of the prospective member state's legislation and court decisions. The second, more indirect, was the EC case law as developed by the ECJ, to which post-communist constitutional courts would have had to engage, even if only tangentially. In the process, these courts may become 'conduits' for democratic consolidation (Maveety and Grosskopf, 2004). It may also be the case, again because of the unique influence the EU (and ECJ) play in the democratization and stabilization of post-communist political systems, that the ECJ had an impact on the relations between institutions, such as national courts and parliaments. Barrett (2008) has argued that from the perspective of strategic interactions between such institutions, the patterns of cooperation and conflict may be at least partly explained by the position of either institution in relation to ECJ rulings. So, in a much broader sense as compared with the western experience, post-communist court interaction with the ECJ in particular, and EC law in general, has many more consequences, especially for political systems in the process of stabilizing and legitimizing their authority.

Conclusion

The impact of the EU on national courts, both in the older and more recent post-communist member states, is a phenomenon to which a Europeanization research framework may be applied. In the first case, what is to be explained are changes in structures and/or behaviour. In this respect, although evidence of intra-organizational change in national courts was not presented, the relationship between national courts, both constitutional as well as lower courts, and other national government institutions such as executives and parliaments, was found to have altered. One can isolate the EU as a factor, specifically the process of legal integration, in the dynamic interaction between national courts and executives and parliaments. The changes are, in themselves, not transformative, but the effect of a slow, incremental 'build-up' of EC case law, with the ECJ acting as the progenitor, has stimulated specific changes through the adoption of 'direct effect' such as litigant access to EC law – thus affecting the decision-making process and conceptual basis of national courts; a 'balancing act' by national courts with regard to the basis on which they *seemingly* accept EC law supremacy; the empowerment of courts *vis-à-vis* other institutions in the national political system, but also between higher and lower courts within the same national political system. The difference between institutional and behavioural change is not so distinct, as empowerment of an institution may alter its relational power position in a political system, and so the ability of national courts to practise judicial review in EU instances – *if taken up* – (to which a social-constructivist approach may be employed) leads to its part in the constitutionalization of the EU treaties as well as its increased position in the national political system. On the other hand, the pressures 'from below' on national courts to adjudicate in EU matters because of increased demand by litigants suggests how resources and interests combine to produce change for which a rational institutionalist approach would seem appropriate. Again, in the case of Europeanization and national courts, both approaches illuminate separate actions and effects. Finally, once national courts do engage with the ECJ, no matter the justification, they act, whether or not intentionally, as channels for the distribution of EC legal norms into national legal cultures. This may be more significant in the case of post-communist courts as they seek both to establish their own legitimate credentials and to ensure the democratization of their respective countries. For both older and newer member states, though, the entry of EC law norms into their political systems has the potential of re-calibrating the respective strength of courts in relation to executives and parliaments.

Finally, apart from the consequences that derive from the formal or procedural engagement of national courts with the ECJ, there are also possible political ramifications. Two potential possibilities are mentioned here, first the politicization of national courts because of their engagement with ECJ decisions, and second the possibility of future European political integration and domestic institutional change. In the first case, two decisions highlight the uncomfortable position national courts are put when an ECJ decision stimulates organized negative reactions. In 2007, the ECJ ruled in matters concerning labour law, in particular collective action, concerning post-communist workers' lower wages and that of western national social protection and collective bargaining systems. In some older member states, for example Sweden, there were claims that in fact the consequences of the single market logic amounted to a potential weakening of collective action practices. In both the *Viking* and *Laval* cases, the ECJ did not produce a clear-cut victory for western trade unions, which protested what they deemed to be cases of social dumping. According to Zahn (2008), the ECJ rulings left the 'justifiability of collective action when it conflicts with the free movement provisions up to the national courts' (12). A consequence of this particular ruling is that national labour relations systems may now have further national judicial considerations intervene, and, as Zahn notes, the outcomes could vary from one member state to another, thus the mobilization of trade unions against the *Viking* and *Laval* ruling. What these cases also exemplify, for purposes of this chapter, is the position national courts are placed in when ECJ rulings become politicized, and the possible ramifications that may develop in national policy areas, not to mention inter-institutional relations.

The second example of national court involvement with the EU, in this case treaty ratification rather than with a specific piece of EU law or the ruling of the ECJ, has to do with national court rulings on the development of the EU itself (or more precisely the impact of the EU's political development on national democratic processes). In June 2009 the German Federal Constitutional Court (FCC) ruled on the compatibility of the EU's Treaty of Lisbon with German law. Although it ruled that there was no fundamental problem with ratification of this treaty, that is, the treaty was compatible with the German constitution, it ruled that the German parliament, both the Bundesrat and Bundestag, should secure a stronger say in EU affairs, in particular when EU leaders agree among themselves to move a policy area from unanimity to qualified majority voting (qmv) using new 'bridging' procedures. The FCC's attention to national parliamentary democracy in this ruling is in line with the logic of its ruling on the Maastricht Treaty noted above, but in this case it has obliged the German parliament to seek closer, *formal* scrutiny of its executive in EU matters; a direct example of Europeanization of domestic institutions. On another level, though, the FCC has also demanded that future attempts at European integration respect the right of self-determination of the German parliament in policy areas such as social policy and the economy. This could prove difficult to secure German ratification for any future European-level advances in these areas, and thus bears heavily on the direction of future EU policy enhancements.

Chapter 6

Political Parties

Searching for evidence of Europeanization and change in the dimension of politics would seem, at first sight, to be a rather straightforward undertaking. After all, high-profile events such as the French and Dutch referendums that sank the EU Constitutional Treaty in 2005 suggest a popular falling out with European integration. In some EU member states, anti-EU parties and public attitudes have become permanent features of national party systems, for example in the United Kingdom, Denmark and the Czech Republic, to name a few. However, as the EU 'is run by party politicians' (Hix and Lord, 1997: 1) and member state governments can also be described as *party government* (Blondel and Cotta, 2000), the centrality of political parties in the context of Europeanization and political change should be significant. All chapters of this book have until now demonstrated evidence of Europeanization in national governmental institutions, in other words in the structure and processes of national political systems. If this finding is correct, and political parties are instrumental actors at both the domestic and European levels, then one can infer that parties themselves must have experienced some degree of change intrinsic to their organization and/or activities. This chapter investigates the question of change in parties, and it is indeed a fundamental issue in the relationship between the EU and its member states, for parties occupy national executives and parliaments and are therefore implicated to some extent in policy decision-making, all of which have experienced EU-related adaptive change. Therefore how 'national' is party government, and what do these potential changes mean for the operation of parliamentary democracy, in particular the act of holding party politicians accountable while operating in the Council of Ministers as well as the European Council? Evaluating the impact of the EU on national parties, therefore, has implications for the nature of how politics is organized in member states.

Parties, politics and the EU

This chapter concerns one of the crucial actors involved in the democratic politics of EU member states – political parties. As such, if one were to advance the argument that there was evidence of the Europeanization of domestic politics, then it would be highly likely that political parties are implicated in this process in some fashion or another. Although an extensive literature on political parties has developed since the Second World War, covering such issues as organization (e.g. elite, mass and more recently cartel), type of party as characterized by its ideology (e.g. catch-all, populist, etc.), links with citizens (e.g. membership characteristics and the decline in the number of members), and so on, it is only recently that attention has turned to the study of political parties and the European Union. The 'turn towards Europe' by political party analysts follows advances in European integration itself, particularly the establishment of direct elections to the European Parliament beginning in 1979. The study of party groups within the European Parliament, e.g. the Socialist group or the European People's Party, and the behaviour of MEPs (Members of European Parliament), e.g. their voting patterns, emerge from this period of the 1980s and continue to the present. Another concern of academic study has been the development of transnational party federations, the extra-parliamentary wings of the party groups within the Parliament. Although much more modest in terms of their visibility and impact, they have slowly become a permanent feature of the European Union party universe, in particular as regards their activities with parties in the post-communist member states (see below).

Even more recent is an interest in Europeanization and political parties and party systems (Ladrech, 2009). It was argued in Chapter 2 that the origins of the Europeanization approach are to be found in the increased influence of the EU beginning with the Single European Act and continuing through the Maastricht, Amsterdam and Nice treaties. The increase in EU supranational institutional influence has had a variable impact on domestic institutions and policies. Can the same be said for domestic politics? There are certainly some obvious examples of EU-related developments in the politics of EU member states, ranging from the emergence of eurosceptic attitudes in almost all member states – though varying greatly in the degree to which they are held in each member state (McLaren, 2006) – to the impact of European Parliament elections

on domestic party fortunes (Marsh, 2007) to changes in mobilization strategies of social movements (see Chapter 7). Political parties,
though, are supposed to exercise a linkage function between citizens
and government, and if the national governmental institutions of
EU member states have experienced Europeanization effects – as
previous chapters have demonstrated – then it is plausible that
parties may have also attempted changes that reflect some aspect of
EU policy- and decision-making dynamics. One could hypothesize
that any such change would be indirect because national political
parties do not formally interact with EU institutions in the same way
as national executives, who are formal participants in EU institutions, nor do they find their position or function in the national
political system challenged in the same manner as national parliaments. Unlike sub-national authorities, national political parties are
not recipients of EU financial resources, usually a powerful incentive for adjusting some element of strategy. In fact, to the extent one
can say that national political parties do interact directly with the
European level of decision-making, it is exercised through their
control over the election campaigns to the European Parliament and
relations with their respective MEPs. One could suggest that as the
national executive is composed of party representatives, then political parties actually influence decision-making in the European
Council and Council of Ministers. This assumption, though, rests
on internal changes within parties to practise either *ex ante* or *ex
post* control over 'their' government ministers' EU activities. But do
these forms of interaction engage any of the mechanisms of change
associated with Europeanization? This chapter explores these questions by first reviewing the Europeanization argument regarding
politics as a dimension of domestic change, then turns to the specific
question of political parties and the EU. As with previous chapters,
the experience of post-communist parties is also evaluated.

Europeanization and domestic politics

Labelling a dimension of domestic change 'politics' casts one's
analytical net quite wide. In fact, it might be argued that politics as
a category for investigation in Europeanization research is simply
too all-encompassing, as it can denote individual as well as group
political dynamics, and sources that are uniquely domestic as well as
international. Consequently, it is necessary to focus on changes in

patterns of organized political behaviour, whether this is expressed in parties (and specific variables such as organization, ideology), interest groups (e.g. organization, lobbying strategy), social movements (e.g. identity, strategy) or public opinion (e.g. emergence of eurosceptic attitudes). In such cases one can explore whether shifts in patterns of activity are related to the influence of the EU, in particular through process tracing and/or counterfactual reasoning. But what places 'politics' as a dimension of change in Europeanization research apart from the general categories of 'polity' and 'policy' is the absence of a direct relationship between authoritative EU legislative output and the actors mentioned above. Further, the mechanisms of change that have been apparent so far in our investigation of Europeanization effects – in particular *misfit* and learning – are much more difficult to conceptualize, for example in the case of parties or public opinion. This does not mean, however, that the increase in the policy competence and institutional decision-making power of the EU since the mid-1980s has had no impact whatsoever in the realm of member states' domestic politics. For our purposes, what needs to be ascertained is exactly what has been changed and in what manner, so that any observed changes can be linked in some way to EU-national government policy and decision-making interaction. Organizational change in parties and interest groups represents a clear example where changes in patterns of activity may be detected and then process traced to uncover whether or not the EU or some aspect of European-level factors have been implicated. How might the EU exercise influence on organizations for which the national political system represents the pre-eminent focus of their activities? In other words, parties and interest groups are not obliged to directly interact with EU institutions if they do not wish to do so. The most likely answer is that the EU has impacted the national political system in such a way that the means to achieving party and interest group goals has been affected, and compensatory adjustments have been undertaken. Let us take this argument and look at it in more depth in regard to parties and interest groups.

Political parties carry out several functions in political systems, such as recruitment of personnel into elected office, as well as having goals specific to their mission, for example gaining government office, influencing public policy and maximizing their electoral support (Strøm and Müller, 1999). If the EU could be said to 'interfere' in a fashion that impacts a party's ability to carry out its systemic function(s) or organizational goals, then one could hypoth-esize some type of response in terms of adaptation to the new envi-ronmental conditions. So the question may then be posed: if the EU does not directly impact parties, what indirect features of the politi-cal system might have been Europeanized to the extent that it trig-gers or causes parties to respond in some manner? First, *mass attitudes* toward the EU may have changed, and political parties may respond to the growth of anti-EU sentiment. Second, *EP elec-tions* necessitate an additional electoral mobilization, and resources are required as well as new rules for candidate selection. Third, with the *development of the EU*, especially in terms of growing policy competence, party programmes with regard to their position on European integration may also evolve. Fourth, as the *policy compe-tence of the EU has broadened*, the consequent narrowing of the scope of national government policy-making may be reflected in the policy proposals of parties. Fifth, as *national parliaments have created European affairs committees*, those MPs sitting on these committees may develop particular expertise in some aspect of EU affairs and thus represent 'expert knowledge' within the party orga-nization. The same principle applies for all those party personnel who occupy positions of leadership and who formally participate in EU institutions, from MEPs to the president of the European Commission. Finally, many but not all national parties are also *members of transnational party federations*, which themselves were originally created in anticipation of direct elections to the EP, and there may be advantages from such affiliation. All of the above are examples of developments that *may* cause national parties to under-take changes in internal organization matters, statutes or manifestos for example, but scarcely affect their functions in the political system or their overall ability to secure their goals.

Interest groups, on the other hand, have different functions and goals in national political systems. These may range from represent-ing their members' interests, from trade associations to trade unions, to actively lobbying on behalf of members' interests in national as well as local and international government institutions, both executive and legislative. Unlike political parties, for which national elections are critical moments in their political and organi-zational existence, interest groups may have the incentive to involve themselves in EU policy-making. The primary reason that may moti-vate interest groups to focus a portion of their activities on the EU legislative agenda – through the gathering of information and lobbying – is that certain EU policies may *directly* impact their members' interests. For example, some member states have opt-outs from the 48 hours' working time directive, and this may have come about from pressure from professional associations that feel unduly or unfairly affected, such as doctors. Producer associations may also see it in their interests to dilute proposed environmental standards that may add costs to their industry. Both examples suggest that the interests represented by such groups may be directly affected by EU policy proposals, though how such organizations react in terms of targeting lobbying activities is not necessarily conditioned by the supranational source of the legislation, namely where lobbying is targeted for maximum efficacy is not predetermined. The EU may also indirectly impact the strategies of domestic interest groups because of *broader changes in national policy-making structures and practices*. In Chapter 8 attention is drawn to the greater expo-sure of national economies to private competitive activity, where the EU's Competition Policy has been responsible at least in part for liberalization of certain utility sectors. In these cases the relationship between the state and producers is altered, both for state-owned (or previous state-owned) and new entrants into a market. This type of change may affect the specific nature of a country's system of inter-est intermediation, and thereby the constraints and opportunities for related interest groups.

In the two examples presented, parties and interest groups may find that changes in their respective operating environments have evolved to some degree because of EU influence, in particular in institutional and policy domains. In both cases, though, there is not a clear pressure or misfit which is created by EU practices that elic-its a response as discussed in previous chapters. Rather, the EU's influence is manifested and interpreted as variously a threat or opportunity, depending on the particular issue at hand. In other words, EU policies and decision-making practices may offer parties' and interest groups' opportunities to advance their goals, but also constraints on the pursuit of their interests; the question is then to understand to what extent this voluntary engagement with the EU results in some degree of change in the actors' organization, ideology, etc. In Chapter 7 Europeanization and interest groups (and social movements) will be discussed in more depth, so atten-tion will centre on the EU and political parties for the remainder of this chapter.

Europeanization and political parties

To the extent empirical changes in political parties can be traced to the influence of the EU, the causal mechanism is less a pressure to adapt than the exploitation of opportunities to advance interests and/or measures taken to resist the spillover of EU issues interfering and thus complicating party leadership goals and activities. Let us begin by asking: what opportunities does the EU provide for national political parties? At first glance, the answer would seem to be 'none'. National political parties do not receive direct financial resources from the EU (although their respective national delegation in the EP will receive funding); the European Commission has no right to intervene in national electoral rules or parties' organizational statutes; and the most prestigious prizes in the EU in terms of political office are appointed rather than contested in competitive elections, for example the post of president of the European Commission. National parties themselves are extremely limited in what they can do at the European level. National parties are in charge of the national campaigns for European Parliament elections, and have, in varying degrees, some influence over the voting decisions of their MEPs. Most EU politicians are also party politicians (Hix and Lord, 1997), although how they act in European-level forums may reflect more a national than partisan behaviour. Finally, political parties can mobilize citizens in their respective member state to support or oppose proposed EU treaty changes where referendums are held on such matters. Although only a minority of EU member states hold such referendums, the 2005 Constitutional Treaty referendum defeats in France and the Netherlands demonstrate the consequences of even one or two such referendum setbacks for EU institutional development. In all, the EU cannot exert direct influence on parties and what a national party can accomplish at the European level is rather modest. As for constraints, or unwelcome complexity, indirectly the EU may, in some member states, contribute to the creation of a new dimension in party competition, in which a pro- and anti-EU axis emerges that is orthogonal to the left–right axis (Hix, 1999). The pro- or anti-EU axis illustrates, at the time of EP elections, the electoral success of small parties in so-called second-order elections, for example UKIP (UK Independence Party) in the United Kingdom. The EU impact on national executive policy-making options – reduced in some respects because of policy transfer to the EU and monetary union –

may affect parties' own policy proposals (Mair, 2008) by limiting their scope. This of course has implications of a normative character for national representative democracy as well as narrowing the scope of competition during national elections. The EU as a potentially politicized issue in domestic political arenas may also represent a form of 'unwanted interference' that may affect the internal equilibrium among a party's different components (or even factions). In this case, party leaderships seek to contain debate over EU institutional reform or specific policy issues in order to prevent internal dissent from undermining electoral credibility (Steenbergen and Scott, 2004). This practice by party leaderships partly explains why campaigns by major parties of the centre-left and centre-right to the European Parliament are mostly devoid of a 'EU' policy content, instead focusing on domestic issues and the record of the incumbent party in national government. What then is the empirical record of change, and how can it be specifically accounted for? Ladrech (2002) suggested five areas of party activity where evidence of Europeanization may be found. Although it is not an exhaustive list, it does engage many of the functions and core activities of national parties. Work published since Ladrech's contribution has taken up the call for more precision in evaluating the impact of the EU on the internal operation of parties as well as on party competition.

Programmatic change

Several studies have employed comparative and national data – both qualitative and quantitative – to see whether the EU and/or its policies have become prominent in party manifestos. There is evidence of (a) a modest rise in references to the EU, but (b) an even lesser increase in specific policy proposals for the EU (e.g. Pennings, 2006). What is evident is that most political parties have devoted a section to addressing their basic stance on their country's membership in the EU. This can take a supportive or sceptical perspective. Specific attention to EU policy content or institutional reform, in the form of proposals for change, is rare except for parties that are animated by the EU as a central feature of their programmatic profile, for example eurosceptic parties. Party programmes and election manifestos, though, may not be the best indicator of the rising profile of the EU or issues related to it within national political parties for several reasons. First, if the EU is not a salient issue in a campaign, there is no incentive for a party to draw attention to it.

Second, it may very well be the case that the EU and related policies are highly politicized in a particular political system, and a specific position may attract and repel voters, so the least said the better. Third, the EU may be a divisive issue within a political party, and the party leadership may, in the interests of containing open dissent, provide as innocuous a statement on the EU as possible. There may, of course, be more country-specific reasons explaining why party manifestos, at least of mainstream parties, do not reflect the policy significance of the EU. In the case of parties at the extremes of party systems, where eurosceptic positions are often found, the EU will be more prominent in campaign manifestos and other party literature as well as during referendum campaigns.

Organizational change

Very few studies have evaluated the extent to which the EU may indirectly influence the organization and internal politics of parties. Raunio (2002) has argued that one consequence of EU membership is increased leadership autonomy (which complements national executive strengthening, see Chapter 2). Poguntke *et al.* (2007) investigated whether the internal equilibrium between the different sections and individual positions of a party may have been influenced, for example the relative weight of those who have direct responsibility for EU affairs. Their conclusion was that although there had been a modest increase in the number of EU affairs positions, mostly confined to the international relations section of a party, this did not result in a relative empowerment of the incumbents. In fact, where organizational change had been apparent, it is in the so-called 'party in central office' (national organization) rather than the 'party in public office' (MPs, etc.) or the 'party on the ground' (constituencies or branches consisting of members). This is not too surprising, as elected party members concentrate on the demands of their positions and re-election, and the members of the party (a declining part of all mainstream parties) are dependent upon specialized information regarding EU policies. That leaves the party apparatus to engage with the European level, whether by having MEPs sit on leadership bodies, providing representation to a transnational party federation of which it is a member, dividing its international relations division into Europe and the rest of the world, or taking charge of drafting party manifestos and other policy documents, for both national and EP elections. As the main task of the party in central office is to support the party's activities in the national arena, only a small amount of resources would be expected to be involved on issues that do not penetrate the domestic issue agenda.

Patterns of party competition

This dimension most closely follows Mair's (2008) discussion of the effect of policy constraints on party competition. With a number of policy areas either transferred to or shared with the EU, parties have a narrow range of policy areas with which to promise change (Mair, 2000). This could, for example, result in the convergence of mainstream centre-left and centre-right parties on economic issues. This could be characterized as a de-politicization, as issues are removed from the national to the supranational level. Another potential change in party competition is the appearance of eurosceptic or anti-EU parties, whether on the left or right. To the extent they have found a permanent niche in some party systems, their percentage of the vote has not been large enough to force the main parties of government to change their positions. However, in the referendums of 2005 in France and the Netherlands, and in 2007 in Ireland, eurosceptic forces were able to influence the results. Finally, as noted above, many political scientists have studied what may be termed a new dimension in party competition, based on the emergence of a pro- and anti-integration axis. As this new axis is considered to be orthogonal to the traditional left v. right axis, its incorporation into national patterns of party competition, that is, national parties adjusting a left or right socio-economic position with support or antagonism for European integration, has not been very well developed. However, evidence of such a dimension in voting behaviour is witnessed at EP elections, where anti-EU parties do substantially better than during national electoral contests, for example UKIP in the United Kingdom.

Party–government relations

Might inter-governmental bargaining and other policy and decision-making activities as part of the EU legislative process precipitate strained relations between the party in public office and the party in central office? This question revolves around the degree to which party activists, who may have a larger or more pronounced voice in the central party organization and take more ideologically pure policy positions,namely mid-level elites, oppose their representatives in government. This phenomenon would depend on the type of central party organization, that is, the internal rules governing leadership selection, and so on, and is more likely to be demonstrated in parties where the 'party in public office' shares control with the 'party in central office', for example the French Socialist Party. This may also be the case where the party leader is not the elected head of government, and so must respond to party-activist sentiment as well as support the party in office, for example the German Social Democratic Party in the late 1990s and after 2005. In general though, this area of party activity, although it presents a challenge for party management, is rare, as it could present a picture of a fragmented party to voters.

Relations beyond the national party system

Many national parties belong to one of several transnational party federations, for example the European Green Party or the Party of European Socialists (PES). (Hanley, 2008). These so-called Euro-parties are the extra-parliamentary party organization whose parliamentary wing is present as a party group in the European Parliament. These Euro-parties play essentially a networking function for national parties, as involvement within their structures reduces the transaction costs of multiple bi-lateral relations (Ladrech, 2000). The leaders of national parties also control the programmatic and organizational development of these Euro-parties. Change in the relations may come about due to a self-perceived need to acquire external legitimacy within a domestic political system, for example the Italian party of Mr Berlusconi, Forza Italia, sought membership in the European People's Party (EPP) in the 1990s as a sign of its acceptance by mainstream centre-right parties in the EU. For some parties, such as the Dutch Labour Party, electing delegates to the congress of its affiliated Euro-party, the PES, rather than the party leadership appointing them, represented an effort to democratize and legitimate positions taken in the Party's name at such occasions. For most national parties, whether they belong to a Euro-party or not, such membership does not impinge on their routine activities, except for the fact that the manifesto drafting process for EP elections does involve the Euro-party, at least for the Greens, Social Democrats, and parties affiliated with the European People's Party (EPP), mostly Christian Democrats and conservatives (but not the UK Conservative party or the Czech ODS). Suggested reforms to the appointment of the president of the European Commission, for example, linking the choice to the outcome of EP elections, would raise the profile of Euro-parties in their member national parties, but this is as yet only a possibility.

These five dimensions of party activity have witnessed modest changes since the mid-1990s, and to some extent the increase in the politics and policy content associated with the EU is responsible. In other words, mainstream national parties have made slight adjustments to their programmes and manifestos which do not do much more than acknowledge the significance of the EU; most parties do not trumpet their position *vis-à-vis* European integration unless they can score electoral points (it has domestic salience); most parties do not make fundamental organizational changes because the primary focus of their activities remains the domestic political system; and national parties' membership in Euro-parties has remained marginal to their basic functions. The lack of national media coverage of EU affairs – except for European Council summits – reinforces the general lack of attention by parties to the EU and its consequences for national political developments. It would then seem that a paradox exists, with the substantial increase in the influence of the EU having little to no impact on most national parties or party systems. National parties continue to go about their activities as if their participation in EU policy and decision-making – in the European Parliament through their MEPs and in the Council of Ministers and European Council through their elected officials and party leaders – has no reverberation in domestic politics. The answer to this apparent contradiction is the attitudes of member states' citizens. Parties respond to shifts in public opinion, but as stated above, opinions on the EU have yet to substantially impact the traditional left–right axis. Parties have therefore had the 'luxury' of compartmentalizing (Aylott, 2002) serious attention within their organization and programme on the EU and its related policies and direction, allowing what mobilization of public opinion that is manifest to seep into marginal eurosceptic parties. If and when public opinion, or the 'sleeping giant', does awake, the consequences for national parties may be unpredictable (van der Eijk and Franklin, 2004; 2007). A glimpse of the possible consequences for parties of a mobilized citizenry in national elections is the case of the Netherlands, which held parliamentary elections before and after the EU referendum in 2005.

De Vries (2009) argues that in the Dutch case referendums do facilitate the development of EU issue voting in national elections. Still, from the perspective of winning office and/or increasing the share of the vote, to the extent that national political parties can be said to have Europeanized, it may be limited but appropriate in terms of the pursuit of their goals (Ladrech, 2007). The discussion has so far concentrated on parties in the older EU member states (pre-2004). A very legitimate question to ask is how far the considerations discussed above pertain to the situation of parties in post-communist member states, where competitive elections and political pluralism have only been in operation since the early 1990s.

Europeanization and parties in post-communist member states

The experience of post-communist political parties in the European Union, or more specifically the impact of the EU on their development and activities, has been of a different order compared with established parties in the older member states. Indeed, as Enyedi succinctly states, 'parties in Eastern Central Europe do not simply adapt to the process of European integration: they are part of it from the very beginning' (2007: 65). The literature on the impact of the EU on post-communist transition and consolidation, and parties in particular, has concerned itself with questions of democratization, the absorption of EU norms, and party development factors deriving from EU political conditionality in general, and the specific role and influence of transnational party cooperation. In general, the party-political terrain in post-communist countries was, and continues to be, challenging for the development of competitive party systems resembling those of older member states. In the process of constitutional development, the position for parties was explicitly acknowledged, no doubt in light of the history of one-party rule under Communist regimes. Party finance rules and regulations were drafted, as well as electoral rules, which because of the low threshold for parties to enter parliament, resulted in a large number of small parties in the emergent multi-party systems. But if these were some of the larger technical factors that had to be put into place early on in order to provide the legal basis for party competition, the development of parties themselves was quite different from the West. Apart from the former regime parties, some of which made the transition to a centre-left, social democratic party, all other parties were created in the wake of the regime change, some inheriting the mantle of anti-regime social movements (many of which then experienced schisms and defections within a few years). Without an existing electoral base, or put another way, without institutional linkages to citizens, whether direct (membership) or indirect (e.g. trade unions or other associations linked to the party), most parties began life as groups of MPs (party in public office) looking to build a 'party in central office' and 'on the ground' (Van Biezen, 2003). In this, at times, chaotic environment the EU exerted a much stronger influence than was the case in older member states' parties.

Democratization

The EU asserted in its Copenhagen criteria political conditions for membership. Among these political conditions was a functioning plural and competitive political system, and, together with the strong desire of political elites and citizens in the region to join the EU as soon as possible, this condition helped the consolidation of the democratic process in these countries. Some have argued that in the case of Slovakia, for example, the EU in fact contributed to the successful mobilization of liberal forces in determining the outcome of the critically important election of 1999 that pitted the authoritarian-leaning government of Prime Minister Meciar against a coalition of democratic parties (Henderson, 2006; Vachudová, 2005). The fear of losing out in terms of candidate status was the extra 'disciplining' factor introduced into the equation.

Transfer of norms

Although the items contained within the political conditionality are broad in scope, the EU monitored the operation of political practices, from legislation on minority rights to the freedom of media coverage in elections. Although new norms are introduced and internalized over a medium- to long-term period of time, in an indirect fashion the EU assisted in several ways in the transfer of certain norms and values as it affected political parties. First, the EU influenced the drafting of regulations for party funding through its promotion of anti-corruption reforms (Walecki, 2007). The legacy of these regulations can be seen in the internal activities related to party funding, where in many countries state financing has become established. Second, the EU's promotion of minority rights in particular, and non-discrimination in general, has meant that extremist parties are not as a rule accepted into government coalitions. Lastly, new party-formation dynamics involved an ideological transfer from the West as regards party programmatic identity (see below for further discussion on this point).

Transnational party cooperation

One of the main differences between the indirect effects of the EU on parties in post-communist member states, particularly during the pre-accession period, and parties in the West is the role that transnational party federations played. Pridham (1996; 2005) has argued that in terms of programmatic development, campaign guidance and ideological profiles, these western party federations, in particular the PES and EPP, contributed significantly to the developmental trajectory of the main centre-left and centre-right parties in these countries (note that the Czech centre-right ODS is the only main party of government to not belong to the EPP or any other transnational party federation). Especially helpful for new parties of government was the recommended policy position they should adopt that was consistent with the policy orientation of the respective transnational party federation. The scrutiny of organizational and political principles of applicant parties in their efforts to gain membership to these Euro-parties also assisted in the establishment and consolidation of western norms on party behaviour (Johansson, 2008). In return, advice in running election campaigns as well as the legitimacy conferred by belonging to one of the main European party families contributed not only in the strengthening of individual parties, but also to the pattern of party competition (Lewis, 2006).

The Europeanization of post-communist parties has been much more profound compared to their counterparts in the West. First, western parties and party systems had been established long before the creation of the EU, and certainly before the strengthening of the EU's influence from the late 1980s onwards. Second, the asymmetric relationship between the EU and the candidate states of east central Europe, coupled with the strong desire to join the EU as soon as possible, meant that fundamental questions regarding political development were heavily influenced by EU norms and western practices (Vachudová, 2008). Third, transnational party federations consciously sought to influence the political trajectory of potential members in the candidate states, as much to see democracy consolidated as to gain members for purposes of their own competition, especially within the European Parliament. The continuing electoral volatility in most of these new EU member states has meant that new party formation and disintegration persists at rates higher than in the West. Higher amounts of eurosceptic attitudes in many of these member states also suggests that perhaps a backlash from the economic conditions that finally allowed membership (a winners v. losers of integration) has taken root, helping to sustain some of the extreme right and left parties found in many of the party systems in the region. In conclusion, Europeanization of post-communist parties has been much more direct in comparison to the experience of parties in the West.

Conclusion

The issue of whether the Europeanization research framework, such as it exists, is applicable to political parties was raised at the outset of this chapter. It was noted that national political parties, as organizations, are removed from direct and legal outputs from the EU. Although the EU may influence certain aspects of parties' operating environment, that is the domestic political system, they are themselves insulated from direct EU rules and regulations. As to whether the activities of party personnel in the European Parliament may have an impact on the national party, research suggests the opposite to be the case (Scully, 2005; Scully and Farrell, 2003). Further, veto players and other domestic variables that have been invoked to explain variability of adaptational response appear to be inappropriate for the study of national parties, though the role of party leaderships in determining the degree to which the party as a whole is 'shielded' from matters related to the EU is critical in any future research agendas. So, despite documented evidence of modest changes in political parties in relation to a more influential EU in general, the exact mechanisms for this phenomenon are under-theorized.

As with all other dimensions of domestic change explored, it is necessary to isolate the EU factor so as to not unjustifiably attribute causal influence where alternative factors may be at work. So too is it the case with political parties, and because of the absence of direct

EU inputs as well as a 'goodness-of-fit' mechanism, process tracing may not be the most fruitful approach. Rather, counterfactual reasoning may lead to some points of departure for future research. For example, new positions within the national party organization, such as a Europe Secretary (in addition to an International Secretary) would not exist were it not for the presence of the EU. What triggers the *timing* of the creation of the position, though, may yield insights as to how the EU's significance is perceived by a party leadership. Similarly, the timing of internal party dissent might be explained by proposed advances in European integration such as the 2005 Constitutional Treaty, or particular legislation such as the 2006 services liberalization directive. Neither of these EU-related actions impinges directly on national parties' electoral fortunes or systemic functions, but the *perception* of their consequences by some party personnel, perhaps from an ideological perspective, is enough to trigger some degree of mobilization. This suggests a social constructivist approach would be useful for uncovering *how* the EU is perceived within a party, namely as a threat or an opportunity. Viewed from this perspective, creating the post of a Europe secretary could then be understood as the means by which a party organization specifies or denotes expertise or 'intelligence gathering' on the possible influence of the EU, that is, the position represents an 'early warning system' for the leadership on developments at the EU level that may have consequences for the party in the near to medium future. At the same time, parties are organizations with specific goals and objectives, and rationalist assumptions of change in structure or behaviour may also have a role to play in understanding party Europeanization. For parties in most older member states, the salience of the EU as an electoral factor has been small and not one that contributes to improving a party's competitive position. There is a tendency in fact for parties to downplay or even suppress the EU as an issue, a decision that rests with party leaders. Party leaderships' perception of interests and evaluation of changing environmental variables and consequent fashioning of new strategies for organizational preservation and development suggest that a combination of rationalist and social-constructivist approaches may yield positive advances in the study of parties and the EU.

Finally, returning to the issues presented at the outset of this chapter, that is, the future of party government in a parliamentary democracy experiencing changes in its structures (institutions) and processes (policy-making), and more narrowly the act of holding party politicians accountable for their actions in EU institutions (Council of Ministers and European Council), what conclusions can be reached? First, if mainstream parties of government are indeed keeping changes to the wider political system at 'arm's length' while they involve themselves with their traditional functions and practices, what does this say about the quality of party government? At the very least, if citizens' interests are to be represented to some degree in government policy output, then the disjuncture between citizen expectations of party responsibility in government (the executive as well as the legislature) and the reality of EU influence in policy which party programmes/manifestos neither address nor are directly informed of by parliamentary groups in national legislatures, leaves unanswered questions as to the accountability and representation of contemporary party government. One possible result of this situation is a form of 'de-politicisation' (Mair, 2007), in which more and more public policy decisions are taken beyond the national political system, thereby emptying a portion of the content of competitive party politics. Of course, one reaction to this state of affairs would be more fundamental opposition to the EU, as no other avenues for citizen choices are available to influence the process at the domestic level, and perhaps one factor explaining the declining turnout at EP elections is precisely the futility felt by many member state citizens that their vote does not translate into policy output, and national parties do not help the situation much by marginalizing European issues during EP campaigns. The party-political aspect of parliamentary government is then one dimension of Europeanization and politics that is increasingly under pressure for change, at least for principled reasons.

Chapter 7

Interest Groups and Social Movements

Collective action in EU member states is reflected in the very fabric or structure of domestic policy-making (interest group activity) and may promote outsider groups' entry into this process or challenge its very legitimacy (social movement mobilization). In either case, this non-electoral political activity involves a more self-directed form of political participation than the more passive act of voting for parties at periodic elections. One of the central aims of either actor is to promote the interests of its members, and in some cases the promotion of 'public goods', so if there is an impact on organization and strategy that impinges on the attainment of these goals, then Europeanization may have positive as well as negative consequences. As Chapter 8 on Policies will demonstrate, a good portion of domestic policy-making is interwoven into the EU policy-making process, so the question of access to this nexus is crucial for organized groups, and issues of resources and long-standing relationships, become important factors for analysis. As for the wider impact on member states' own interest intermediation systems, the possibility the EU may indirectly stimulate more societal demands on national governments, that is, EU policy content being lobbied or protested at the doors of national government, raises issues of how this type of demand is dealt with by national governmental actors.

Organized interests such as trade unions, business interests and professional associations on the one hand, and social movements on the other, represent two very general types of collective actors. In the former category, activities are directed at appropriate levels of government that are responsible for controlling or coordinating resources and legislating policies that are of significance to the members of such organizations. Depending on the particular national system of interest intermediation, relations between interest groups and government may range from open and cooperative to confrontational. The activity itself may be highly structured between groups and government, as in neo-corporatist systems, or display a high degree of competition between groups as they seek to influence government policy, as in pluralist systems. As for social movements, their *modus operandi* is most likely to bear the characteristics of protest, whether demonstrating for a 'new politics' issue or to defend or protect the survival of an occupation. In both cases, it is clear that the EU may influence the strategy of actors as they seek to promote their interests, owing to the policy domain in which the EU may have competence – ranging from agriculture to transport – and the particular level of territorial authority at which this is exercised, namely exclusively or shared with the national and/or sub-national levels. In other words, the development of multi-level governance in the EU has potential consequences for collective action. This chapter explores the extent to which the EU has had a direct or indirect impact on the strategy and organization of domestic interest groups and social movements. As the previous chapter on Political Parties demonstrated, the EU has virtually no *direct* impact on domestic actors for which the EU has no formal or legal connection or is in a position to transfer resources that are integral to the goals of the domestic actor. However, the EU may *indirectly* affect the domestic political system in ways that provide domestic actors such as parties and interest groups with an incentive to direct a portion of their activities in either a proactive or defensive stance *vis-à-vis* the EU. In Chapter 6 we saw that political parties, except in limited ways, have not engaged with the EU primarily due to the lack of incentive to do so. Exceptions were anti-EU or eurosceptic parties, for whom politicizing the EU in negative terms serves to draw attention to themselves during election campaigns, and small parties such as Greens that have secured some representation in the European Parliament, from which resources may be critical to their financial survival. Political parties consequently continue to operate almost exclusively within the domestic political system from which they secure all of their key resources and exercise their basic functions. Interest groups, and to a limited extent social movements, relate to the EU by way of maximizing and defending their resources and key objectives. In this context, the EU represents a 'political opportunity structure' that may be exploited by interest groups. This chapter investigates this political opportunity structure 'mechanism' in order to understand why and in what manner certain groups engage the EU. This encompasses a discussion of the EU policy output, lobbying strategies and resources, the appropriate level of lobbying, and in the specific case of social movements, the manner in which politicizing their issue affects their relationship to the EU and their domestic political system.

How does the EU affect interest group behaviour?

The policy output of the EU means that many domestic groups have a stake in influencing EU decision-making in order to protect and/or advance their goals. Greenwood (2007) notes that the variety of such interests is vast: 'It includes firms, professions, employers and labour groups, consumer, cause, social/community, citizen and environmental interests, at European, national and sub-national levels of organization, and territorial interests themselves, such as regional and local government' (9). All of these different organized interests have developed over the years a particular relationship with their respective domestic institutions, whether these are legislatures, executive agencies and ministries, and in federal systems, sub-national levels of government, all depending on the policy domain. Considering that the EU may be characterized as a regulatory actor, especially regarding Single Market issues, it is not too difficult to expect that domestic interest groups may find, at any time, that proposed EU legislation may affect their activities. The key issues then, from a Europeanization perspective, are *when* do domestic interest groups divert a portion of their attention to the EU in the pursuit of their goals, and *how* do they do so? In order to explain the behaviour of domestic interest groups *vis-à-vis* the EU, we should consider, first, the nature of EU policy output, and second, the degree to which domestic interest groups are embedded in their national political systems. When we speak of the EU as a 'political opportunity structure' for domestic interest groups, a double meaning is implied. First, the EU generates directives and regulations in policies that may have an impact on domestic groups, so there exists a potential or possibility that groups will organize themselves in such a way as to influence the final legislation. Second, if we consider that over time interest groups have developed repertoires of action suited to the level which is most efficacious for their activities, then the EU represents a possible field of action within an overall multi-level governance structure for domestic groups, which may choose to operate as 'branches' at the sub-national, national, or supranational level, depending on the 'return' on the investment of resources. When we turn to the nature of interest groups' place or ties in their respective national political systems, we are interested in determining how these relations affect groups' adaptation to EU influence (EU output). Following Beyers and Kerremans (2007), one can conceptualize the Europeanization of interest groups as being dependent on 'the immediate organizational environment of domestic groups' (463), and 'how organizations are structurally connected or tied to their environment' (464) will determine how they respond to EU policies. In sum, they argue that critical resource dependencies are key to understanding whether domestic groups do in fact Europeanize, and a

> simple resource-based perspective that ignores critical resource dependencies ... assumes that interest groups are always prepared to modify and Europeanize their strategies as soon as their material self-interests would require or their interests would enable them to do so. Such a perspective neglects the possibility that actors refrain from going beyond the domestic level because they are in need of, identify with or are loyal to their local or domestic resource suppliers. (464)

The nature of interest group critical resource dependency acts as a mediating factor in the Europeanization process, so that although a particular group may recognize the significance of a proposed EU policy on their activities, how they react will vary according to the nature of their domestic embeddedness.

How does the EU affect social movements?

Similar to the manner in which the EU may encourage interest groups to develop strategies to influence EU policy-making where this has the potential to impact their goals, social movements also may react to the policy output of the EU. However, since social movements consist of both occupational and non-occupational groups, for example farmers (occupational) and ecologists (non-occupational), EU policy output varies greatly in stimulating a response. For example, proposed cuts in subsidies to EU farmers as part reforms to the Common Agricultural Policy (CAP) may directly threaten the livelihood of certain groups of farmers across EU member states. On the other hand, proposed EU legislation on carbon emissions may invite environmental groups to lobby for or against the legislation (depending on the specific details). In the first case, farmers' income is directly affected, if not survival, whereas in the case of environmentalists, although all citizens may be affected by changes in carbon emissions, only a small segment of those affected may mobilize. Social movements, both occupational and non-occupational, are characterized by 'political protest', and in the context of EU policies, the protest is most likely to be directed against the EU and its decisions. This being said, the difference between occupational and non-occupational social movements may have an impact on the precise nature of the protest. Princen and Kerremans (2008) have argued that the 'actual effects of political opportunities on social movements depend on (1) the identification of those opportunities, (2) the existence of collective identities and frames that are favourable to specific forms of political activity, and (3) organizational resources and capabilities that allow social movements to take advantage of those opportunities' (1132). Occupational groups, because of the clearly identifiable profile of membership, usually with organizational structures of long standing – trade unions, farmers' collectives and unions, and so on – may feel 'targeted' by certain EU policies and thus stimulate a defensive reaction compared to non-occupational groups, for whom the diffuse nature of the EU policy output that in principle may engage their members may not be felt as strongly (i.e. not have immediate consequences). For example, in a study of protest and the EU covering the years 1984 to 1997, Imig and Tarrow (2001: 38–9) found that in comparing

> the propensity of occupational and nonoccupational groups across Europe to protest against the EU ... through 1997, the former initiated a much larger share (82.1 percent) of the total than the latter. It appears that those issues most likely to affect the livelihood of workers are also likely to encourage their contentious political action against the EU.

In both cases, groups may identify the significance of a proposed EU policy, but the mobilizing potential may be greater for occupational groups.

For both interest groups and social movements, the policy output of the EU is a necessary but not sufficient factor in itself to cause adaptational change. Still, several sets of factors may be said to condition their responses to EU policy. Eising (2008) suggests four sets of such factors. First, the widening scope of EU policy competence, especially in Single Market matters (linked with the absence of the national veto), brings EU regulatory actions into direct contact with these actors' activities and goals. As in the distinction between occupational and non-occupational social movements, so too with interest groups the particular policy domain – related to the Single Market or not – reveals a second dimension of potential mobilizing power. Thirdly, resources of groups may also contribute to their capacity to operate at different levels – supranational as well as national and sub-national. Finally, the ability of individual interest groups or social movements to attract support or align with other actors and political institutions may also contribute to their success in successfully focusing efforts at the European level. All of these factors may explain the variability of groups, within and across member states, to successfully engage the EU, from lobbying to protest. What is now required is an understanding of how these actors respond to the EU policy output that impacts their goals and activities.

How do interest groups and social movements respond to EU policy outputs?

The policy output of the EU has the potential to trigger responses from domestic interest groups and social movements because they are either threatened by the proposed policy or else they perceive opportunities for advancing goals. This being said, the response of those groups or movements that perceive themselves either threatened or with a possible opportunity to exploit the EU, may not actually result in directly engaging EU institutions. In fact, one of the most striking characteristics of the Europeanization of interest groups and social movements is how little their targets in terms of mobilization are actually EU institutions, whether one speaks of lobbying the European Parliament or protesting in front of the European Commission. Let us be clear: although there is indeed evidence of domestic groups adapting their organization and strategies to involve themselves at the European level, and further, that European-level interest associations have indeed emerged (whose members are national-based), when domestic identities, goals and interests are affected by EU policies, more often than not the response is targeted within the national arena. The following section explores this issue of the (self-perceived) appropriate venue for reactions to EU policy input. Most studies on the phenomenon distinguish between interest groups and social movements when considering the degree of involvement at either the European or national level, with the former more likely to adapt a portion of their organization and resources to directly influence EU decision-making while the latter centring their more limited resources on national governments.

Interest groups

A list of the types of domestic interests that may be affected by EU policy output was presented at the outset of this chapter. Of course, the resources necessary to undertake new or additional activities at the European level would favour larger organizations over smaller ones, and narrowly defined interests over those more diffuse or cross-sectoral. According to Mazey and Richardson (2003), discussing the institutionalization of interest intermediation within the European Commission, 'notwithstanding the Commission's efforts to integrate the so-called civil society interests into the policy process, the most powerful European lobbyists are producers interests, notably multinational firms, whose interests (and policy frames) are deeply embedded within the Commission' (225). Coen and Dannreuther (2003) also note that large firms have more options to influence Brussels than small businesses, as they have the resources and organizational capacity 'to express the clearly defined interests that are required to cut through the noise of opinions at the European level, as nation states do' (271). Even so, as discussed above in regard to the EU as a political opportunity structure – and the effort by the Commission and Parliament to attract civil society actors makes it inviting at least in principle – it remains the case that the nature of domestic interest groups is tied to their national political system, ranging from relations with executive agencies and parliamentary actors, support from one or another political party, access to ministers, membership strength, and so on, all combining to present interest groups with a choice of venue when seeking to influence the EU policy-making realm. Consider the relationship between large producers, for example a car manufacturer, and the government(s) of the member state where its plant(s) is(are) located.

Policy proposals from the Commission requiring better fuel mileage by a certain date may mobilize the manufacturer to present evidence at a European Parliament committee arguing that the standards are either too high or the target date is too soon, or both. At the same time, because of the critical position of such a business actor for the national economy, lobbying the national executive may be a more cost-effective method for diluting the Commission proposal. This is because lobbying on its behalf in Brussels by national executive actors, such as its Permanent Representative (COREPER) and ultimately support from the appropriate minister in the context of inter-governmental bargaining, may pay greater dividends. Certainly in the case of car manufacturers, the same perceived threat from Commission proposals will be shared in all member states with such business interests. The greater return on resource expenditure, in other words, comes from (multi-) national lobbying. In this example, greater resources do not necessarily translate into a predisposition for European-level activity. Lobbying at the European Parliament is episodic, whereas relations with national government officials are ongoing. This suggests, as Beyers and Kerremans (2007) argue, that '[w]ithout denying the potential importance of the role played by resources and EU-level opportunity structures, we demonstrated that an interest group's embeddedness in its immediate environment as well as critical resource dependencies play a crucial role' (477). So domestic ties, or the 'national route' (Greenwood, 2007), may offer the more rational channel to responding to or influencing EU policy development, from a cost–benefit analysis. According to Greenwood, 'reliance upon "tried and tested" channels through a domestic host government may reduce the incentive to develop a "Brussels route", while the lack of practical resource means to find direct representation in Brussels means that a "national route" remains the principal outlet for many domestic interests' (2007: 29).

Europeanization of interest groups, to be precise, must encompass a reaction – either defensive or proactive – to EU policy outputs that are understood to affect their goals or ability to acquire certain goods. However, the evidence to date suggests that adaptive change – either in strategy or organization, or both – is not necessarily reflected in the development of a European presence, whether in terms of direct lobbying or through the efforts of a European-level association. Rather, resources – to enable European-level activity but also in terms of intelligence on the potential impact of EU policies, as well as ties to the domestic arena, and the nature of the institutions – both European and national, account for the variation in utilizing either the national or 'Brussels' route (or a combination of both). What is clear is that Europeanization involves interest groups' response to a perception that the EU level is or will generate potential changes in their specific operating environment, and that they act upon this finding. How they do so, especially at the European level, contributes to an understanding of how bottom-up Europeanization builds a European system of interest intermediation (Wessels, 2004). But even with the proliferation of Euro-associations since the Single European Act, many of them exist solely as 'information-gatherers' for their national membership, with modest secretariats. Additionally, the needs of their national members in regard to most EU legislation that could possibly generate some level of mobilization, is episodic, thus the provision of a rudimentary organization in Brussels is all that most Euro-associations encompass. At the domestic level, which is our central concern, continued focus on national government for support in responding to EU policy output may mask these groups' 'internal' Europeanization, in other words, the perception of an EU impact exists, but the response is incorporated into traditional routes of influence, or, as Beyers and Kerremans (2007: 477) put it, 'they are still able to realize many of their political goals at the domestic level'. Europeanization research could benefit from further exploration of this 'internal' dimension of change within interest groups, for as Eising (2008: 177) states, 'to date EU scholars do not pay great attention to the *structure and internal politics of domestic interest groups* or to the inter-organizational dynamics of co-operation and competition that emerge in *multi-level networks*' (original italics). Finally, even as domestic interest groups lobby national governments over potential EU policy concerns, does the nature of this activity indirectly affect national government–domestic interest group relations? That is, does increased lobbying of national government over EU-policy related issues have any consequences for a national interest intermediation system? In a study of four Nordic countries – Sweden, Denmark, Norway and Finland – Pedersen (2007) suggests that 'with European integration the number of channels between administration and interests has increased; the means of managing interests have been combined; contacts are more intensive and extensive; and representation has taken new forms (i.e. has become more informal than formal)'

(105). More research addressing this phenomenon across different types or clusters of EU member states would perhaps detect patterns of change that are related to the type of national interest intermediation system.

Social movements

If protest, rather than lobbying, is the expressive means of many social movements, whether occupational or non-occupational, then the impact of the message – namely the publicity it derives – may be at least as important as the specific content of the protest. For social movements, not only is the EU policy output of critical significance for potential mobilization, but also the need for publicity is crucial because the route used by governments and interest groups, i.e. direct engagement with EU institutions, is not a suitable recourse for many social movements. The multi-level arrangement of the EU puts a premium on resources, and consequently, together with the absence of routine access to policy-makers in Brussels, social movements focus on attracting attention. Put together, this means that social movements, which are comparatively poorer in terms of resources than large producers and firms, must determine the appropriate level – national or supranational – for the most effective use of their efforts in creating publicity for their cause. Kriesi *et al.* (2007) state, when considering the importance of public-oriented strategies of political actors, that 'the struggle for public attention and, conversely, the use of public-oriented strategies, is important for all types of actors, but to various degrees' (54). In the case of social movement organizations, they 'typically lack routinized access to the decision-making arenas and can therefore be expected to primarily rely on public strategies' (55), unlike state actors, political parties or even interest groups. Further, social movement organizations tend to rely on 'a combination of two kinds of public-related strategies – a combination of "*protest politics*" (mobilizing for protest events) and "*information politics*" (the collection of credible informations [*sic*] and their introduction into the public sphere as well as in the decision-making arenas)' (55). Bearing in mind, then, the relative resource weakness of social movements compared to other actors, the target arena for their public-related strategies must be carefully chosen to maximize their political claim (Koopmans, 2007). A political claim may be defined as: 'the purposive and public articulation of political demands, calls to action, proposals, criticisms or physical attacks, which, actually or potentially, affect the interests or integrity of the claimants and/or other collective actors' (Koopmans, 2007: 189). The question of social movement Europeanization is similar in part to that of interest groups, that is, the appropriate venue. Unlike interest groups, which may have, depending on the resources and access, the option of adding European-level lobbying to their routine national activity, social movements, the evidence demonstrates, are more reliant on the national arena for their public-related strategies, and in fact, 'are clearly the least able to profit from the opening up of Europeanised discursive spaces' (Koopmans, 2007: 199).

There are two general sets of factors that explain the domestic focus of social movement responses to EU policy output, bearing in mind the important dependence on public-related strategies to attract attention to their cause. The first is the nature of EU institutions as a target of protests, and the second is the rootedness or institutionalization of social movements in their domestic setting. First, the EU institutions, or more specifically Brussels (and Strasbourg) as sites for protest, are not conducive to attracting attention that can be useful for a cause. These institutions are 'media poor' from a social movement perspective. Since protest activities are dependent on publicity, meaning simply that media coverage should be transmitted to the appropriate audience or audiences, activities in Brussels or Strasbourg covered by a Belgian or French press do little to help if the protesters are Spanish or Slovenian. Where there may be a European press or television, such as the European Voice or Euronews, they reach only small audiences, and transnational media such as CNN 'have a global, rather than European profile and audience' (Koopmans, 2007: 185). In other words, protests and demonstrations in European Union capitals ill serve social movements if maximizing media coverage is part of their repertoire. Second, in addition to the drawback of low media coverage, the opposite of what is intended for a particular audience of supporters and sympathizers, the object of the protests, that is, European institutions and decision-makers, are themselves not ideal targets. For example, a Commission proposal will be decided by the Council of Ministers and the European Parliament, so demonstrations in front of the Berlaymont building in Brussels (the Commission headquarters) is not directing pressure at the correct decision-maker. As for the Council of Ministers, apart from its secretariat and COREPER, the ministers are in their national governments most of the time, and particular Council meetings, which may not last usually more than one day, put an extra effort on the social movement in question for intelligence on dates, coordination of members' travel from different member states, etc. And finally the European Parliament, made up as it is of representatives from the member states, and arrayed in a partisan manner, is not a cohesive body on policy issues. Third, the EU institutions, therefore, are not ideal candidates for 'outsider' activities such as protests, and in the end, although the EP can make amendments, it is inter-governmental bargaining that characterizes most decision-making, and so one-dimensional protests are ineffective. Lastly, if the intent of protests, other than to influence the decision-makers, is to mobilize public opinion to their cause, there is very little in the way that this potential support can be expressed. Elections to the EP occur every five years, and European issues have featured very little in each member state's EP election campaigns (the so-called 'second-order' nature of these electoral contests focuses on mostly national issues). The electoral cycles in the member states are not uniform, so even an electoral sanction of a national government will do little to change the array of political forces in inter-governmental bargaining. The combination of these factors and the complexity of EU decision-making make these institutions a suboptimal choice in terms of social movements' strategic mobilization. As a set of institutions, therefore, the EU is not a very effective political opportunity structure for domestic social movements.

If EU institutions are a poor choice as a platform for protests by social movements, the ties to their domestic surroundings, resource capabilities, and perception of opportunity explain why domestic-situated protest, even if it is aimed at EU policies, is a more conducive environment. Ties to domestic venues are as important to social movements as they are for interest groups. Many social movements have grown out of grass-roots activism, and membership is therefore a critical resource. Existing networks of smaller groups that can converge on an issue is a hallmark of domestic social movement protest. The nature of these ties suggests that the domestic arena presents the optimum venue for 'contentious claims'; the issue is how an EU-inspired response can be articulated in a domestic setting with any effect. Here research on the Europeanization of protest has produced consistent findings in what Imig and Tarrow (2001) label '*domesticated protests*', as a category of '*Europrotests*'. Europrotests are 'all incidents of contentious claims-making to which the EU or one of its agencies is in some way either the source, the direct target, or an indirect target of protests and the actors come from at least one member state' (32). Domesticated protests, in particular, are 'examples of contentious claims-making in which the EU or one of its agencies is either the source or an indirect target of a protest by domestic actors, but the direct target of the action is either the state, its components, or other actors present on its territory' (32). Finally, Imig and Tarrow do acknowledge that there exist 'transnational European protests', the difference with domesticated protests being the fact that 'actors from more than one EU member state take part' (32). Although there is evidence of a growth in the number of transnational European protests (Imig and Tarrow, 2001; Imig, 2004), the overwhelming type of protest in which the EU is the target are of the domesticated type, attesting to the centrality of domestic settings as the best possible venue for reactions to EU policy output. In the Imig and Tarrow study, which covered the years 1984 to 1997, domesticated protest accounted for 82.8 percent of protests against the EU, while transnational protest made up 17.1 percent. Within these domesticated protests, occupational groups make up the largest share. To date, 'the largest proportion of protests concerning the European Union have taken domestic rather than transnational shape, indicating that while Europeans are increasingly troubled by the policy incursions of the EU, they continue to vent their grievances close to home – demanding that their national governments act on their behalf' (Imig, 2004: 233). An illustration of this phenomenon was a three-day protest by French fishermen in March 2009, who blockaded a few key ports on the French coast preventing ferries from the UK from either entering or departing, causing consternation for individuals as well as freight. According to a spokesperson for the protesters (BBC News reporting), the target of their protest was what they considered to be unfair EU fishing quotas, which he argued favoured large corporate fishing fleets over small fishermen. The dispute was finally resolved when the French Government, unable to unilaterally change EU guidelines, agreed to pay compensation for losses incurred by small fishermen. The example demonstrates that changing the EU policy may not necessarily be the intent of the protest but seeking national protection or relief is ultimately, in light of the nature of EU decision-making, the rational approach for these actors. Della Porta (2007) reports another dimension, the 'externalization' of protest at the EU level with the 'aim to change national policies' (205). In 'this case actors who are feeling weak at home try to mobilize allies at the supranational level: protest addresses the EU institutions in order to push them to intervene in domestic affairs' (196). Environmental campaigns are examples of such mobilizations. Thus Europeanization of social movements, as with interest groups, certainly involves a response to an EU policy output, but a European or transnational response is not necessarily, in light of resources and domestic grounding, the rational response when confronted with the supranational and inter-governmental nature of EU decision-making. Nevertheless, as studies indicate, the EU is becoming a target of social movement activism, though demonstrated primarily by occupational groups who perceive themselves at the short end of EU policy developments.

The Europeanization of interest groups and social movements is a documented phenomenon in many studies. Two generalizations can be made: first, the growing scope of EU policy competence has stimulated a response in terms of the action repertoires of both actors. In the case of interest groups, critical resource dependencies and pre-existing links and relations to domestic governments, national and sub-national, very often represent the best focus for lobbying over proposed EU policies; more as a complement than as an alternative, activity at the European level, either as direct engagement with EU institutions and actors, or through Euro-associations, has increased since the Single European Act, though again resources and information are critical in this respect. The openness of the Commission and European Parliament presents the EU as a political opportunity structure, but only for a limited number of domestic interest groups. For social movements, multiple factors mitigate against EU institutions as an ideal location for protests. Although there is a slowly rising number of transnational EU protests, where protests are organized with actors from more than one EU member state, it remains the case that 'the salience and accessibility of the decision-making process of the EU is much lower than that at the national level, which explains why they [domestic actors] are still predominantly focused on influencing the national political process' (Kriesi *et al.*, 2007: 69). Where occupational groups may sense that the national government may respond to protests through compensation for the debilitating effects of EU policies, then these types of domesticated protests will persist.

Europeanization and post-communist interest groups and social movements

One of the general characteristics often used to describe the societies emerging from the communist experience was the lack of a developed civil society. It was expected that the post-communist regimes would evolve in a direction roughly similar to their Western European neighbours, and this included creating organized groups in society and corresponding channels to government for their interests to be articulated. The legacy of the communist era, that is, the underdeveloped nature of civil society, makes comparisons with western counterparts inappropriate, especially within the context of Europeanization. However, some patterns have been noted, and this section describes some of the activity that one can trace to EU influence. First, labour and employers' organizations are discussed with reference to EU inputs. Second, the nature of organized business interests is addressed. Finally, the existence of social movement activity and the relationship with EU policy output is presented. The common denominator in all cases is the weakness of civil society actors and the influence of EU political conditionality and the rapid downloading of the *acquis communautaire* on state–society relations. Communist one-party rule and the lack of autonomy afforded organized groups, many of which were initiated by the state, such as trade unions, meant that apart from some of the grass-root groups that quickly emerged in 1989 to challenge communist governments (an exception being Solidarity in Poland which began nearly ten years earlier), there was a virtual vacuum of autonomous organized interests to assist in the reconstruction of society under the new regimes. From the mid-1990s onwards, with the decision taken by government elites with the presumed support of the citizenry to achieve EU membership as swiftly as possible, any policy developments that could have elicited support or input from (dis)affected interests were tied to the efforts to download the EU's *acquis communautaire*. Thus the development of civil society groups was indirectly influenced by pre-accession dynamics, which, broadly speaking, affected a range of interests from business and labour to environmental and minority rights. The development of a national civil society was therefore indirectly affected by external factors, in this case the policy orientation of the EU and its asymmetric relationship with post-communist prospective member states. These nascent groups would need to absorb (i.e. learn) both domestic and

EU institutional and policy norms. This is one dimension of their Europeanization.

The relations between the main social actors in western societies, employers, labour and the state often represent the foundation upon which a national interest intermediation system rests, as well as characteristics such as pluralist or neo-corporatist. The legacy of communist rule meant that independent trade unions had to be established anew, and the privatization of the economy, which unfolded differently among post-communist countries, affected the nature of enterprise ownership. Rates of unionization have declined in most post-communist states faster than in the West (with exceptions), although this may partially be explained by the abolition of compulsory communist-era union membership. However, as Avdagić and Crouch (2006) explain, other factors have influenced this decline, including 'a generally negative image of the unions in the new democracies, and particularly their low effectiveness in protecting the interests of their members during the process of economic transformation' (206). As for employers' organizations, they have been characterized as relatively fragmented and organizationally weak, and this fact helps to explain why wages in most post-communist states are predominantly determined at the enterprise rather than the sectoral level (as they are in Western Europe): 'despite the existence of peak-level tripartite structures ... the weakness or virtual absence of bargaining at the sectoral-level in the CEECs is directly related to the weakness of employers' organizations' (Avdagić and Crouch, 2006: 206–7). Essentially, interest groups representing employers and labour are still evolving, and in their absence the state, guided in many areas of socio-economic development by EU policies, proceeds with policy development without an active and authoritative input from these actors. The formation of business interest associations has had an additional obstacle, a feature found in many post-communist governments especially during their early years: corruption. Duvanova (2007), on the other hand, suggests that in fact corruption among new state bureaucracies may actually be an impetus for the creation of business associations, because 'protection from corruption is a relative benefit provided by associations to their members ... [by making] ... their members less vulnerable to arbitrary regulations and extortions on the part of bureaucrats' (444). As business interest associations developed, the impact of the EU on the direction of economic development also affected their lobbying strategies, primarily to produce a model of interest mediation 'where the exchange and ownership of information are more important than the actual impact on policy-making' (Pérez-Solórzano Borragán, 2004: 262). Finally, despite the role that grass-roots social movements played in the final year or so of the communist regimes, often under the broad label of environmental movements, 'one of the most surprising aspects of post-communist politics is the lack of large-scale political protests' (Mudde, 2007: 221). Apart from protests as a means for articulating a reaction to actual or proposed legislation, certain civil society organizations, with assistance from European sources, do maintain a voice especially where minority rights are involved. Here the EU's Copenhagen criteria give such organizations their external-generated legitimacy, for example in defence of the rights of Roma minorities in the Czech Republic, Slovakia, etc. This development and maintenance of an organizational profile hand-in-hand with EU norms and criteria also characterize aspects of Europeanization in the region.

Conclusion

The study of the influence of the EU on national systems of interest intermediation and collective actors, both in the older and newer member states, is relatively recent. Indeed, as Saurugger (2007) exclaims, it 'is therefore astonishing that scholars concerned with developments in the EU have only slowly become interested in the particular aspect [in particular collective action]' (482). As for post-communist member states, 'analyses of the Europeanization of interest groups are still particularly rare' (Sedelmeier, 2006: 16). The tentative conclusions one can draw from this chapter are: (1) national systems of interest intermediation and the ties of interest groups to government agencies and the resource dependencies that have evolved over years prevent an automatic 'turn towards Brussels' when EU policy output is perceived to affect group interests. In the case of post-communist member states, the transition period and pre-accession political and economic dynamics produced an environment somewhat inhospitable for the formation and activity of civil society organizations; (2) for interest groups in older as well as newer member states, aiming activity at the EU institutions is a complement rather than an alternative to their 'tried and tested' national routes for articulating their interests to decision-makers; (3) a reason for the persistence of the national route, even when the specific issue is European, is that in many cases national government (executive) actors, operating in EU institutions, may be able to achieve some or all of the goals of the domestic interest group; (4) social movements are more dependent on their domestic environments for mobilization potential and resources, and are more often inclined to use domestic sites to protest against EU policy output, and further, occupational groups are more active in reacting to EU legislation they believe threatens their way of life, e.g. farmers, fishermen, workers; and (5) future study of Europeanization and interest groups and social movements can benefit from more intra-organizational studies of the impact of EU legislation. On this final point, it is clear that the EU does influence the behaviour of these domestic actors, but a response manifesting itself in terms of EU-level activity and organization is only a small part of the evidence of Europeanization. The studies cited above, for example noting the significance of critical resource dependencies, make use of both rational actor approaches and constructivist understandings of learning. For actors in both the older and newer member states, combining both approaches should yield interesting results.

Finally, considering whether the degree of changes documented above add up to either positive or negative consequences for national systems of interest intermediation, the simple answer in the case of interest groups is that the development of EU policy competence in a range of policy domains has not fundamentally altered their role and practices; slight adjustments to conventional behaviour seem to be the overall outcome of change. This being said, there are certain occupational groups for whom EU policy outputs may have more fundamental repercussions, and sometimes conventional lobbying is complemented by protest – using the national government at the site for venting displeasure and opposition to EU policies. As for social movements, although there has been a modest increase in transnational movement mobilization, the national arena remains the central site for action, whether by choice or necessity. There is a clear difference in the Europeanization of parties, on the one hand, and interest groups and social movements on the other, all actors in the dimension of *political* change. Whereas in the former case, parties' immediate concerns allow them to ignore or at best 'compartmentalize' the EU as an issue, thereby leading to situations where individual party personnel acknowledge changes in the domestic political system generated by

EU membership but at the same time resist responding to this state of affairs, interest groups and social movements have adjusted where the costs and benefits of such change makes sense to the achievement of their goals. Overall, the outcome of domestic change in politics, as measured by these actors, is modest in terms of the persistence of political system characteristics.

Chapter 8

National Policy

The chapters up to this point covering Europeanization and institutional change have illustrated, in the case of the pre-2004 member states, widespread but modest degrees of change (although the changes in relations between national institutions may have longer-term impacts). In the realm of Europeanization and policy change, the question of state evolution again comes to the fore, as the spectrum of change runs from modest adjustments of individual policies to pressure on national policy styles. In this regard, Europeanization and policy change implicates private actors as well as public institutions and modes of participation, and can potentially stimulate public reaction to changes in policy direction, especially in economic policy. Where leadership in policy change is located, and how this has changed over time is also a feature of the impact of the EU in domestic policy domains and policy-making. Chapter 9 will specifically treat the classically inter-governmental area of foreign policy. This chapter casts a wider net over the myriad ways in which the EU, probably in its most characteristic fashion of intensively engaging member states on a continuous basis, hits domestic 'ways of doing things'.

EU policy and national policy-making systems

The causes of policy change in EU member states are many; however, before we delve into this subject, we should be clear about exactly what we are referring to. When one speaks of policy change, one can mean wholesale or fundamental change, for instance a shifting of emphasis from regulation to de-regulation (or vice versa) in one or more sectors, or even a fundamental change in philosophy with regard to state–economy relations. A change of government representing a major partisan shift is one of the traditional ways that such policy change occurs, for example when the Conservative

Party under Mrs Thatcher entered British government in 1979. Literature regarding the differences between centre-left and centre-right spending on social welfare policies, even in an era of globalization, supports this finding (Garrett, 1998). On the other hand, there is also incremental policy change, which may come about for a variety of reasons, for example budgetary retrenchment, especially affecting policies that a government has some discretion in funding. Feedback in terms of how well a policy is implemented and maintained can also alter practice. Organized interests may have an influence on the development and implementation of certain policies, and in some cases competition between organized interests may affect the evolution of public policies. In such cases concerning societal interests, the nature of the national interest intermediation system – for instance neo-corporatist or pluralist – may offer further insights as to the degree of influence of interest groups. Finally, although this is not an exhaustive list of possible causes of incremental policy change, reforms to national administration may cause changes in the contours of policy; here the New Public Management approach, especially in the UK and Scandinavia, had an effect on public sector administration, and thereby the delivery and maintenance of certain policies. Our concern in this chapter is with the impact of the EU on national policy and policy-making. One therefore needs to carefully distinguish between the normal or routine EU policy-making process that includes national interests ranging from governments to organized domestic interests, with its legislative output formally transposed into national law, from the effects or consequences of this process and outputs. Top-down Europeanization as policy change – our specific concern – is not reflected in the formal output and implementation of the EU policy-making process; rather, it is about what happens during the process and its implementation inside the member states.

It is widely accepted that the content as well as the means by which national policy is developed has been significantly affected by the European Union. In the area of Europeanization studies, it is also fair to say that the bulk of research has focused on EU-influenced change on national policy and policy-making. However, this very general statement of fact does not help us to understand *how* the EU exerts influence nor on *what types of national policy* this influence may be felt. On the one hand, it is not too difficult to imagine that the influence the EU has accumulated in certain areas of policy can have a possible effect upon corresponding domestic domains. This is because the member states have themselves transferred policy competence to the EU. Second, changes in the decision-making process, especially in regard to Single Market policies, namely the use of qualified majority voting in the Council of Ministers, as well as the development of co-decision between the European Parliament and the Council of Ministers, have meant that the range of policies and the manner in which they are decided upon amplify the influence of the EU. On the other hand, there are sets of policy to which the EU has a more direct – if not directing – influence and a set in which the EU may attempt to influence, but the final say resides with the member states. This distinction between two general sets of policy is crucial for understanding how EU-induced changes in national policy occur and where, namely the policy area, and what in particular is changed. Any such discussion is therefore concerned expressly with the consequences that derive from the implementation of EU policy (or even the attempt to implement such policy). To be clear, this means that Europeanization is not a reflection of how well national governments implement EU policies – slowly, badly, and so on – as this would be an issue of compliance, and a matter for which member state governments are legally obliged to conform due to treaty obligations. Reasons for non-compliance are not simply a refusal to accede to legal obligations, and some of the same factors that explain Europeanization outputs may also explain non-compliance, for example the varying administrative capacities of national government (Falkner *et al.*, 2005). Nor is Europeanization of national policy simply the downloading of an EU policy into a domestic area that was previously absent such a policy, for example certain aspects of environmental policy. In this case, formal adoption of a EU policy belongs to the area of EU and national governance or even European integration more broadly construed. Instead, the aim of this chapter is to demonstrate the varying degree to which the EU impacts or changes national policy or policy sectors, and explain the variation across national policy areas, and the exact nature of the changes. To give a simple example of the phenomenon: assume some member states may struggle to implement a certain agreed EU regulation – and in fact may have argued for longer periods for implementation. Nevertheless, in the course of building the capability to carry out their obligation, national regulatory law or agencies may be modified in their content or operation, a process reflecting the pressure deriving from the nature of the EU regulation, not a specific demand by the EU to reorganize a national administrative structure or wider regulatory emphasis. The evidence of Europeanization is reflected in the various means by which a member state adapts its policy or policy instruments to meet the challenge of implementation. Europeanization of national policy is therefore reflected in the consequences that derive from national governments' attempt to implement EU policies, whether this emanates in the form of directives and regulations or in the form of policy recommendations made by the Commission. In this chapter, the distinction between EU policies that member states must implement and those policy suggestions and ideas promoted by the EU will be designated 'hard' and 'soft' respectively.

Types of EU policy influence on member states: 'hard' and 'soft'

There are a variety of ways in which the policy output of the EU may have an impact on its member states' policies. One should first distinguish between the EU policy output that follows the legislative process resulting in binding legislation in the form of directives and regulations, and the policy ideas or recommendations promoted by the EU, whether they originate with the Commission, the European Council, or from one or a set of member states. Concerning the first type of policies, what we shall label 'hard' policies, there are two broad sets that affect national governments: those that are involved in 'market correcting' (positive integration) and the other in 'market making' (negative integration). With positive integration, for example environmental policy, however broad or specific the legislation in terms of actions – especially the case with directives – the agreed policy that is to be 'downloaded' by member states can be said to represent a template for policy activity in the stated sector. It is, of course, the case that during negotiations over this type of policy output, member state governments as well as other domestic actors may have 'uploaded' their preferences and compromises secured, that is, competition will have taken place to shape the EU agenda. Negative integration, for example through the EU's Competition Policy, has as its intent the removal of barriers to market transactions, and the liberalization of 'closed' sectors is one of the primary means by which this is articulated. However, unlike the 'template' that is downloaded in regard to positive integration policies, the consequences of negative integration tend to influence member state economies in terms of 'a much more horizontal process of policy adjustment associated with Europeanization' (Bulmer and Radaelli, 2005: 345). Our concern, though, is what happens after the process is complete at the European level and the implementation into domestic law as regards positive integration, and the wider consequences of national economic adjustment to competition among national rules and market actors with negative integration.

The second type of EU activity that may impact national policies are policy ideas or proposals that, even if promoted by the European Commission, do not have the same binding or legal jurisdiction as those policies which derive from first pillar (Community) policies, what we shall label 'soft' policies. In other words, the Commission may suggest certain examples of best practice for member states or a sub-set of member states, but is in no position to have this proposition channelled through the regular decision-making process involving the European Parliament and the Council of Ministers. The member states themselves determine whether or not the policy idea promoted by the Commission is something they would countenance, and then develop to the degree of becoming a shared practice. Such ideas may originate from a variety of sources, for example from the Commission, acting as a 'policy entrepreneur'; a practice by one or a number of member states that the Commission thinks should be more widely disseminated; by one or a number of member states themselves, using the Commission to circulate and promote the idea or practice (so as to lower the transaction costs of bi-lateral meetings); and finally from domestic actors whose benefit would be enhanced if such ideas or practices were more widely in use. Formally, the two pillars of Common Foreign and Security Policy (CFSP) and Justice and Home Affairs (JHA) are policy areas where the Commission does not take a leading position; indeed, these are inter-governmental policy areas (see Chapter 9 for a discussion of foreign policy). To the extent the Commission may have suggestions for initiatives in either policy area, it is still the member state governments who act as gatekeepers and control any eventual policy development process. What has arisen since the mid-1990s is another dimension of activity in which the activities described above have taken place, that is, where member state governments remain in control but engage policies not normally associated with either CFSP or JHA. The best example of this phenomenon is the so-called Open Method of Coordination

(OMC). Originally set up in order to develop and implement the agenda of the Lisbon Strategy, the OMC, according to the March 2000 European Council Conclusions, is a

> means of spreading best practice and achieving greater conver-
> gence towards the main EU goals. This method, which is
> designed to help Member States to progressively develop their
> own policies, involves, *inter alia*, a) fixed guidelines with specific
> timetables, b) quantitative and qualitative indicators and bench-
> marks, c) setting specific targets, and d) periodic monitoring,
> evaluation and peer review which can aid in mutual learning.

Radaelli has characterized the OMC, at least in its intent, as a means by which the EU is employed 'as a policy transfer platform rather than a law-making system' (2003: 43). Economic, employment and social policies have been broad areas in which the OMC has been applied (see Heidenreich and Bischoff, 2008 for an evaluation of the OMC as regards social and employment policy institutionalization). The means of diffusion of the policies that we shall label as 'soft' – where national governments control the process – has been termed 'facilitated coordination' by Bulmer and Radaelli (2005), which will be employed below in the discussion of the impact of such policies.

The discussion so far has touched on, in the broadest sense, the main dimensions of policy change from the position of the EU, or mode of governance. To recap, the EU 'hits' member state policy areas by virtue of the formal downloading of directives and regula-tions (first pillar; positive integration). EU legislation also affects member states' policy areas through the legislated removal of barri-ers to Single Market activity (e.g. Competition Policy; negative inte-gration). More recently, the EU acts as a medium through which member state governments may seek to spread certain policy prac-tices, ideas, and goals without the binding nature of first pillar legis-lation as well as the directing role of the Commission, with the best example of this practice being the OMC (some have suggested the OMC itself represents an inter-governmental direction for EU policy-making in general). The mode of governance in which 'hard' policies are transmitted has been referred to as hierarchical due to the authoritativeness of the EU in its mandate, while the mode of governance in which member states set the agenda and the horizon-tal exchange of ideas, etc., has been labelled one of 'facilitation' (see Bulmer and Radaelli, 2005 for the theoretical discussion; and

Bulmer *et al.*, 2007 for its application in case studies of the regulation of utilities). Having established how, in general, the EU is in a position to influence or induce policy change in member states, it is now necessary to examine the mechanisms by which change may occur. Here we are back in familiar terrain, that is, the explanatory factor is the misfit arising from the pressure that is produced between EU demands – positive or negative integration (hard) or through spreading policy ideas and practices (soft) – and the pre-existing situation or structures in a member state. As concerns domestic policy and related implementation practices, a misfit may manifest itself in two basic fashions. A policy misfit is, in the first instance, the incongruence between a EU and a domestic policy. There is thus, on the face of it, adaptational pressure on the national government in question to achieve compliance with the EU directive or regulation by the appropriate means necessary, and in so doing, some member states may find that overall standards in the particular area have been affected (i.e. raised) and/or new policy instruments have been developed in order to meet compliance requirements. A misfit between an EU policy area in more general terms and that of a member state may, in some cases, produce Europeanization effects that engage wider dynamics, in some cases becoming politicized. Here we are speaking of an incremental misfit pressure on a whole policy sector, not only in terms of a mismatch in policy outputs, but also in the general direction of the domestic policy-making style (e.g. challenges to French public services by EU liberalization directives, or a shift in public–private labour relations in Denmark). The adaptational pressure, which may ignite resistance in early stages, goes beyond the policy misfit creation of new policy instruments, and instead may lead to shifts in the national policy paradigm. This dimension of policy change then may stimulate changes in the polity itself.

The misfit argument, while a key precondition for change, does not explain the variation in policy change or even *if* such change were to occur. In most cases of EU legislation transmitted to member states, there will be some degree of latitude in which domestic institutions and actors shape the policy content of the legislation, and here we should expect a variety of national positions. For example, it may be that an EU policy may either weaken or strengthen a particular domestic constituency, and the implementation phase of a policy may therefore influence the 'balance of power' among groups, which in some circumstances might be labelled traditionalists and modernizers. The 'political opportunity structure' opened up for some groups by an EU policy may serve to shift coalitions of organized interests, again a political effect of Europeanization. Héritier *et al.* (2001) argue that in order to understand why change happens in some member states and not others, or why it may be reflected in different forms – adaptation or resistance for example – the degree and direction of domestic change should be seen as depending on the 'distinctive constellation of three factors: the stage of the national policy process (pre-reform, reform, post-reform), the level of the sectoral reform capacity, as well as the prevailing belief system' (288–9). Their framework helps one to understand why, for example, a particular directive concerning liberalization of a public utility will generate internal resistance by public sector trade unions in one member state (the prevailing belief system and level of sectoral reform capacity) and perhaps run into compliance problems, but another member state may experience no such dilemma. This framework necessarily enriches the Europeanization research agenda by focusing on the pre-existing national characteristics that explain differential Europeanization outcomes.

Having established the main outlines of the Europeanization of policy change, we now proceed to illustrate in more depth the dynamics of how the EU hierarchical mode of governance results in 'hard' policy impact and domestic change followed by a presentation of how facilitated governance results in 'soft' policy triggering domestic change. In the former category, two cases are presented that capture the essence of the more direct impact the EU may have on domestic policy, one representing positive integration and the other negative integration; in the latter category two cases are presented demonstrating that despite the fact member state governments strive to control the process of policy diffusion, consequences in terms of policy change may nevertheless occur. The two examples chosen to exemplify this phenomenon are policies in the area of the Open Method of Coordination (OMC).

The domestic impact of 'hard' EU policies

Positive integration

Positive integration represents the set of EU policies that aim to correct for market deficiencies or problems that arise from the development of the Single Market and national market processes (market-correcting). Examples would include negative externalities such as air pollution and its movement across borders that call for supranational regulation and national legal compliance. Positive integration EU policies have the legal weight of EC law, so the final adoption of the directive or regulation at the EU level – after sometimes protracted negotiation – is not in question as to whether or not a member state must comply. This is the hierarchical nature of positive integration policies in relation to member state obligations. EU policies that fall under this area include, among others, environmental policy, social policy, and Economic and Monetary Union.

Environmental policy has emerged since the 1980s as an area in which the EU 'template' for domestic implementation has developed a distinct profile and for which one can also observe Europeanization effects. The EU's competence in this policy area first began in the early 1970s, but at this time and until the late 1980s the Commission had to rely mostly on a market regulation justification for environmental policy, and, due to various member states' suspicion of different proposals, the Council often prolonged the time needed to produce legislation. With the adoption of the Single European Act, environmental policy-making could be made more efficacious by the fact it was now connected to the Single Market, and accordingly qualified majority voting (QMV) could be invoked. The Maastricht and Amsterdam treaties extended the range of issues in which QMV could be used, and along with co-decision with the European Parliament (EP), environmental policy rose to certain prominence (especially as the EP had been a proponent of environmental policy since the 1970s). Environmental policy directives and regulations range from limits on emissions from large combustion plants (1988), controlling pollution through urban waste water (1991), a habitats directive intended to conserve national habitats of wild flora and fauna (1992), to a directive establishing a scheme for greenhouse gas emissions allowances trading within the Community (2003). Together with the establishment of a European Environmental Agency in 1994, environmental policy has become one of the central goals of the EU (Lenschow, 2005). The development of new Treaty articles and ECJ case law gives EU environmental policy a firm footing with which to expect compliance from member states. With this brief background, we turn now to a consideration of the Europeanization effects.

Most studies on EU environmental policy and Europeanization

focus on policy content, administrative structures, and regulatory style. *Policy content* refers to the specific type of problem-solving, which can be precautionary (e.g. policies to prevent release of toxins at source) or reactive (e.g. policies dealing with the effect of climate change); the policy instruments, which can be substantive (e.g. product standards) or procedural (e.g. the regulation of incentive structures); and the policy standards. *Administrative structures* encompass the relationship between government ministries (horizontal) and between different levels of government (vertical), that is, the degree to which they are centralized or de-centralized. *Regulatory styles* denote the different national patterns of interest intermediation in the making and implementation of environmental policy (hierarchical, adversarial v. discretionary, consensual) (Börzel, 2008: 227). The evidence of Europeanization in these three areas is, as to be expected, differential across member states, but also weighted in one area in particular, namely policy content. In this area, there is evidence of the precautionary problem-solving approach being adopted, along with incentive-based policy instruments and tighter standards. Although some areas are more impacted than others, for example air and water pollution control in relation to the precautionary problem-solving approach, tighter standards have been effective in nearly all areas of environmental policy. Administrative structures and regulatory styles, rooted as they are in member states' institutional and political traditions, would most likely be the least amenable to externally driven change. Instead, 'absorption' or 'accommodation' (to use Börzel's terminology) of EU directives into existing national policy and regulatory styles – however appropriate or not from an EU perspective – has been a more common outcome.

In a 10-country (older member states) study, Jordan and Liefferink (2004) are careful to note that not all change with regard to member state environmental policy content, much less administrative structure or regulatory style, can be put at the door of the EU. Nevertheless, they suggest that the EU has had the effect of promoting development in some member states whose purely domestic initiatives might have resulted in legislation far later than was the case. Their project records tighter standards in Ireland and Spain, and policy goals on a more source-based basis in Finland, France and the United Kingdom. As for the structure of national policies, they find a general strengthening of central coordination mechanisms and national environmental ministries (even their creation, as in Spain). The differential outcome of environmental policy Europeanization may also be explained by widening the intervening variable of pre-existing domestic institutions and policy patterns. Knill and Liefferink (2007) argue that national institutional capacity in relation to EU policy requirements affects implementation success, and therefore also indirect change. In addition, the domestic constellations of actors and interests contribute to implementation success, in both basic implementation and the quality of the domestic legislation (which may have missed the 'intent' of an EU directive). The degree of adaptational pressure is then engaged by these two factors, helping to explain how a directive on environmental information access, for example, may be effective in the UK and France, but not in Germany and Spain. Although Börzel (2008: 227) argues that the Europeanization of environmental policy is perhaps 'more subtle and indirect than the Europeanization literature would lead us to expect', or as Jordan and Liefferink (2004) characterize it – 'a slow and steady adaptation' – it does represent a significant EU policy area. Environmental policy exemplifies positive integration, the 'template' that is downloaded into member states, and the resulting variation in implementation as well as its effects, all the while highlighting aspects of misfit, adaptational pressure, and intervening variables that have become hallmarks of Europeanization analysis.

Negative integration

Negative integration, in contrast to positive integration, involves the removal of barriers to trade, which was the intent of the Single Market programme launched by the SEA. Over the subsequent years, measures by the Commission to create a common policy for the free movement of goods, services, capital and people have been deemed to be 'market-making' (as opposed to positive integration's 'market-correcting' policy intent). The intent of negative integration is not to promote new policy templates for member states, but rather to allow market mechanisms to perform as free from uncompetitive practices and blockages as possible, whether these negative dynamics are in the private or public sector. Where there are economic sectors that remain 'closed' to competitors, for example a state-owned industry monopoly, negative integration promotes the opening of such a sector by way of directives aimed at 'liberalizing' activity, whether through deregulation, privatization, etc. One policy that exemplifies negative integration is the EU's Competition Policy, to which we now turn.

Competition Policy rests on a vision of economic integration that draws its underlying principles from free market capitalism, and has therefore been implicit since the creation of the European integration project from the late 1950s. However, with the variety of state–economy relations that characterize the member states – including among the founding Six – Competition Policy has been viewed with varying degrees of support or enthusiasm. Although Competition Policy was implicit from the beginning, in the 1960s and 1970s only minimal developments took place such that the policy had an impact on member states. For example, the first major decision by the Commission in the area of antitrust or restrictive practices came in 1964 (Art. 81 TEU, ex Art. 85 EEC), with the ECJ upholding the decision in 1966 (*Constern and Grundig* v. *Commission*). Four of the five components of EU Competition Policy were articulated in the early treaties but were activated only later. The first four components are:

(1)   *Antitrust*: concerns restrictive and therefore anti-competitive practices between firms.
(2)   *Antitrust*: concerns the abuse of dominance and therefore anti-competitive position due to a dominant position by one or more firms.
(3)   *State aid*: concerns the potential anti-competitive position of firms given state aid.
(4)   *Liberalization of utilities*: measures such as deregulation and privatization to open often nationalized industries or sectors to European competition.

The fifth component came into effect only in 1990:

(5)   *Merger control*: concerns the oversight and control of mergers that could produce a dominant and therefore anti-competitive position by a firm.

What is clear from the components of the Competition Policy is that the Commission is dedicated to introducing free market principles by way of enhancing the competitive nature of market transactions, and if this means controlling for private firm collusion or illegal state aid, it will act (often with ECJ rulings to strengthen its hand).

The major change in the Competition Policy, that is, its more assertive and far-reaching powers, resulted from both the Single Market initiative and a general ideological shift with regard to state intervention in the economy, and in many respects the source of such ideological positions was the United Kingdom (and to a certain extent the United States). Together these changes promoted a belief in a more wide-ranging and enforceable competitive playing field for European firms, and a consequent pruning back of state intervention. The consequences of a more 'beefed-up' Competition Policy have been stark, not only in terms of high-profile cases brought by the Commission against giant multinational firms that had abused a dominant position (for example Microsoft in 2008) or in the prevention of certain mergers (American Airlines and British Airways in 2001), but also of Europeanization dynamics manifested in the pressure generated on certain member states whose state–economy relations have come under intense scrutiny from a Competition Policy perspective. The fact that the state aid component became a priority only in the late 1980s (along with merger control) attests to the convergence of elites and the Commission to pursue a more robust neo-liberal policy (however reluctant some national leaders were with certain competition policy components). Competition Policy, as a form of negative integration, shares with those policies under the rubric of positive integration, the same force of law or compliance requirement; the difference is that a template of policy targets or content is not employed. Rather, the Europeanization mechanism is horizontal rather than vertical (as with positive integration), in which the target – market competition free from market-distorting practice – 'affirms that competition creates wealth through the generation of economic efficiency, both productive efficiency (making more goods for the same cost), and allocative efficiency (giving consumers what they want)' (Wilks, 2005: 115). This goal is spread through a process of policy adjustment by firms and national regimes to the competition rules.

The specific evidence of Europeanization resulting from the Competition Policy has emerged on two fronts. The first, more general, is in the area of policy style and in some rare cases policy paradigm change. The second is in regard to policy instruments. EU Competition Policy rules concerning the constraints on state aid reflect the latter, and directives on liberalization in the public utilities sector reflect the former. The issue at hand is the pressure that is generated on the member state to introduce more competition in specific economic sectors – e.g. utilities – as well as how the state interacts financially with state-owned industries and/or those financially subsidized to a critical extent, making them virtual 'public-interest monopolies'. On the other hand, as we have seen in the previous discussion, pre-existing structures – which include governmental as well as the interest intermediation system – and domestic political belief systems, explain the variety in output despite the binding nature of a directive. One member state in particular, the UK, has been an uploader of policy ideas in both of these specific components of Competition Policy, if not the general thrust of its underlying principles. Its policy of privatizing nationalized industries, beginning with the Thatcher Government in 1979 and throughout the 1980s and continuing with the liberalization of certain utilities under New Labour governments, has been upheld as a model for continental member states to emulate. EU Competition Policy then reflects its (British) domestic interests. Competition Policy thus complements elite belief systems, both from the centre-right and the centre-left, as well as reinforcing deregulated and competitive market sectors. The pluralist interest intermediation process also facilitated the creation and subsequent promotion of new and multiple firms competing for market share in former monopolized sectors. But the evidence of Europeanization is most likely to occur where there is some pressure arising from a misfit between domestic policies and institutions and EU policies. In the case of state aid, the EU directly confronts member state governments over their role in subsidizing domestic industries (M. Smith, 1998: 57), and in so doing may challenge entrenched practices, and so the pressure can be both political as well as policy-oriented (state aid policy is a mix of soft and hard law, with the latter emerging in the second half of the 1990s; see Cini, 2001). The practices include, in addition to direct subsidies, tax breaks and other allowances, preferential loans, etc., all of which are not available to competing private actors, and therefore such state–industry relations may distort competition. Member states whose industrial policy had included provision of financial assistance – whether to keep a company or whole industry from collapse, to protect employment as part of a regional development policy, or to develop so-called 'national champions', – found that the Commission could either overrule the aid or a portion of it as incompatible with competition in the sector. The process is one in which member states must provide the Commission with their state aid plans, and await a verdict as to its amount and applicability (Cini and McGowan, 1998). The result has been the elimination of state aid in certain areas and its diminution where it continues to exist. Wilks (2005) reports that in 1988 'state aid accounted for about 10 per cent of public expenditure or 3–5 per cent of GDP', but by 2002 'the figure had fallen to about 1.2 per cent of public expenditure and 0.6 per cent of GDP' (124–125). What have been the consequences of this shift in expenditure for those member states that have more pronounced state-interventionist policies? Certainly, on the issue of state rescue of certain industries, for example steel, a painful adjustment to European and global competition meant the withdrawl of state support, followed by spending on re-training schemes and regional development to respond to the subsequent unemployment (Smith, 1998).

Even though member states with relatively high proportions of state aid as part of their industrial policy did seek to circumvent Commission rules, either by not reporting all or portions of the aid they were considering, or developing elaborate ways in which to provide the assistance (thus violating the spirit of the rules at the very least), the general decline in amounts has had an effect on these member states' policy instruments in that state aid which had been used for redistributive uses (e.g. Germany) or market-correcting purposes, such as aid to small and medium-size businesses (e.g. Sweden), developed alternatives in the pursuit of their policy objectives. In France, the state aid regime has been a factor in the changing French industrial policy of *dirigisme* (state-led model of regulatory coordination) to its more contemporary mix of state and market, or what Thatcher terms a 'regulated competitive market model of coordination' (2007: 159–63, for the discussion on France).

As for the liberalization of utilities, Europeanization effects also vary from member state to member state, in some cases becoming highly politicized (e.g. France). Essentially, the monopoly powers developed by national governments over public utilities – or what are also labelled 'network' industries – during the 1950s have been challenged by the logic of the Single Market and concerted actions of the Commission since the late 1980s. Directives have been employed as the means by which to open these industries – telecoms, water, post, energy, transport, and airlines – to competitors, both domestic and European. Again, as in the case of state aid, the UK served as a promoter for such a liberalized market, and the 1990s witnessed directives, especially in telecoms, which led to the end of government monopolies. The issue of misfit pressure for some member states arises from the more fundamental role and commitment by a state as it developed a principle underpinning its 'attachments' to many of these industries, such as universal provision. Some member states have legislation promoting them as public goods or in the public service, and the notion of subjecting such an enterprise to competition has aroused political backlashes, especially from industries with strong public sector trade union membership. In France, where such industries are referred to as '*les services publics*', the commitment to their universal access is linked with concepts of the state's social contract with citizens, supported by most on the left and right of the political spectrum (Cole, 1999). Domestic political pressure is not the only reason that a member state government may find itself opposing the details of a directive in its development phase, but the domestic structure of the specific industries as well as the interest intermediation system also account for the ways in which liberalization directives are implemented and the subsequent effect on national policy styles. Thus the pressure arising from a misfit with EU directives varies in nature from member state to member state as well as in different policy sectors. In the French case, in particular, such pressure, while not resulting in inertia or resistance (to use Börzel's terminology), has led to a singular attempt to influence EU policy on a fundamental basis, that is, to upload to the EU level the socio-political legitimation for the protection of public services that has been enshrined in the French Constitution. This has occurred at the same time that the state sector is transformed in its domestic setting by EU and global forces. In a comparative context, evidence does suggest a 'domestication' of EU directives into domestic norms, as well as the differences in the various sectors to be liberalized. Humphreys and Padgett (2006), in a comparative study of telecoms and electricity liberalization in Germany and France, conclude that pressure arising from the EU (and beyond) varies in degree, such that the EU plus international market pressure in telecoms helps to explain the relatively more rapid domestic adjustments in both countries as compared to electricity. However, they point to the different manner in which both countries domesticated EU policy, depending upon the degree of misfit as well as their domestic institutional settings – stressing the presence of multiple veto points – and national policy norms. Both Germany and France experienced domestic resistance to change in telecoms, arising from the *service public* ethos and strong public sector unions in France, and the defence by the *länder* of their prerogatives in the sector as well as union opposition in Germany. Market pressure and the manner in which the EU constructed the directive allowed these veto players to be neutralized to a certain extent; the political opportunity created by the combination of EU and global market pressure (Bulmer *et al.*, 2007) and the directive allowed other domestic forces to challenge the opposition, and together with government preferences, engage the telecoms liberalization in a timely manner. In the case of electricity, Germany's pluralist domestic interest structure presented multiple veto points, ranging from land governments to competing government ministries; in France the more 'closed' and statist interest structure allowed the government, together with Electricité de France (EdF), to shape the resulting legislation, although political opposition from public sector unions caused delays in implementation during the Socialist-led government after 1997. In the French case, the principle of *service public* again came under pressure, yet as Bauby and Varone state, the liberalization directive paradoxically 'forced the French authorities to define, for the first time, in a piece of legislation, a precise description of the mandate and obligations of public service in the electricity sector' (2007: 1052). Bauby and Varone also suggest that the manner in which the French state changed its control over EdF – no longer 'the sole shareholder and leader of a company that had become a European, if not global, operator' – actually 'contributed to furthering the process of privatization' (1055). Liberalization in telecoms and electricity, though propelled differently by the EU and having more explicit political opposition with regard to electricity implementation, nevertheless has added to the shift in French economic policy style, from statist/dirigiste to a mixture of state and market. In Germany, the pluralist structure allowing multiple veto points, plus the lesser pressure of market forces, resulted in lesser consequences, institutionally as well as in policy styles.

Positive and negative integration, demonstrating EU 'hard' policy input into member state's domestic policy structures, is most indicative of 'top-down' Europeanization, where the EU legislation triggers adaptational pressure and subsequent (potential) change. In the example of environmental policy, an example of positive integration was shown to have had adaptation consequences in terms of institutional change as well as policy instruments. Competition Policy presented an opportunity to evaluate how the EU (and global dynamics mediated by the EU) may contribute to incremental changes in state–economy relations, illustrating the intervening variables of veto players and domestic policy structures. With both positive and negative integration, member states are obliged to respond to EU legislative inputs into their domestic systems; in other words, the potential Europeanization effects result from the legal obligation to comply with EU law. Turning to a discussion of 'soft' EU policy influence, the immediate difference is the absence of a EU mandate; rather, the member states themselves direct policy promotion and diffusion, what Bulmer and Radaelli (2005) term *facilitated coordination*. The mechanisms by which possible Europeanization may occur is therefore one not based on the consequences of compliance, and therefore a misfit cause, but rather through learning and emulation (among other processes to be discussed below). This section on 'soft' EU policy will focus on an issue that is placed under the label of Open Method of Coordination (OMC), for this is the means of dissemination for a policy initiative, rather than the Community legislative route that gives the Commission the authoritative position *vis-à-vis* the member states.

The domestic impact of 'soft' policies

Facilitated coordination

Member states have for a number of years employed different means by which to frame policies that do not fall under the authority of the Commission, as we discussed in the cases of positive and negative integration. This so-called 'soft law' consists of non-binding forms of regulation, which includes recommendations, declarations and resolutions. This policy instrument was given more structured influence when at the 2000 Lisbon Summit the member states agreed to formalize their efforts to meet Lisbon targets in an intergovernmental fashion known as the Open Method of Coordination (OMC). Examples of soft law were expanded to include peer review and 'activities such as benchmarking, attempts to spread "best practice", studies, conferences, and encouragement of reform' (Thatcher, 2006: 312). Policy learning is the expected or desired outcome of these endeavours, which may range from efforts to promote macroeconomic coordination to immigration policy. In the example below, initiatives in the area of employment policy will be presented to demonstrate the type of approach that characterizes OMC as well as to evaluate how Europeanization effects may develop from a non-hierarchical form of integration, or a horizontal mechanism.

A major initiative that emerged from the 1997 Amsterdam Treaty was the launch of a European Employment Strategy (EES), intended to develop an approach that was oriented more toward employment-creation rather than simply employment-protection. As can easily be imagined, member states were not keen on delivering up to the supranational Commission responsibility for employment policy, for reasons that stretch from the near impossibility, due to very different policy approaches in member states, to the sheer practical electoral benefits that accrue to a national government which can claim positive results in this area. Originating as it did shortly before the more formal unveiling of OMC, the EES represents an early form of this new mode of governance based on soft coordination. Rhodes (2005) points to its 'policy coordination' function. From 1997 to 2002, an annual agenda-setting process began the policy cycle, initiated by the Council and supported by the Commission. An indicator of the inter-governmental nature of the approach is illustrated by a 2003 reform, which in addition to making it a more mainstream OMC approach, 'was also in response to complaints from the member states over the excessive complexity and high levels of detail in EES guidelines, the considerable overlap between the EES and other processes, and the duplication of work for national officials' (Rhodes, 2005: 293). The number of guidelines was reduced from 20 to 10, and the number of technical indicators and targets were also somewhat reduced. After the agenda-setting stage, policy objectives are decided. In phase three, member state governments – mostly employment and social affairs ministers – draw up national action plans (NAPs) stating how they will meet outlined objectives. From this point onward, the Commission is involved in assessing the European-wide employment situation as it prepares a joint employment report. The Commission also makes individual recommendations, and together with the joint report are endorsed by the Council. Finally, in a fourth phase, member state governments prepare their NAPs in response to the Commission recommendations. Rhodes notes that the Commission ability to make recommendations 'is a key element that distinguishes the EES from other areas covered by OMC' (2005: 295). Nevertheless, the EES has made only modest progress in its stated objectives, resulting in mostly better coordination among ministries and, according to Zeitlin (2005), a shift in national policy orientation from reducing unemployment rates toward increasing employment, in other words, processes rather than policy content.

In light of the fact the EES involves recommendations rather than binding directives or regulations, how could Europeanization occur without pressure? Evidence does suggest that, depending on the nature of the national policy regime, such as political ideology, role of domestic actors, and so on, even persistent recommendations may have an effect. The case of Denmark in this respect is striking. Ordinarily one would not suspect that Denmark was a member state in need of new policy ideas in respect to employment; in fact, due to the popularity of the Danish employment policy of *flexicurity*, one would imagine Denmark to be an active 'uploader' of employment 'best practice' for the rest of the EU. Even so, as Mailand (2008) states from the findings of a four-country comparative analysis of the influence of the EES on member states' employment policies, a shift to a preventive approach to unemployment did occur, despite initial reservations from the Danish government. Danish activation policy had focused on long-term unemployed, whereas the EES prioritizes preventing the unemployed becoming long-term unemployed in the first place. Denmark did not reach endorsed targets, and though it did not receive 'official recommendations', the fact that Denmark's record – through its NAP – was common knowledge appears to have motivated the social democrat prime minister Rasmussen and other government officials to 'use the EES in their argumentation for a more preventive approach' (Mailand, 2008: 356). So although evidence has been demonstrated of changes to Danish policy content, it came about less from pressure, and rather from the political opportunity it afforded certain domestic actors to push for changes in an area that the EES had highlighted as deficient. In terms of policy learning, the 'secondary recommendations' voiced at Council meetings to Danish representatives point to the diffusion of ideas through the EES 'platform'. In this way, best practice was communicated to receptive domestic actors for whom this European policy helped legitimize their position *vis-à-vis* other critical actors, for example sceptical civil servants (Mailand, 2008). This Danish example exemplifies the fact that the OMC 'potential for learning does not hinge on sanctions but on convictions' (Bulmer and Radaelli, 2005: 351).

Facilitated coordination leaves the initiative for specific integration projects in the hands of the member states. The example of the
EES demonstrates that even where the Commission is involved, the
national governments control the process, going so far as to reform
it as they see fit. And yet, as the case of Denmark demonstrates, even
where the misfit pressure is absent – Danish employment policy was
broadly in line with the main features of what became the EES – the
recognition on the part of select political elites that a practice urged
by fellow member states could contribute toward strengthening
Danish practices illustrates how peer review may also act as a
contributing element in this mechanism of change.

Post-communist experience of policy change: adaptation or transformation?

The experience of the post-communist member states differs greatly in
terms of the impact of EU policy on their domestic policy content and
processes. There are a number of reasons why the post-communist
member states have had a fundamentally different experience with
regard to EU influence in the policy domain in general, not the least
of which is the fact that changes began *before* membership (what
Ágh, 2003 has termed 'anticipatory europeanization'). The impact
of the EU was more immediate for these countries, explained by the
fact that their structures – both institutional and policy – had yet to
firmly stabilize in their transition from the communist regime. We
have already touched on the findings of a strengthening of the core
executive in post-communist states (Chapter 2); more generally, as
these post-communist regimes were moving from a transition to a
consolidation phase – in terms of political stability, economic structures, policy orientations and patterns of interest intermediation –
their 'pre-existing' structures were comparatively weak in comparison to older or Western European member states, or put another
way, settled 'ways of doing things' had yet to solidify. Patterns of
interest group activity and relations with state officials were still
unfolding; the party systems of most post-communist states had high
and continuing rates of electoral volatility; institutional norms were
developing; and so on. In this environment, the presence and influence of veto points would be small and/or weak. This would explain
the relatively more rapid adjustments by candidate states to the
downloading of the *acquis communautaire*. However, a significant

additional element was present in the relationship between post-communist candidate states and the EU (the Commission in particular). This was the explicit intrusion into candidate countries' development toward membership by way of political conditionality, which, in addition to mandating a working market economy, also required political conditions or standards in the area of human rights (in particular minority rights) and free and competitive elections. The incentive structure between the EU and post-communist states 'locked-in' these states' efforts at meeting the conditions and different chapters of the *acquis* as fast as possible (Schimmelfennig and Sedelmeier, 2005). The asymmetric nature of the relationship – the post-communist states were in need of aid, assistance in economic development, dependency on EU markets, etc. – also facilitated this process (Vachudova, 2005). Indeed, the more immediate changes in these countries together with the intrusive Commission behaviour, suggests that Europeanization in the post-communist experience most resembles Börzel's (2005) 'transformation' as an outcome of Europeanization, where fundamental change in core features of structures and policies occurs. The literature on Europeanization and post-communist states arose from the evidence produced during their candidacies, from the late 1990s to 2004. As member states since 2004 (and 2007 for Bulgaria and Romania), one can ask if they continue to experience the influence of the EU differently in terms of policy from their western neighbours.

Based on the assumption that the desire to join the EU as soon as possible was a rational and instrumental policy on the part of political elites in post-communist countries, how 'deep' have the changes been, or put differently, how sustainable is the commitment to EU norms and rules by political elites in these countries once membership had been achieved? Some speculation on this matter has occurred under the label of 'shallow Europeanization', specifically to characterize the nature of the changes during the pre-accession period. The argument is basically that too little time elapsed for socialization processes to have brought about a 'deep' commitment to EU practices and the norms upon which they rest. Instead, a rational-institutional argument explains the relatively rapid adjustment by post-communist elites by virtue of the material incentives that membership would bring. Consequently, post-accession membership could very possibly produce compliance problems as domestic interests and preferences have not been fully transformed. The evidence of such behaviour is sketchy, as not enough case studies or cross-national studies have had enough time to present results on activities since 2004. What studies do exist focus on compliance and related effects from the years between 2000 and 2004. Whereas Mailand (2008) demonstrates Europeanization effects in Polish policy processes with regard to the 'soft' EU policy programme of the European Employment Strategy, where certain actions began even before the legislation was approved, Leiber (2007) suggests, also in the case of Poland, that at least in the area of EU social policy a 'fourth world of compliance' consisting of post-communist member states does not seem justified (that is, problems with compliance do not deviate substantially from those countries in the older member states). She concludes that although there is no strong evidence of a 'domestic culture of law observance' having developed, it would be expected that Poland lies within the compliance cultures of the 'world of domestic politics' (e.g. Austria, Belgium and the UK) and the 'world of neglect' (Italy, France and Portugal). Yet other anecdotal evidence since 2004 suggests that the lack of socialization may explain certain negative occurrences, such as the treatment of Roma minorities in the Czech Republic (e.g. ECJ rulings concerning the nature of reformed education policies) or the Bulgarian government's failure to meet Commission targets with regard to judicial corruption (which resulted in the Commission withholding approximately 200 million euros in development aid to Bulgaria in early 2009). In any case, misfit as a mechanism for Europeanization is certainly present in the examples given of post-communist policies, both in content and processes. Compliance issues may range from the same feature consisting of veto points, a low degree of administrative capability, as well as a lack of socialization. In this regard, it may very well be that a post-communist member state category for Europeanization and policy change will persist for some time after accession.

Conclusion

Policy change is the most investigated category of phenomena in the Europeanization research agenda. Policy change, by which a causal link can be traced to the EU, is both widespread and yet contested as the sole explanation in explaining the dependent variable. This is because the EU itself may act as a regional 'filter' mediating the type of policy responses to unfolding global or extra-European dynamics, such as trade liberalization, international climate conferences and agreements, etc. Nevertheless, once the negotiation at the European level has concluded over a piece of proposed legislation – involving the Commission, the European Parliament and national actors including national ministers and domestic interest groups – the consequences for domestic adaptation are contingent upon a host of factors, not the least of which is the 'goodness of fit' (misfit) between domestic policy content and processes and those articulated by the EU. Yet as misfit is only a precondition for change, this chapter has demonstrated that particular attention must be given to the pre-existing structures, belief systems, internal power configuration among domestic interest groups, the administrative capability of the state, the presence and number of veto points, as well as what Héritier *et al.* (2001) labelled 'the stage of the national policy process (pre-reform, reform, post-reform)'. Together, these factors not only account for Europeanization effects, but also explain the differential nature of Europeanization in policy matters.

The chapter also drew attention to the different methods by which the EU transmits or puts into effect its policies in the member states. The manner in which EU policies are received by member states greatly influences the mechanism of domestic policy change. Positive integration, in which a 'hard' EU policy in the form of directives or regulations must be implemented, by providing a compulsory policy template, may stimulate pressure for change in all those member states' policy domains that have some degree of difference from the EU model. Negative integration, by contrast, affects the nature of national economic and regulatory arenas by enhancing the possibility of increased competition between firms. Those member states with pronounced degrees of state economic intervention – whether through tight regulation or state subsidies – must adjust to this state of affairs, and in the process redefine the principle upon which such state economic activism rests. Thus Europeanization effects may be reflected in altered national policy styles and instruments as well as in the results of enhanced competition (between firms and also national regulations). Another way in which Europeanization as policy change occurs, but in which the European Commission is not the authoritative lead, is through what has been termed 'facilitated coordination'. Member states agree among themselves certain policy initiatives and goals, and also control the process through which such policy proposals are diffused and engaged by national governments. These sets of 'soft' policies, which may include the Commission as a facilitating institution, are designed to allow member states to set the pace of implementation. The Lisbon process, agreed by the member states in 2000, is the most ambitious initiative, and the method chosen to promote policy development, exchange and adoption best exemplifies facilitated coordination, namely the Open Method of Coordination (OMC), with its emphasis on peer review, benchmarking, the use of conferences to spread ideas and appeal to national policy experts, etc. Yet even with such soft laws as have been promoted, there is evidence of indirect policy change, thus suggesting that whereas hard EU policy Europeanization may best be explained by a rational institutionalist approach, the influence or impact of soft law may be better explained by a social-constructivist approach. In either case, the differential nature of Europeanization in the area of policy change continues to be a rich vein of study, with an interesting variation deriving from the post-communist experience of membership.

Finally, this chapter demonstrates that in the debate concerning Europeanization and member state policy change, convergence is not a likely outcome. Rather, the initiative of member states to promote OMC suggests a learning curve of wider proportions, that is, member state reassertion of policy competences from what has been authorized for the Commission (i.e. hard policy direction). Whether considered in light of realist arguments about the primacy of the state, it does suggest a desire for the benefits of European integration without some of the costs. This may be better illustrated by M. Smith's assertion, in the context of member state attitudes toward the Commission's autonomy and vigorousness in Competition Policy, that 'were Member States given the choice today, they would probably not delegate the same powers to the Commission as they did 40 years ago' (1998: 76).

Chapter 9

Foreign Policy

An underlying premise of this book is that the mechanisms of change, that is, the specific ways in which EU influence may cause or trigger a response in terms of institutional or policy change, involves some form of relationship between a domestic actor or institution and the EU. Whether this relationship is of a hierarchical nature as in the case of 'hard' EU policy or where the EU itself represents a political opportunity structure for domestic actors, there is some evidence of a causal link. In Chapter 8, a particular dimension of EU–domestic relations in the area of 'soft' policy was discussed, where the hierarchical arrangement was replaced with a member state-led process such as the Open Method of Coordination (OMC). When one turns to the area of national foreign policy (and security policy), the last bastion of national sovereignty occupies centre stage of analysis, and it is therefore understandable that member states have been most reluctant to cede any policy authority to the Commission in this area (at least most member states). Nevertheless, policy change that derives from such processes as the OMC suggests that even where member states assert the right to lead in policy developments, the nature of the interaction between themselves and through EU institutions such as the Council of Ministers may elicit some degree of adaptation to the method of interaction. If national foreign policy were to experience changes in somewhat the same manner, even if only better coordination among member state foreign ministries, state sovereignty in the context of EU membership, especially where exposure on a daily basis to information and policy options through common structures for its dissemination had become routine, is again subject to reconsideration.

Member states continue to control their foreign policies in such a way that the European Union's institutions remain marginal to their formal development and operation. To the extent that member states have allowed national foreign policy to be given a European dimension, especially through the establishment of the Common

190

Foreign and Security Policy (CFSP), it has been defined in the Treaties as a clear inter-governmental pillar (Pillar 2). Owing to the fact that member state governments have remained committed to an inter-governmental approach in the constitution of a 'common' foreign and security policy, studies on a possible Europeanization effect have been few. Nevertheless, since the late 1990s, a view as to how the influence of the EU may impact national foreign policy supported by empirical evidence has slowly emerged. This chapter outlines the main points put forward in explaining how the EU affects national foreign policy (the mechanism of domestic change), focusing primarily on national adaptation of institutions and policy, as well as arguments that world-view or identity of a member state's foreign policy elites may also experience subtle changes over time. A rationalist approach has usually been invoked for the former, while social-constructivist approaches have been common for the latter (concerning social constructivism and CFSP in particular, see Glarbo 1999). In both cases, as Chapter 8 has illustrated in the case of soft law and facilitated coordination (e.g. OMC), the supranational institutions of the EU take a back seat in the engagement of national foreign policy actions and CFSP. Further complicating – or perhaps diluting – the influence and thereby the causal link between the EU and national foreign policy change is the presence of and membership in NATO by most member states, which for many is an alternative if not competitor to CFSP. Before turning explicitly to a discussion of Europeanization and national foreign policy, it is necessary to briefly describe the manner in which vertical and horizontal mechanisms of change operate, especially the operation of CFSP. Although CFSP is not the sole example of a European-level architecture for national foreign policy establishment to come into contact with dynamics having the potential to generate adaptive change, it is the centrepiece of collective coordination and action since the mid-1990s. Subsequent initiatives such as the European Security and Defence Policy (ESDP) follow from evaluations of the efficacy of CFSP. In addition to high-profile inter-governmental undertakings such as CFSP, one should also bear in mind that other EU activities and decision-making processes may also contribute to an element of change in a member state's foreign policy perspective, for example holding the rotating Presidency of the Union. All of these factors are explored below, beginning with a presentation on member states' efforts in launching CFSP.

Developing a European foreign policy?

The inter-governmental nature of CFSP contrasts with the 'hard' positive integration impact of EU policies upon domestic policy arenas and practices. In the latter, the EU institutions, primarily the Commission, act in an authoritative manner *vis-à-vis* member states (that is, after the negotiation and legislative phase). The creation and subsequent development of CFSP reflects the fact that member states control its agenda and institutional development while formal institutions such as the Commission are relegated to the sidelines; yet CFSP is more than an informal networking among national foreign ministries. In order to determine how this example of facilitated coordination may contribute to change among its members, a brief sketch and highlights of CFSP and related events are necessary.

Common foreign and security policy

A full recounting of the history of efforts to create an EU foreign policy would occupy too much space in this chapter, but several points should be considered that weigh heavily on the subsequent development of CFSP. First, there has never been a unanimous agreement among the member states, even among the founding Six, that the EC or EU should have a well-defined foreign and especially security policy profile. Second, as mentioned above, a politico-military alliance already existed: NATO, to which many – but not all – member states belonged. This fact has complicated efforts by those member states wishing to see a more European defence identity emerge, such as France, as it encounters more entrenched Atlanticist views by other member states. Third, those member states not belonging to NATO practised some form of neutrality (a position affected by the end of the Cold War). Finally, at least during the Cold War, NATO and American military guarantees – no matter the intermittent 'crises' in transatlantic relations – meant that any urgency for a more European (if not EU) foreign and security identity was absent from most member states' agendas. Taken together, it is not surprising that the first concerted effort at creating an EU foreign and security identity since the launch of European Political Cooperation (EPC) in the early 1970s – however much under the thumb of national governments – should emerge only in the early 1990s, that is, after the end of the Cold War and when the purpose of NATO itself was being questioned. The experience of how EU member states responded to the crisis and war in the break-up of the former Yugoslavia, the subsequent hostilities in Kosovo, and involvement in Iraq have all added extra impetus to better coordination among member states.

Formally, CFSP made its debut in the Maastricht Treaty (1992), with subsequent developments in the Amsterdam Treaty (1997) and Nice Treaty (2000). A central feature of CFSP was an emphasis on *foreign* rather than *security* policy, with the latter emerging in the context of the European Security and Defence Policy (ESDP). The ESDP took shape after a key meeting between British and French government leaders in December 1998 at St Malo, France, which produced a declaration stating that 'the Union must have the capacity for autonomous action, backed up by credible military forces, the means to decide to use them and a readiness to do so, in order to respond to international crises'. The other central *organizational* feature was the clear control maintained by the member state governments, which would act together as a network of continuous information transmission and cooperative efforts. Within the member state governments themselves, it is primarily the respective foreign ministries that are involved in these arrangements. Despite the clear inter-governmental character of this horizontal arrangement between governments, certain EU institutions play a role, most notably the European Council and the Council of Ministers. As the CFSP has as its central mission the pursuit of common policies and the development of properly coordinated policy actions and policy instruments, it follows that the Council of Ministers would play an active role in reducing the transaction costs of maintaining communication and coordinating declarations and common policy development. The CFSP architecture that brings together foreign ministers and other officials on a regular basis consists of the General Affairs and External Relations Council (GAERC), which makes most of the routine CFSP decisions concerning common positions and the adoption of joint actions. As the Council of Ministers is also the EU body through which a (rotating) Presidency is exercised, foreign policy statements or initiatives will be announced through the Council. As the CFSP evolved over the 1990s, two other actors chosen by the member states have come to the fore in working with the Council Presidency: the High Representative for the CFSP and the Commissioner for External Relations. Together these three actors make up the EU common foreign policy face to the rest of the world. Apart from further technical groups and committees within the Council of Ministers, the other actor of note is the European Commission, of which the Commissioner for External Relations is a member. Although the Commission as a body is not formally influential in CFSP, the occupant of the portfolio for External Relations may exert leadership qualities, and in circumstances when 'CFSP actions involve the use of EC policy instruments, such as the use of economic sanctions ... the Council can only act on the basis of Commission proposals' (Nugent, 2006: 509).

CFSP was intended to foster common policies, and Article 11 of the Maastricht Treaty states objectives such as 'to promote international cooperation', 'to strengthen the security of the Union in all ways', and 'develop and consolidate democracy and the rule of law, and respect for human rights and fundamental freedoms', among others. Article 12 sets out how these objectives are to be achieved, and here the discussion in Chapter 8 is pertinent as regards soft policies, facilitated coordination and OMC: 'defining the principles of and general guidelines for the common foreign and security policy; deciding on common strategies; adopting joint actions; adopting common positions; strengthening systematic cooperation between Member States in the conduct of policy' (taken from Nugent, 2006: 501). The means to achieve the objectives and actions are the constant communication and networking through the Council of Ministers, Council Presidency and the European Council, in other words through horizontal exchanges between governments. Due to the nature of such a process, the impact of CFSP on a national foreign policy would most likely be manifested in *learning* as the Europeanization mechanism of change. The next section explores the issue of whether the jealously guarded area of national foreign policy may in fact be susceptible to a non-hierarchical process such as CFSP.

Europeanization and national foreign policy: dimensions and mechanisms

Michael Smith (2000) presented one of the first theoretical formulations with which to analyse how sustained interaction under the auspices of CFSP may affect national foreign policy. He suggested that the indicators of change – namely, national adaptation – would be: (a) elite socialization; (b) bureaucratic adaptation; (c) constitutional changes; and (d) changes in public opinion (i.e. increase in support for European political cooperation). The process by which change may occur is based on 'prolonged participation in the CFSP [which] feeds back into EU member states and reorients their foreign policy cultures along similar lines' (614). This process reflects the same dynamics apparent in facilitated coordination as well as a multi-level governance approach (Smith, 2004a). Encapsulated in Smith's account is institutional and cognitive change, conforming to rational institutionalist and social-constructivist approaches to understanding Europeanization. Tonra (2000) defined Europeanization in regard to foreign policy emphasizing the change arising from interaction at the European level rather than any 'hard' top-down pressures by the EU: 'a transformation in the way in which national foreign policies are constructed, in the ways in which professional roles are defined and pursued and in the consequent internalisation of norms and expectations arising from a complex system of collective European policy making' (229). More recent accounts of Europeanization and national foreign policy have not strayed from this characterization, and have categorized changes into three areas that resemble the Europeanization dimensions of domestic changes, i.e. polity, policy, and politics (see, *inter alia*, Keukeleire and MacNaughtan, 2008; Tonra 2001; Wong, 2005, 2008). The first is domestic institutional change; second, policy change in terms of new policy content; and third, identity change, involving elite and possibly mass opinion. Although it is fair to say that there is an absence of 'hard' top-down dynamics involved in foreign policy Europeanization, one can still conceptualize an uploading and downloading process of policy positions and practices circulating through such mechanisms as CFSP.

Domestic institutional change

The process of continual communication and the need to promote and receive other member state positions on foreign policy issues may have an indirect effect on the national foreign policy machinery (or 'bureaucratic adaptation': Smith 2000). The increased involvement of the national executive in EU activities such as Council summit decision-making (see Chapter 2), in particular by the prime minister, has had the effect of making domestic oversight by parliaments more difficult, and has contributed to the overall strengthening of the executive (see Chapter 2). Signs of this strengthening may also affect foreign ministries, as the need for coordination has shifted responsibility from the foreign ministry to the prime minister's office (Smith, 2004a; Spence, 1999; 2002). Concerning institutional change within foreign ministries themselves, Allen and Oliver (2006) point to shifts within the British Foreign and Commonwealth Office (FCO) for example where they note changes in, among other areas, 'the structure of the FCO in terms of both the Political Director and the PUS; the management of desks for EU member states and the growing importance of the European command ... the increased prominence of "Europeanists" in the FCO' (63–4). Of course, in the case of such a prominent member state in the areas of foreign and security policy, a more intense degree of interaction occurs within CFSP as well as bilaterally. Other institutional changes may also include the relations between a foreign ministry and other national ministries, as agenda items may fall outside traditionally defined foreign and security policy, such as transport or immigration policy. The need for coordination among national ministries, especially in the context of security matters, may draw foreign and defence ministries closer together. Smith (2000) also notes that, on some occasions, constitutional change may be fostered, as in the case of Germany and the involvement of its armed forces in the Balkans and beyond. Apart from historic debates on the use of armed forces beyond a strictly defined geographic role within NATO, as in the German example, most of these changes are incremental, and suggests adaptation is intended for better projection of national preferences through CFSP, and to do requires more efficiency, internal coordination, expertise and resources for the executive ministries involved.

Policy change

Policy content may change over time as a result of consultations, coordination and joint policy-making under the auspices of CFSP. Member states may also develop a policy on an issue or toward a third country where one did not previously exist. This may occur over time as other member state positions are engaged in European political cooperation and CFSP; for example, the position of certain member states has evolved over time with respect to the Arab–Israeli issue. In some cases, especially during the occupancy of a Council Presidency, the member state in question may find that a relatively rapid response is required in the event of a crisis on which previous experience or even relations were nil. Finally, a member state may formulate new positions with regard to third countries or regions where it has historic relations, but for which EU membership now introduces new considerations. For example, Spain's historic relationship with many Latin American countries gives it a more distinct voice and profile in EU–Latin American bi-lateral conferences. Policy change may also be reflected in the choice of CFSP as an appropriate forum to engage or project a member state's interests rather than or in addition to other organizations such as NATO. Gross (2007), for example, argues that for German involvement in post-9/11 Afghanistan, the German government deemed the CFSP as an appropriate platform 'for exporting and reinforcing national preferences, thus providing evidence of europeanization' (514). In this example, CFSP provides a 'political opportunity structure' for Germany, where promotion of CFSP allows foreign policy development that might have encountered more domestic resistance had it been attempted either as a unilateral or NATO medium for action. Indeed, Miskimmon and Paterson (2003) note that for Germany, perhaps 'the most important positive factor has been firm support from public and elite opinions for CFSP as a process' (343). Interestingly, Gross (2007) suggests that in the case of Germany, change (Europeanization) occurred with regard to CFSP – that is, political policy evolution – but not in military matters, where Germany continued to regard NATO rather than ESDP as the preferred organizational medium.

Identity change

Values or identity, or more specifically, policy preferences, may change as a result of the continual interaction of political elites within the various points of the CFSP process. Wong (2005) refers to this dimension of change as 'identity reconstruction', by which he means the socialization of interests and identities, and policy indicators of such change represented by (a) the emergence of norms among policy-making elites, and (b) shared definitions of European and national interests. Gross (2007) adds that an indicator of Europeanization 'as a result of identity formation can be expected to include the recourse to the European option as an instinctive choice or the value attached to a European approach in a particular policy decision' (506). Socialization of elite officials is the key mechanism of change (Manners and Whitman, 2000; Smith, 2000, 2004a,

2004b), though it implies a slow, incremental process that may occasionally be impacted or accelerated by a foreign policy crisis (a form of 'punctuated equilibrium'). It is the dynamic interface between EU officials (e.g. High Representative and other Council secretariat members) and national foreign ministry officials (vertical), the structured relationships between different national officials under the auspices of CFSP (horizontal), and the processing of European and other national views and EU declarations by national foreign ministry staff that structures the socialization process. Even so, Keukeleire and MacNaughtan (2008) warn that 'the 'socialization effect' of Europeanization tends to be exaggerated' (146). They point to the fact of so many different foreign policy cultures co-existing within the EU, especially after the 2004 enlargement, the large differences in size among the national foreign policy establishments, especially between those of France, Britain and Germany and the rest, and finally the differences between national officials in contact with the CFSP process directly and those 'with more limited or no involvement in EU networks and with a dominant focus on bilateral relations or on other multilateral fora' (146–147). The question of changing national policy preferences is represented in the choice of CFSP as a more 'natural' format to promote foreign policy goals, and this 'instinctive habit' would arise not only among a member state's foreign policy establishment but also in conjunction with the country's political leadership. This being said, certain values and norms informing national action in the international arena change slowly, and even promoters of change are careful to construct linking justifications. A case in point is President Sarkozy's justification for taking France into NATO's integrated military command (from which his predecessor President De Gaulle removed France in 1966). Dissent from opposition parties was also echoed from some within the President's party, though in the end a parliamentary vote was never in doubt due to the size of the majority. Nevertheless, this 'breach' of a consensual (left and right support for) Gaullist policy, which appeared to undermine French support for a European, if not EU, military evolution, for example support for ESDP (Irondelle, 2008), necessitated President Sarkozy to define this change as in step with French foreign policy goals and identity:

> If France shoulders all her responsibilities in NATO, Europe will have more influence in NATO. And so NATO will not be an exclusively US-dominated organization.

The Lisbon Treaty itself establishes the link between European defence and the Atlantic Alliance. It stipulates that the Allies collective defence will be conducted in the Atlantic framework. And this link, I would remind you, was formally noted in 2003, by the Convention on the Future of Europe, and then by the foreign affairs ministers at the Intergovernmental Conference. I wasn't president of the Republic at the time.

Finally, European defence will be stronger. Because, by ending ambiguity as to our goals, we are creating the necessary trust to develop a strong and autonomous European defence. I believe more than ever in European defence ...

If this choice is a break with the past, it isn't so much as regards its substance, which is the result of a long maturation process. It's as regards the method. (Sarkozy, 2009)

Europeanization and foreign policy change: methodological issues

As in the mechanisms of domestic change discussed in previous chapters, Europeanization research in the area of foreign policy must account for two substantive methodological issues. The first is explaining differential outcomes, and the second is isolating the EU factor. On the question of differential outcomes, attention is drawn to those mediating factors that qualify domestic responses, either in promoting or resisting change. It is clear that institutional change, in particular within foreign affairs ministries – organizational change and resource enhancement – has occurred due to the great weight put upon coordination between national and European policy development. Smith (2000) notes that, especially in the case of a Council Presidency, enormous pressure is put upon the coordination capability of the member state in question, and for those with historically smaller foreign ministries, in most cases rapid expansion occurred. Since the benefits of EU membership encompass many policy areas, including foreign policy goals, increasing resources for a foreign ministry to enhance a country's leadership during a Presidency, for example, is difficult to resist even in times of budgetary constraint. On the other hand, the 'spillover' of other domestic policies into an EU and even international context has meant more competition between foreign ministries and other ministries for the 'lead' in international and EU affairs. Within the context of CFSP, though, Hocking (2002) suggests that here 'foreign ministries emerge as having the greatest scope for initiative' (278). The traditionally understood special nature of foreign policy – linked as it is to issues of peace and war – have allowed foreign ministries to adjust to the EU environment despite bureaucratic competition. Differential outcomes are also explained by pre-existing institutional frameworks, and as mentioned earlier some member states – Britain and France in particular – have endowed their foreign ministries with special advantages and power relations that are absent in other member states. Thus one would not expect great changes in the British and French foreign ministries' position *vis-à-vis* other ministries or a new privileging of its position; on the other hand evidence of significant change arising from coordination pressures have been marked in countries such as Ireland (Tonra, 2002).

With regard to changes in policy content and policy instruments, differential Europeanization outcomes may be understood as the result of internal power relations among epistemic groups; in such circumstances the policy positions of EU and other member states may strengthen the relative influence of a group arguing for a policy change by linking their position with an 'external majority' practice. In other cases, the wider EU position fits into pre-existing practice, so there is an absence of outward change. CFSP may also be seized upon as a complement for foreign policy projection by small states more than the larger member states. Finally, identity change is susceptible to public opinion constraints, as government elites may find existing national positions have a deep resonance in public attitudes that limits their room for manoeuvre. Neutrality is a case in point, where government and other foreign policy elites may have argued for NATO membership and CFSP (and ESDP), but were constrained at least in their pace of change by public ambivalence or even opposition to abandoning a hallmark of national identity. This position would vary also among the different types of neutrality practised during the Cold War, and conditioned public responses to arguments made for joining alliances and CFSP, for example the difference between Austria and Ireland. There are, then, many variables that explain why changes in national foreign policy institutions, policies and identity vary among member states, and pre-existing institutional patterns, veto players and elite as well as public attitudes and identity are part of the Europeanization research tool-kit.

Turning to the other critical methodological issue in Europeanization research – isolating the EU factor – process tracing takes on an added significance because of competing sources. Indeed, the 'EU factor' operates in a process of facilitated coordination far different from the more authoritative and top-down manner one finds in first pillar policies. CFSP, as an example of the open method of coordination (but far more structured), represents a process of interaction involving policy positions, information, attempts at coordinated declarations and even action, with the member states themselves the instigators. The changes that can be detected from this process over time, with particular foreign policy events generating reactions that feed into substantive shifts in development of the process (CFSP) itself, affect primarily the internal organization of foreign affairs ministries, and then in more variable instances, policy content and identity. These changes result from the structuring of the collective interests and perceptions that initially emerged to underpin CFSP (Hill, 1997). Attributing the source of change to the EU as a set of institutions or political system is then highly problematic. What CFSP does undoubtedly provide is a structured pattern of interaction, with rules and norms reinforcing and/or promoting values. Another complication in the exercise of isolating the EU factor is that even though we may assert that CFSP has had an impact on foreign affairs ministries, most EU member states belong to other international organizations and alliances (e.g. NATO) that also generate adjustment changes in organizational terms. Especially in the case of NATO membership, coordination between foreign affairs and defence ministries on security issues, especially in the context of ESDP, blurs the causal trail in terms of influence, that is, commitments (financial and otherwise) to NATO affect national decision-making when confronted with prioritizing either the EU or NATO as a venue for action. OSCE (Organization for Security and Cooperation in Europe) and even UN membership may, in exceptions, also intrude on national foreign policy development. In addition to the potential competition for influence from multiple international organization memberships, there is the wider issue of secular trends that have affected state structures. It was noted at the outset of this chapter that the national executive, in particular the office of the prime minister, has strengthened its position due to the need for greater coordination across policy areas. This has affected to some degree the primacy of foreign affairs ministries in diplomatic relations, and thus its position of relative influence within the national executive. Globalization dynamics such as complex interdependence may be connected to such domestic government restructuring, and thus also compete with more narrowly defined EU causes of change. It is also quite plausible to suggest that public opinion support for CFSP (or more basically, collective EU action) – however varied between member states – is itself a reaction to perceptions about the capability of small and medium-sized states in an interdependent world. All of this discussion is by way of warning that efforts in tracing changes in national foreign policy – both policy and institutions – back to the EU, or EU-attributed processes such as CFSP, must be particularly aware of external actors and trends that may compete for causal influence. Indeed, as Hurrell and Menon (2003) stress, 'Europe and the North Atlantic area constitute the most densely institutionalised region on earth and we would expect this to have important implications for the character and functioning of the European state' (396).

Europeanization and foreign policy change: is there a singular post-communist dimension?

Previous chapters have highlighted a singular Europeanization effect with regard to post-communist member states, and in the area of foreign policy we also witness fundamental differences in comparison with the older member states. Many changes in policy and institutions began during accession negotiations, thereby again highlighting the notion of 'anticipatory europeanization'. In the specific case of CFSP, although this is a second-pillar, inter-governmental policy of the EU, it was included as a chapter in the accession negotiations between the Commission and the applicant governments. Looked at in the broader perspective of political conditionality, post-communist foreign ministries were under pressure to reorient their norms and values as well as their institutional design. According to the Commission, CFSP, or Chapter 27 of the accession negotiations, because of the

> particular nature of the *acquis* in the chapter, no transposition into the national legal order of the candidate countries is necessary. Nevertheless, as member states they must undertake to give active and unconditional support to the implementation of the common foreign and security policy in a spirit of loyalty and

mutual solidarity. Member states must ensure that their national policies conform to the common positions and defend these common positions in international fora. (European Commission, 2004)

It is clear that in the process of downloading the *acquis communautaire*, post-communist foreign policies were obliged to adapt to the CFSP, and Commission monitoring (in the context of political conditionality) was the additional external pressure absent from the experience of older member states. Although the mechanism of domestic change identified for older member states – facilitated coordination – represents the means by which norms, ideas, benchmarking, etc. within the CFSP are diffused, and is also pertinent for post-communist member states, the pre-accession period represents a more intense relationship with the EU that puts a premium on accelerated institutional adaptation. With most institutional adaptation undertaken by 2004 – with some additional changes to the role of EU coordination committees' relationship to other ministries – it could be expected that change in norms and values would proceed along lines more similar to those of the older member states. In the case of Poland, for example, Pomorska (2007) argues that the pre-accession negotiation period had a concrete effect on roles and staffing and resources within the Ministry for Foreign Affairs (MFA); inter-ministerial relations also changed due to the fact that the task of overall coordination of Polish European policy was given to an Office of the Committee for European Integration (UKIE), which challenged the position of the Ministry for Foreign Affairs. Indeed, Pomorska states that this 'development was not welcomed by the MFA's officials and soon competition with UKIE became a vivid illustration of the MFA's struggle to retain its role' (2007: 33–4). Once Poland became an 'active observer' in 2003 – when its diplomats were able to attend Council meetings – the socialization process involving a transfer of norms began. The Polish case is not unique, especially the institutional adjustments made within foreign ministries.

Isolating the EU factor, though, presents a specific challenge in the case of post-communist states in the area of foreign policy for at least two reasons. One, regime change and integration into global politics as fully sovereign states (that is, post-Brezhnev Doctrine/Soviet influence) would have undoubtedly begun a process of institutional but also political elite cultural evolution into western norms to some degree. Attributing this solely to the EU or CFSP is unwarranted. Second, many of the Central European post-communist states joined NATO *before* the EU, and so the learning or internalization of new practices, concepts and norms would have already commenced from this source, at least in defence ministries. Nevertheless, CFSP provides a specific channel through which a state undergoing transformation in its relative position in global politics may have its whole range of foreign policy perspectives affected. Certainly there are also additional factors that account for greater or lesser socialization into the CFSP, for instance strong bilateral relations with the United States, as in the case of Poland or the Czech Republic. Process tracing may therefore help to tie certain administrative and organizational changes within post-communist foreign affairs ministries to the CFSP process – and during the pre-accession period in a more intensive manner than for older member states, but in the realm of elite socialization there are supplemental sources of norm and value transfer.

Conclusion

The Europeanization of national foreign policy proceeds through the highly structured and frequent interaction of national foreign ministry officials – diplomats and other officials – with EU Council personnel. This interaction introduces the perspective of other member states into each national world-view, and introduces elements that may be internalized or learned, especially in situations where no prior position has been established. Much as COREPER has been suggested to act as a supranational socializing experience, the constant communication between EU and national foreign policy officials on a wide range of issues may be seen in the same manner. The CFSP, in particular, complements national foreign policy-making while also being viewed as an extension of such policy in terms of the projection of a member state's interests. Although clearly an inter-governmental pillar, the CFSP as a form of facilitated coordination diffuses information and norms in such a way that an EU sub-system of foreign policy-making has evolved. Hill (1997) characterizes this process as one in which the member states are actors 'shaped and constrained by structures over time, and the structure as well as the context of European foreign policy has changed considerably in the last decade, increasing both the actual centripetal pressures and the expectations of progress' (96). In the case of post-communist member states, as in so many other dimensions of domestic change, their historical experience and the singular manner in which the EU decided to manage the accession process, in particular the monitoring of political conditionality, has meant that the initial change in institutional terms was much more rapid than for older member states. CFSP, for states redesigning the whole of their foreign policy identity, became a vital part of their desire to join the EU, and therefore the urgency for administrative reform was far stronger for these states. Actual membership and generational turnover may also accelerate socialization dynamics. At the same time, it must be noted that foreign policy and defence policy may overlap considerably depending on the issue at hand, for example EU policy toward the western Balkan states. In this context, membership in NATO and bi-lateral relations with the United States are also factors that must be considered in any Europeanization analysis.

The Europeanization of national foreign policy was an inter-governmental initiative that was intended to develop as national political elites saw fit, that is, without authoritative supranational influence. Yet the evidence provided by numerous analyses of CFSP and national actors leads us to confirm a Europeanization effect, mainly one of socialization and to a limited degree institutional, especially in the cases of post-communist states. Despite foreign policy representing one of the last bastions of state sovereignty, 'socialization and learning processes have taken place and actually brought integration forward in this policy area originally designed to avoid supranational integration' (Wong, 2008: 333). Although this chapter has concentrated on the top-down or national adaptation and horizontal mechanisms of change, one of the legacies of national foreign policy Europeanization may be the creation of an EU foreign policy, that is, a complementary exercise in bottom-up Europeanization (Hill and Smith, 2005; Smith, 2004b). In this case, the efficacy of CFSP would be a crucial element in the identification and evaluation of such a common policy. At the very least, our understanding of state sovereignty in the area of foreign policy continues to evolve, and perhaps the meaning of 'inter-governmental' with it. As the development of CFSP demonstrates, intense and continual interaction of national governments in an area that had been initially understood as a 'supranational-free zone' has from the beginning produced change both within states and between them.

Chapter 10

Conclusion

Membership in the European Union implies costs as well as benefits, and all member governments believe the benefits outweigh the costs. Benefits can vary from the quite narrow, such as a particular project involving EU Structural and Development Funds, to more profound, such as contributing to the stabilization and democratization of post-communist regimes. By costs we do not simply mean the revenue transfer to the EU budget that has sometimes set the scene for budget rebate arguments during European Council summits, but also the trade-offs in autonomous policy development, especially in the area of the Single Market. But the notion of cost–benefit analysis to measure the utility of membership in the EU completely misses another dimension, which is the domestic adjustment or adaptation of political and institutional practices, conventions, understandings, or 'ways of doing things' (Radaelli, 2003), to the policy and practices of the EU, labelled as *Europeanization* throughout this book. However, as much as we have documented (and put into an explanatory framework) the changes that membership in the EU has instigated in the member states, it nevertheless remains the fact that Europeanization has not produced any seismic shifts in the operation of national policy-making and institutions. That being said, the net result of Europeanization effects in various domestic policy domains, institutions and political actors, may still lead one to conclude that membership in the EU does have consequences, perhaps not dramatic but nevertheless indicative of the influence of the EU on the evolving nature of the state. This is a valid conclusion, although from a narrow perspective. A broader reading, especially for the Politics dimension, may suggest deeper dynamics at work. In this concluding chapter, we shall evaluate some of these consequences from three perspectives, each broad in its scope of critical evaluation: first, how have the changes documented in the previous chapters altered the relationship between the member state and the EU? Second, in terms of the evidence of Europeanization, what can we say about the cumulative impact of the EU on its member states, that is, the nature of contemporary 'member state'? Third, are there normative considerations emerging from the Europeanization of national politics? The final section of the Conclusion will briefly discuss and summarize the main arguments and findings presented in the book.

Relations between member states and Brussels

Does the relationship between the EU – its institutions and policy-making process – and member states change over time by virtue of Europeanization effects? In other words, even as member states have strengthened the EU from the SEA to the Nice Treaty (and possibly the Lisbon Treaty), have corresponding changes within member states allowed them to upload and/or defend their interests more efficiently as well as exploit the EU for resources? The assumption is that as organizational ties between EU institutions and policy-making process on the one hand, and member state governments (especially the executive) and interest groups on the other have become both more sophisticated and dense, the changes in domestic institutions and actor behaviour that have resulted from adjusting to EU policy outputs strengthen the linkage-relations between the various levels of multi-level governance. These developments within member states and their corresponding relations with the EU may also be seen as building a multi-level polity in Europe, that is, the interdependence of the various levels contributes toward developing the EU as a polity (Bulmer, 2008). Following Egeberg's (2007) argument that a new executive centre at the European level is emerging, in which parts of national governments 'seem to some extent to have become parts of a kind of European government as well' (16), Bulmer suggests that the 'transformation of executive politics in Europe is therefore part of a broader, multi-faceted development ... [involving] ... political transformation in EU–member state relations' (2008: 183). Although Egeberg identifies a number of causes for the 'double-hattedness' of national agencies, for instance New Public Management reforms, one consequence of Europeanization within national executives may also be a contribution to a general transformation in EU–member state relations. The major examples presented in this book substantiate adjustments by member states that allow for more efficient uploading of their preferences in the EU policy-making process. This is reflected in the alignment of domestic institutional practices with EU decision-making, for example the enhanced coordination within national executives, national regulatory agencies increasingly incorporating EU norms, the creation of EU policy experts in the relevant ministries, the expertise gained by efforts at many territorial levels to seek EU development funds, and the activities of certain types of domestic interest groups in Brussels to press their concerns at appropriate institutional venues, to name a few. In other words, domestic actors and government institutions have become more sophisticated in their relations with the EU, and although we do not define Europeanization as convergence, each member state in its own manner has adjusted, often in an incremental manner, its domestic practices to more effectively upload its preferences to the EU level. Although the perspective that we have focused on in this book has been the top-down direction of EU influence in the discussion of Europeanization, the refinement of member states' EU-aimed activities as they attempt to minimize adaptation costs indirectly demonstrates the 'feedback' nature of the mutual supranational–national dynamic informing the Europeanization process, that is, bottom-up as well as top-down. The net effect is to subtly redefine the nature of EU–member state relations, and in the process contribute toward the creation of a distinct EU polity.

Europeanization and national state transformation

Utilizing three broad dimensions for the investigation of domestic change – polity, policy, and politics – and a variety of specific areas within each dimension, for example executives within the institutional dimension, foreign policy within the policy dimension, and parties within the politics dimension, this book has evaluated how changes in each of these specific areas have been influenced by EU inputs. Börzel's (2005) summary list of the outcomes of change, that is, inertia, retrenchment, absorption, accommodation and transformation, has been useful as a descriptive measurement of Europeanization effects. Apart from examples of change in post-communist member states, where transformation or 'deep impact' may be the more exact defining characterization, corresponding to Grabbe's (2003) conclusion that 'europeanization can penetrate

deeply into policy making in the region, given the fundamental trans-
formations taking place in post-communist polities and the importance of EU models in CEE political discourse' (323), the predominant
scope of domestic change has been within the medium range, namely
absorption and accommodation. To what extent does the cumulative
nature of these changes signal anything of significance about the
evolving nature of the contemporary EU member state? The previous
section briefly discussed the effect of Europeanization on EU–member
state relations, and how this redefined relationship may be contributing to the construction of the EU polity. But have national polities –
the member states – changed at the systemic level? Let us consider
each dimension of domestic change from a general perspective along
with a specific discussion of the post-communist experience.

Polity

This chapter began by noting that there have not been any seismic
shifts in national policy-making and politics from the evidence
produced so far from Europeanization research. Nevertheless,
certain issues can be raised relating to the nature of national inter-
institutional relations, bearing in mind the differential impact of
Europeanization. First, although the executive–legislative relationship may appear, from a certain distance, to be intact in formal
terms, the EU has indirectly contributed to the already growing
executive bias in parliamentary government. Secondly, despite the
fact that the partnership principle of the EU's regional policy may
not, in itself, trigger changes in centre and sub-national relations,
where such trends or established relations gave a prominent position to the sub-national level, i.e. constitutional regions, EU influence has strengthened this level of territorial authority (thereby
highlighting the path-dependent nature of intra-state territorial relations). Thirdly, although forms of 'resistance' continue to challenge
the relationship, national courts have become as much an agent of
change through the institutionalization of EU legal norms as defend-
ers of national constitutional orders.

Policy

Much of the evidence supporting the Europeanization thesis arises
from domestic policy change. It has been noted that under the label
of policy change one may present changes in standards, policy

instruments, and so on. Comparative analysis of policy change has also benefited the Europeanization research approach more generally by offering reasons for the differential impact of the EU. As for the specific presentation in this book between hard and soft polices, as well as foreign policy, we highlighted the difference in mechanisms of change, from the misfit thesis most associated with EU-directed (hard) policies, such as environmental policy, to actor-learning experiences (soft) associated with, for example, the Open Method of Coordination. What can be said with some degree of certainty is that convergence has not been a product of Europeanization. However, despite the fact that Europeanization of domestic policy impacts different policy domains at different times within and across member states, the simple fact is that EU policy output has been an unceasing and constant process. Whatever the exact outcome of change, whether inertia, absorption or adaptational change (using Börzel's terms) – and even if in some cases the origin of a specific policy development is domestic – member states' structures as well as policy traditions are exposed to a degree of intensity (i.e. compliance expectations) that is a signal characteristic of EU membership.

Politics

Findings regarding political parties have emphasized the very modest outward or formal changes that have taken place which are traceable to EU influence. Studies on the influence of MEPs within their national parties demonstrate no appreciable increase in influence (and in some cases no increase in recognition). Apart from the UK and the Czech Republic, avowedly eurosceptic parties are confined to the margins of most party systems, and with an exception or two, never form governments (either alone or in coalition). However, some indication of intra-party dissent over EU issues has been detected, thereby indicating a possible new avenue for party Europeanization research, that is, how the EU is 'played out' within parties. The discrepancy between political elites and the public over positions on EU issues and the direction of European integration does not seem to affect the role of national parties within their respective political systems, at least in any outward sense. How long this situation will persist is difficult to say, but the likelihood of the 'sleeping giant' of public opinion over European integration to awake and transform domestic party politics is ever-present, and the presence of eurosceptic parties may indicate only the tip of an iceberg in this respect. As for interest groups, the establishment of Euro-associations continues, but still supplements the national arena as the primary focus for group activities. This being said, there is some evidence of subtle shifts in certain policy domains where the result of EU liberalization has triggered changes in the role of government and private interests, for example in France in the area of public utilities. More generally, the French and Dutch referendum rejections of the EU Constitutional Treaty do appear to have politicized the EU as an issue, both from the left-right and the pro- and anti-EU axis. Although this politicization of public opinion is not reflected across all member states, public opinion in selected older and post-communist states may have led to a constraint on national political elites in regard to further EU institutional developments. Perhaps intended as such, the 2009 ruling on the Lisbon Treaty by the German Federal Constitutional Court may set into motion more explicit domestic political mobilization around the impact of the EU on domestic affairs, which could have reverberations across other member states.

Europeanization as a normative concern

Are there any concerns expressed as to the impact of the EU with regard to issues such as democracy? There has certainly been a concern about what has become labelled a 'democratic deficit'. This discussion usually considers two dimensions of the alleged problem, representation and accountability at the EU level, that is, the relative power of the European parliament *vis-à-vis* the Commission and the Council of Ministers, and a problem generated within the member states, i.e. deparliamentarization (O'Brennan and Raunio, 2007a). The former category is not of immediate concern here as we are interested in the impact of the EU on national democratic processes. However, some proposals for both an additional 'dose' of democracy and strengthening the legitimacy of the EU involve some degree of increased national parliamentary influence and enhanced politicizing of European Parliament elections, for example Hix's *What's Wrong with the European Union and How to Fix It* (2008). Such proposed actions could have consequences for national politics. Nevertheless, the impact of the EU on the quality of national democracy has implications for both institutional trends as well as broader concerns of participation. From an institutional perspective, the privileged position of the national executive with EU decision-making and its near total monopoly on information is said to disadvantage the accountability and representation function of national parliaments; this is in short the deparliamentarization thesis. The de-parliamentarization thesis can also reach 'down' into central and sub-national relations, where even constitutional regions may see a relative loss of influence for their parliaments while their executives gain in some 'co-decision' rights with the national executive over EU policy-making.

In addition to purely institutional relations, the role of the media in framing European integration has been debated, but a greater amount of attention has been drawn to the nature of elections – both to the European Parliament and national parliaments – which have been criticized for lack of a European dimension when the significance of the EU for domestic policy is so substantial. This line of argument combines the descriptive analysis of EP elections as second order and the corresponding lack of attention to European issues – policy or institutional – in national elections. For some, the net result is a de-politicization of national politics (Mair, 2007), a turn toward a technocratic operation of policy-making. Within political parties, leaderships are wary of treading into EU affairs lest dissent and division within the party ignite; better to ignore the European level, thereby rendering it 'foreign policy'. The lack of a 'communicative discourse' (Schmidt, 2006) is probably intentional rather than an inherent weakness. The lack of media attention coupled with apparent party disinterest (the major parties of government) combine to render national citizens unaware of the importance of the EU to domestic policies except where a particular occupational group feels threatened by an EU policy directive, regulation or reform, for example dairy farmers and proposed reforms to the CAP. Ignorance about the EU features as a factor in the declining turnout to EP elections, and so the circle is complete: national political strategies have the effect of marginalizing knowledge of the impact and authority of the EU in most policy domains, and so member state citizens are not mobilized to participate in the one opportunity they have to express positions on EU issues. The growth in the percentage of domestic legislation affected by the EU since the Single European Act, and the evidence of Europeanization in the dimensions of polity and policy especially, means that the EU has had a profound effect on national politics in terms of distancing access to decision-makers by marginalized groups affected by EU policy, the inequality in resources among interest groups in general, and public-interest groups in particular, and so on, yet perception of this situation is generally absent in public opinion. Ironically, much of the anti-EU sentiment expressed through parties is gathered at the extreme ends of the party-political spectrum, and especially on the far right the position is EU rejectionist, that is, withdraw from the EU (on the far left, anti-EU sentiment is bound up more with policy disagreement, leaving some far-left parties in favour of integration, but calling for a different EU). All of these considerations have implications for the quality of national democracy, and domestic changes that are essentially responses either to misfit pressures or even policy learning, where these do not include a compensatory broadening of input and participation from those intended to receive the new policy product, may be storing up pressure that could serve to undermine the legitimacy of domestic politics. The Europeanization of domestic politics may, in the first instance, de-politicize politics, but at the cost of aggravating already present anti-politics sentiment.

Concluding remarks

This book has had two intentions, first, introduce readers to the concept of Europeanization, providing a distillation of the methods and approaches that have developed over since roughly the mid-1990s, and second, apply Europeanization as a general analytical approach to the three dimension of changes, namely polity, policy and politics. A brief re-cap may be useful in order to situate the study of Europeanization in its wider intellectual context. Europeanization research does not seek to predict either specific outcomes or trends; in fact, the emphasis that has been placed on explaining the variable or differential output of Europeanization should disabuse one from this expectation. The Europeanization framework begins from the observation that the policy output of the EU has an effect on member states, but more specifically this effect may generate pressures for a domestic response arising from the degree of misfit between the logic of the EU policies and/or policy-making process and the corresponding domestic policy and/or institution. As noted above, there may be a variety of responses to such pressure, where in some cases it is simply absorbed into domestic styles of behaviour with very little consequences for innovative change in institutional design and resource capacity. However, to also understand the differential response in comparative perspective, that is, where one might ascribe similar pressure but observe different patterns of change (or no change), mediating institutions are also incorporated into the Europeanization framework, illustrated by such factors as veto points (rational institutionalism) and informal institutions such as political culture (social constructivism). Europeanization research is open to matching the appropriate analytic approach to the type of phenomenon under study. So, for example, a rational-institutionalist approach may help explain formal institutional change by providing an understanding of how actors react to new political opportunities, as presented in the chapter on national executives. A social-constructivist approach may better explain how actors learn new policies or norms, as presented for example in the discussion of the Open Method of Coordination (OMC). As 'the two logics of change are not mutually exclusive' (Börzel and Risse, 2003: 59), they may be used to characterize different stages in a process of change, for example the spread of ideas through best practice and subsequent mobilization of actors in changing a domestic policy in which they had previously been only a vocal minority. Finally, the research strategy of process tracing as a central method in the Europeanizaton framework is of critical importance, for external inputs and pressures on national political systems may arise from non-European sources (aspects of globalization) as well as purely domestic, and so potentially multiple causal factors must be disentangled, or the combination clearly posited.

The second intention of the book was to apply the Europeanization framework to a number of examples from each of the three dimensions of change. Although not exhaustive, the examples provided draw on published research since roughly 2000 and fulfil the aim of providing an illustration of the potential for Europeanization research to explain clear evidence of institutional, policy and political change, and trace these changes to EU policy output. In trying to provide a comparative perspective as well, the reasons given to explain the differential impact of the EU on national politics (broadly defined) are highlighted; thus the EU's Regional Policy does not necessarily lead to empowered sub-national regions *vis-à-vis* the national centre, contrasting the cases of the UK and Germany; nor are all national executives, in particular prime ministers, necessarily strengthened at the expense of the foreign minister, as demonstrated in the cases of Sweden and Hungary. An additional perspective was added to each chapter that addressed the three dimensions of change, this being the distinctive impact of the EU on post-communist member states. The intention was to isolate the unique pressures on these states that, even before they became members of the EU beginning in 2004, had begun to transform their national executives, policy-making styles, etc. It may be that over time a form of 'normality' will eventually come to pass, as these states learn to play the Brussels game (upload national preferences in a more efficacious manner) and various parts of their political system consolidate the changes brought about by the relatively rapid downloading of the *acquis communautaire*. The differences in the Europeanization process and outcomes between the more established, older member states and the newer, post-communist member states again draws attention to the manner in which the EU penetrates its national components. One incontestable finding regarding Europeanization and the pre-2004 member states is the incremental nature of change, while in the case of the post-communist states, the rapid and transformational effects of the EU are attributable – beyond the explicit desire of the political elites in these countries to join the EU as swiftly as possible – to the unprecedented intrusive measures taken by the EU such as political conditionality, administrative twinning, the essentially public 'scorecards' on progress toward completing the chapters of the *acquis*, together with the historic position of these new regimes *vis-à-vis* the EU: the clearly asymmetric relationship, development funding dependency, and so on.

The EU and its policy-making process were created by and for the interests of its founding members, and subsequent enlargements in membership have always been predicated on the notion that membership has benefits that outweigh any costs. As mentioned in Chapter 1, there are various reasons specific to each European state that motivates them to apply for membership, and so the benefits themselves may be varied. The Europeanization process reflects the fact that the EU's scope in terms of policy competence and the nature of its post-SEA decision-making process has produced certain consequences as a by-product of this membership. Although undetected as regards its cumulative effect, the degree of penetration by the EU into its member states' political systems has resulted in a myriad of adjustments that, while perhaps not formally redefining national statehood, does imply that twenty-first-century EU membership commits a state to a continuous process of Europeanization, whatever the exact nature of the outcomes.

Bibliography

Ágh, Attila (2003) *Anticipative and Adaptive Europeanization in Hungary* (Budapest: Hungarian Centre for Democracy Studies).

Allen, David and Tim Oliver (2006) 'The Foreign and Commonwealth Office', in Ian Bache and Andrew Jordan (eds), *The Europeanization of British Politics* (Basingstoke: Palgrave Macmillan), 52–66.

Alter, Karen (1998) 'Explaining National Court Acceptance of European Court Jurisprudence: A Critical Evaluation of Theories of Legal Integration', in Anne-Marie Slaughter, Alec Stone Sweet and J. H. H. Weiler (eds) *The European Court and National Courts – Doctrine and Jurisprudence: Legal Change in Its Social Context* (Oxford: Hart Publishing), 227–252.

Alter, Karen and Jeannette Vargas (2000) 'Explaining Variation in the Use of European Litigation Strategies: European Community Law and British Gender Equality Policy', *Comparative Political Studies*, 33 (4): 452–482.

Andeweg, Rudy B. (2007) 'A Comment on Auel, Benz, and Maurer', in Beate Kohler-Koch and Berthold Rittberger (eds), *Debating the Democratic Legitimacy of the European Union* (Lanham: Rowman & Littlefield), 102–109.

Andeweg, Rudy B. and Lia Nijzink (1995) 'Beyond the Two-Body Image: Relations between Ministers and MPs', in H. Doering (ed.), *Parliaments and Majority Rule in Western Europe* (New York: St Martin's Press), 152–178.

Armstrong, Kenneth A. and Simon Bulmer (2003) 'The United Kingdom: Between Political Controversy and Administrative Efficiency', in Wolfgang Wessels, Andreas Maurer and Jürgen Mittag (eds), *Fifteen into One?: The European Union and its Member States* (Manchester: Manchester University Press), 388–410.

Auel, Katrin and Berthold Rittberger (2006) '*Fluctuant nec merguntur*: The European Parliament, National Parliaments, and European Integration', in Jeremy Richardson (ed.), *European Union: Power and Policy-Making* (Abingdon: Routledge), 121–145.

Auel, Katrin and Arthur Benz (2007) 'Expanding National Parliamentary Control: Does it Enhance European Democracy?', in Beate Kohler-Koch and Berthold Rittberger (eds), *Debating the Democratic Legitimacy of the European Union* (Lanham: Rowman & Littlefield), 75–101.

Avdagić, Sabina and Colin Crouch (2006) 'Organized Economic Interests: Diversity and Change in an Enlarged Europe', in Paul M. Heywood, Erik Jones, Martin Rhodes and Ulrich Sedelmeier (eds), *Developments in European Politics* (Basingstoke: Palgrave Macmillan), 196–215.

Aylott, Nicholas (1999) *Swedish Social Democracy and European Integration: The People's Home on the Market* (Aldershot: Ashgate).

Aylott, Nicholas (2002) 'Let's Discuss this Later: Party Responses to Euro-Division in Scandinavia', *Party Politics*, 8 (4): 441–461.

Bache, Ian (2007) *Europeanization and Multilevel Goverance: Cohesion Policy in the European Union and Britain* (Lanham: Rowman & Littlefield).

Balme, Richard and Cornelia Woll (2005) 'France: Between Integration and National Sovereignty', in Simon Bulmer and Christian Lequesne (eds), *The Member States of the European Union* (Oxford: Oxford University Press), 97–118.

Barrett, Kathleen (2008) 'Collaboration versus Confrontation: A Comparison of Post-Communist Constitutional Courts under the Influence of the European Union', paper presented at the Annual Meeting of the American Political Science Association, 28–31 August 2008.

Bauby, Pierre and Frédéric Varone (2007) 'Europeanization of the French Electricity Policy: Four Paradoxes', *Journal of European Public Policy*, 14 (7): 1048–1060.

Beyers, Jan and Bart Kerremans (2007) 'Critical Resource Dependencies and the Europeanization of Domestic Interest Groups', *Journal of European Public Policy*, 14 (3): 460–481.

Blondel, Jean and Maurizio Cotta (2000) *The Nature of Party Government: A Comparative European Perspective* (Basingstoke: Palgrave Macmillan).

Börzel, Tanja A. (2002) *States and Regions in the European Union: Institutional Adaptation in Germany and Spain* (Cambridge: Cambridge University Press).

Börzel, Tanja A. (2005) 'Europeanization: How the European Union Interacts with its Member States', in Simon Bulmer and Christian Lequesne (eds), *The Member States of the European Union* (Oxford: Oxford University Press), 45–76.

Börzel, Tanja A. (2006) 'Deep Impact? Europeanisation meets Eastern Enlargement', in Attila Ágh and Alexandra Ferencz (eds), *Deepening and Widening in an Enlarged Europe: The Impact of the Eastern Enlargement* (Budapest: 'Together for Europe' Research Centre of the Hungarian Academy of Sciences), 161–170.

Börzel, Tanja A. (2008) 'Environmental Policy', in Paolo Graziano and Maarten P. Vink (eds), *Europeanization: New Research Agendas* (Basingstoke: Palgrave), 226–238.

Börzel, Tanja A. and Thomas Risse (2003) 'Conceptualizing the Domestic Impact of Europe', in Kevin Featherstone and Claudio M. Radaelli (eds),

The Politics of Europeanization (Oxford: Oxford University Press), 57–80.

Börzel, Tanja A. and Thomas Risse (2007) 'Europeanization: The Domestic Impact of European Union Politics', in Knud Erik Jørgensen, Mark A. Pollack and Ben Rosamond (eds), *Handbook of European Union Politics* (London: Sage), 483–504.

Börzel, Tanja A. and Carina Sprungk (2007) 'Undermining Democratic Governance in the Member States? The Europeanization of National Decision-Making', in Ronald Holzhacker and Erik Albæk (eds), *Democratic Governance and European Integration: Linking Societal and State Processes of Democracy* (Cheltenham: Edward Elgar), 113–136.

Bourne, Angela K. (2003) 'The Impact of European Integration on Regional Power', *Journal of Common Market Studies*, 41 (4): 597–620.

Bruszt, László (2008) 'Multi-level Governance – the Eastern Versions: Emerging Patterns of Regional Developmental Governance in the New Member States', *Regional and Federal Studies*, 18 (5): 607–627.

Bulmer, Simon (1983) 'Domestic Politics and European Policy-Making', *Journal of Common Market Studies*, 21: 349–363.

Bulmer, Simon (2008) 'Building a Multi-level Polity in Europe', in Ulf Sverdrup and Jarle Trondal (eds), *The Organizational Dimension of Politics: Essays in Honour of Morten Egeberg* (Bergen: Fagbokforlaget), 170–185.

Bulmer, Simon and Christian Lequesne (2005) 'The European Union and its Member States: An Overview', in Simon Bulmer and Christian Lequesne (eds), *The Member States of the European Union* (Oxford: Oxford University Press), 1–20.

Bulmer, Simon and Claudio M. Radaelli (2005) 'The Europeanization of National Policy', in Simon Bulmer and Christian Lequesne (eds), *The Member States of the European Union* (Oxford: Oxford University Press), 338–359.

Bulmer, Simon and Martin Burch (2006) 'Central Government', in Ian Bache and Andrew Jordan (eds), *The Europeanization of British Politics* (Basingstoke: Palgrave), 37–51.

Bulmer, Simon, David Dolowitz, Peter Humphreys and Stephen Padgett (2007) *Policy Transfer in European Union Governance* (Abingdon: Routledge).

Burch, Martin and Ricardo Gomez (2006) 'The English Regions', in Ian Bache and Andrew Jordan (eds), *The Europeanization of British Politics* (Basingstoke: Palgrave), 82–97.

Burgess, Michael (2006) 'Territoriality and Federalism in EU Governance', in Michael Burgess and Hans Vollaard (eds), *State Territoriality and European Integration* (Abingdon: Routledge) 100–119.

Bursens, Peter (2008) 'State Structures', in Paolo Graziano and Maarten P. Vink (eds), *Europeanization: New research Agendas* (Basingstoke: Palgrave Macmillan), 115–127.

Chiva, Cristina (2007) 'The Institutionalisation of Post-Communist Parliaments: Hungary and Romania in Comparative Perspective', *Parliamentary Affairs*, 60 (2): 187–211.

Cini, Michelle (2001) 'The Soft Law Approach: Commission Rule-Making in the EU's State Aid Regime', *Journal of European Public Policy*, 8 (2): 192–207.

Cini, Michelle and Lee McGowan (1998) *Competition Policy in the European Union* (Basingstoke: Palgrave).

Claes, Monica (2006) *The National Courts' Mandate in the European Constitution* (Oxford: Hart Publishing).

Coen, David and Charles Dannreuther (2003) 'Differentiated Europeanization: Large and Small Firms in the EU Policy Process', in Kevin Featherstone and Claudio M. Radaelli (eds), *The Politics of Europeanization* (Oxford: Oxford University Press), 255–275.

Cole, Alistair (1999) 'The *Service Public* under Stress', *West European Politics*, 22 (4): 166–184.

Conant, Lisa (2001) 'Europeanization and the Courts: Variable Patterns of Adaptation among National Judiciaries', in Maria Green Cowles, James Caporaso and Thomas Risse (eds), *Transforming Europe: Europeanization and Domestic Change* (Ithaca: Cornell University Press), 97–115.

Conant, Lisa (2002) *Justice Contained* (Ithaca: Cornell University Press).

Conant, Lisa (2007) 'Review Article: The Politics of Legal Integration', *Journal of Common Market Studies: Annual Review*, 45: 45–66.

Craig, Paul P. (1998) 'Report on the United Kingdom', in Anne-Marie Slaughter, Alec Stone Sweet, and J. H. H. Weiler (eds), *The European Court and National Courts – Doctrine and Jurisprudence: Legal Change in its Social Context* (Oxford: Hart Publishing), 195–226.

Craig, Paul P. (2003) 'National Courts and Community Law', in Jack Hayward and Anand Menon (eds), *Governing Europe* (Oxford: Oxford University Press), 15–35.

De Vries, Catherine (2009) 'The Impact of EU Referenda on National Electoral Politics: The Dutch Case', *West European Politics*, 32 (1): 142–171.

De Witte, Bruno (1999) 'Direct Effect, Supremacy, and the Nature of the Legal Order', in Paul Craig and Gráinne de Búrca (eds), *The Evolution of EU Law* (Oxford: Oxford University Press), 177–214.

Della Porta, Donatella (2007) 'The Europeanization of Protest: A Typology and Empirical Evidence', in Beate Kohler-Koch and Berthold Rittberger (eds), *Debating the Democratic Legitimacy of the European Union* (Lanham: Rowman & Littlefield), 189–208.

Dimitrova, Antoaneta (2006) 'Not "New" Anymore? The States from Central and Eastern Europe as Member States: Effects of Enlargement Governance and the Post-Enlargement Research Agenda', in Attila Ágh and Alexandra Ferencz (eds), *Deepening and Widening in an Enlarged*

Europe: The Impact of the Eastern Enlargement (Budapest: 'Together for Europe' Research Centre of the Hungarian Academy of Sciences), 101–116.

Dimitrova, Antoaneta and Dimiter Toshkov (2007) 'The Dynamics of Domestic Coordination of EU Policy in the New Member States: Impossible to Lock In?', *West European Politics*, 30 (5): 961–986.

Duvanova, Dinissa (2007) 'Bureaucratic Corruption and Collective Action: Business Associations in the Postcommunist Transition', *Comparative Politics*, 39 (4): 441–462.

Egeberg, Morten (2007) 'European Government(s): Executive Politics in Transition?', ARENA Working Papers WP/05, University of Oslo.

Eising, Rainer (2008) 'Interest Groups and Social Movements', in Paolo Graziano and Maarten P. Vink (eds), *Europeanization: New Research Agendas* (Basingstoke: Palgrave Macmillan), 167–181.

Enyedi, Zsolt (2007) 'The "Europeanisation" of Eastern Central European Party Systems', *THE NET Journal of Political Science*, 5 (1): 65–74.

European Commission (2004) *Enlargement: Negotiations of the Chapter 27: CFSP* (Brussels: Enlargement Archives, December).

Exadaktylos, Theofanis and Claudio M. Radaelli (2009) 'Research Design in European Studies: The Case of Europeanization', *Journal of Common Market Studies*, 47 (3): 507–530.

Falkner, Gerda, Oliver Treib, Miriam Hartlapp and Simone Leiber (2005) *Complying with Europe: EU Harmonisation and Soft Law in the Member States* (Cambridge: Cambridge University Press).

Featherstone, Kevin (2003) 'Introduction: In the Name of "Europe"', in Kevin Featherstone and Claudio M. Radaelli (eds), *The Politics of Europeanization* (Oxford: Oxford University Press), 3–26.

Fink-Hafner, Danica and Damjan Lajh (2003) *Managing Europe from Home: The Europeanisation of the Slovenian Core Executive* (Ljubljana: Faculty of Social Sciences, University of Ljubljana).

Franck, Christian, Hervé Leclercq and Claire Vandevievere (2003) 'Belgium: Europeanisation and Belgian Federalism', in Wolfgang Wessels, Andeas Maurer and Jürgen Mittag (eds), *Fifteen into One?: The European Union and its Member States* (Manchester: Manchester University Press), 69–91.

Gallagher, Michael, Michael Laver and Peter Mair (2006) *Representative Government in Modern Europe*, 4th edition (New York: McGraw-Hill).

Garrett, Geoffrey (1998) *Partisan Politics in the Global Economy* (Cambridge: Cambridge University Press).

Geddes, Andrew (2004) *The European Union and British Politics* (Basingstoke: Palgrave).

Georgopoulos, Theodore (2003) 'The 'Checks and Balances' Doctrine in Member States as a Rule of EC Law: The Cases of France and Germany', *European Law Journal*, 9 (5): 530–548.

Gerstenlauer, Hans-Georg (1995) 'German *Länder* and the European Community', in Barry Jones and Michael Keating (eds), *The European Union and the Regions* (Oxford: Clarendon Press), 191–213.

Glarbo, Kenneth (1999) 'Wide-Awake Diplomacy: Reconstructing the Common Foreign and Security Policy of the European Union', *Journal of European Public Policy*, 6 (4): 634–651.

Goetz, Klaus H. and Jan-Hinrik Meyer-Sahling (2008) 'The Europeanisation of National Political Systems: Parliaments and Executive', *Living Reviews in European Governance*, 3 (2): www.livingreviews.org/lreg-2008-2.

Grabbe, Heather (2003) 'Europeanization Goes East: Power and Uncertainty in the EU Accession Process', in Kevin Featherstone and Claudio M. Radaelli (eds), *The Politics of Europeanization* (Oxford: Oxford University Press), 303–327.

Graver, Hans Petter (2002) 'National Implementation of EU Law and the Shaping of European Administrative Policy', *Arena Working Papers*, no. 17.

Graziano, Paolo and Maarten P. Vink (eds) (2008) *Europeanization: New Research Agendas* (Basingstoke: Palgrave).

Greenwood, Justin (2007) *Interest Representation in the European Union*, 2nd edition (Basingstoke: Palgrave Macmillan).

Gross, Eva (2007) 'Germany and European Security and Defence Cooperation: The Europeanization of National Crisis Management Policies?', *Security Dialogue*, 38 (4): 501–520.

Guiraudon, Virginie (2004) 'Immigration and Asylum: A High Politics Agenda', in Maria Green Cowles and Desmond Dinan (eds), *Developments in the European Union 2* (Basingstoke: Palgrave Macmillan), 160–180.

Hanley, David (2008) *Beyond the Nation State: Parties in the Era of European Integration* (Basingstoke: Palgrave Macmillan).

Haverland, Markus (2006) 'Does the EU *Cause* Domestic Developments? Improving Case Selection in Europeanisation Research', *West European Politics*, 29 (1): 134–146.

Haverland, Markus (2008) 'Methodology', in Paolo Graziano and Maarten P. Vink (eds), *Europeanization: New Research Agendas* (Basingstoke: Palgrave), 59–70.

Hayes-Renshaw, Fiona and Helen Wallace (2006) *The Council of Ministers* (Basingstoke: Palgrave Macmillan).

Heidenreich, Martin and Gabriele Bischoff (2008) 'The Open Method of Co-ordination: A Way to the Europeanization of Social and Employment Policies?', *Journal of Common Market Studies*, 46 (3): 497–532.

Henderson, Karen (2006) 'Slovak Political Parties and the EU: From Symbolic Politics to Policies', in Paul G. Lewis and Zdenka Mansfeldová (eds), *The European Union and Party Politics in Central and Eastern Europe* (Basingstoke: Palgrave Macmillan), 149–168.

Héritier, Adrienne, Dieter Kerwer, Christoph Knill, Dirk Lehmkuhl, Michael Teutsch, and Anne-Cécile Douillet (2001) *Differential Europe: The European Union Impact on National Policymaking* (Lanham: Rowman & Littlefield).

Héritier, Adrienne and Christoph Knill (2001) 'Differential Responses to European Policies: A Comparison', in Héritier *et al.*, *Differential Europe* (Lanham: Rowman & Littlefield), 257–294.

Hill, Christopher (1997) 'The Actors Involved: National Perspectives', in Elfriede Regelsberger, Philippe de Schoutheete de Tervarent and Wolfgang Wessels (eds), *Foreign Policy of the European Union: From EPC to CFSP and Beyond* (Boulder: Lynne Rienner Publishers), 85–97.

Hill, Christopher and Michael Smith (2005) 'Acting for Europe: Reassessing the European Union's Place in International Relations', in Christopher Hill and Michael Smith (eds), *International Relations and the European Union* (Oxford: Oxford University Press) 388–406.

Hix, Simon (1994) 'The Study of the European Community: The Challenge to Comparative Politics', *West European Politics*, 17 (1): 1–30.

Hix, Simon (1999) 'Dimensions and Alignments in European Union Politics: Cognitive Constraints and Partisan Responses' *European Journal of Political Research*, 35 (1): 69–106.

Hix, Simon (2008) *What's Wrong with the European Union and How to Fix It* (Cambridge: Polity).

Hix, Simon and Christopher Lord (1997) *Political Parties in the European Union* (Basingstoke: Palgrave Macmillan).

Hocking, Brian (2002) 'Conclusion', in Brian Hocking and David Spence (eds), *Foreign Ministries in the European Union: Integrating Diplomats* (Basingstoke: Palgrave Macmillan), 273–286.

Holmes, Michael and Nicholas Reese (1995) 'Regions within a Region: The Paradox of the Republic of Ireland', in Barry Jones and Michael Keating (eds), *The European Union and the Regions* (Oxford: Clarendon Press), 231–246.

Holzhacker, Ronald (2008) 'Parliamentary Scrutiny', in Paolo Graziano and Maarten P. Vink (eds), *Europeanization: New Research Agendas* (Basingstoke: Palgrave Macmillan), 141–153.

Hooghe, Liesbet (1996) *Cohesion Policy and European Integration: Building Multi-level Governance* (Oxford: Oxford University Press).

Hooghe, Liesbet and Gary Marks (2001) *Multi-Level Governance and European Integration* (Lanham: Rowman & Littlefield Publishers).

Howarth, David J. (2001) *The French Road to European Monetary Union* (Basingstoke: Palgrave Macmillan).

Hughes, James, Gwendolyn Sasse, and Claire Gordon (2004) *Europeanization and Regionalization in the EU's Enlargement to Central and Eastern Europe* (Basingstoke: Palgrave Macmillan).

Humphreys, Peter and Stephen Padgett (2006) 'Globalization, the European Union, and Domestic Governance in Telecoms and Electricity', *Governance*, 19 (3): 383–406.

Hurrell, Andrew and Anand Menon (2003) 'International Relations, International Institutions, and the European State', in Jack Hayward and Anand Menon (eds), *Governing Europe* (Oxford: Oxford University Press), 395–412.

Imig, Doug (2004) 'Contestation in the Streets: European Protest and the Emerging Euro-polity', in Gary Marks and Marco R. Steenbergen (eds), *European Integration and Political Conflict* (Cambridge: Cambridge University Press), 216–234.

Imig, Doug and Sidney Tarrow (2001) *Contentious Europeans: Protest and Politics in an Emerging Polity* (Lanham: Rowman & Littlefield).

Irondelle, Bastien (2008) 'European Foreign Policy: The End of French Europe?', *European Integration*, 30 (1): 153–168.

Jeffrey, Charlie and William E. Paterson (2003) 'Germany and European Integration: A Shifting of Tectonic Plates', *West European Politics*, 26 (4): 59–75.

Jensen, Henrik (2007) 'A Model for the Strictest Scrutiny? The Danish European Affairs Committee in a Party Group Perspective', in Ronald Holzhacker and Erik Albæk (eds), *Democratic Governance and European Integration: Linking Societal and State Processes of Democracy* (Cheltenham: Edward Elgar), 207–228.

Johansson, Karl Magnus (2008) 'External Legitimization and Standardization of National Political Parties: The Case of Estonian Social Democracy', *Journal of Baltic Studies*, 39 (2): 157–183.

Johansson, Karl Magnus and Jonas Tallberg (2008) 'Explaining Chief Executive Empowerment: European Union Summitry and Domestic Institutional Change', Paper presented at the Fourth Pan-European Conference on EU Politics, Riga, September 25–27 2008.

Jones, Barry and Michael Keating (eds) (1995) *The European Union and the Regions* (Oxford: Clarendon Press).

Jordan, Andrew (2006) 'Environmental Policy', in Ian Bache and Andrew Jordan (eds), *The Europeanization of British Politics* (Basingstoke: Palgrave Macmillan), 231–247.

Jordan, Andrew and Duncan Liefferink (2004) 'Europeanization and Convergence: Comparative Conclusions', in Andrew Jordan and Duncan Liefferink (eds), *Environment Policy in Europe: The Europeanization of National Environmental Policy* (Abingdon: Routledge), 224–243.

Jupille, Joseph and James A. Caporaso (2009) 'Domesticating Discourses: European Law, English Judges, and Political Institutions', *European Political Science Review*, 1 (2): 205–228.

Kassim, Hussain (2003) 'Meeting the Demands of EU Membership: The Europeanization of National Administrative Systems', in Kevin Featherstone and Claudio M. Radaelli (eds), *The Politics of Europeanization* (Oxford: Oxford University Press), 83–111.

Kassim, Hussain (2005) 'The Europeanization of Member State Institutions', in Simon Bulmer and Christian Lequesne (eds), *The Member States of the European Union* (Oxford: Oxford University Press), 285–316.

Kassim, Hussain, B. Guy Peters and Vincent Wright (eds) (2000) *The National Co-ordination of EU Policy: The Domestic Level* (Oxford: Oxford University Press).

Keating, Michael (1995) 'Europeanism and Regionalism', in Barry Jones and Michael Keating (eds), *The European Union and the Regions* (Oxford: Clarendon Press), 1–22.

Keating, Michael (2006) 'Territorial Government in the New Member States', in Wojciech Sadurski, Jacques Ziller and Karolina Zurek (eds), *Après Enlargement: Legal and Political Responses in Central and Eastern Europe* (Florence: Robert Schuman Centre for Advanced Studies, European University Institute), 249–267.

Keating, Michael and James Hughes (eds) (2003) *The Regional Challenge in Central and Eastern Europe: Territorial Restructuring and European Integration* (Brussels: Peter Lang).

Kelemen, R. Daniel (2006) 'Suing for Europe: Adversarial Legalism and European Governance', *Comparative Political Studies*, 39 (1): 101–127.

Keukeleire, Stephan and Jennifer MacNaughtan (2008) *The Foreign Policy of the European Union* (Basingstoke: Palgrave Macmillan).

Knill, Christoph and Duncan Liefferink (2007) *Environmental Politics in the European Union: Policy-Making, Implementation and Patterns of Multi-level Governance* (Manchester: Manchester University Press).

Koch, Henning (2008) 'A Legal Mission: The Emergence of a European 'Rationalized' Natural Law', in Hanne Petersen, Anne Lise Kjær, Helle Krunke and Mikael Rask Madsen (eds), *Paradoxes of European Legal Integration* (Aldershot: Ashgate).

Koopmans, Ruud (2007) 'Who Inhabits the European Public Sphere? Winners and Losers, Supporters and Opponents in Europeanised Political Debates', *European Journal of Political Research*, 46: 183–210.

Kopecký, Petr (2007) 'Structures of Representation', in Stephen White, Judy Batt and Paul G. Lewis (eds), *Developments in Central and East Eurorpean Politics 4* (Basingstoke: Palgrave Macmillan), 145–160.

Kriesi, Hanspeter, Anke Tresch and Margit Jochum (2007) 'Going Public in the European Union: Action Repertoires of Western European Collective Political Actors', *Comparative Political Studies*, 40 (1): 48–73.

Kühn, Zdenek (2006) 'The Judialization of European Politics', in Paul M. Heywood, Erik Jones, Martin Rhodes and Ulrich Sedelmeier (eds), *Developments in European Politics* (Basingstoke: Palgrave Macmillan), 216–236.

Ladrech, Robert (1993) 'Parliamentary Democracy and Political Discourse in EC Institutional Change', *Journal of European Integration*, 17 (1): 53–69.

Ladrech, Robert (1994) 'Europeanization of Domestic Politics and Institutions: The Case of France', *Journal of Common Market Studies*, 32 (1): 69–88.

Ladrech, Robert (2000) *Social Democracy and the Challenge of European Union* (Boulder: Lynne Rienner Publishers).

Ladrech, Robert (2002) 'Europeanization and Political Parties: Towards a Framework for Analysis', *Party Politics*, 8 (4): 389–403.

Ladrech, Robert (2007) 'Europeanization and National Party Organization: Limited but Appropriate Adaptation?', in Thomas Poguntke, Nicholas Aylott, Elisabeth Carter, Robert Ladrech and Kurt Richard Luther (eds), *The Europeanization of National Political Parties: Power and Organizational Adaptation* (Abingdon: Routledge), 211–229.

Ladrech, Robert (2009) 'Europeanization and Political Parties', *Living Reviews in European Governance*, 4 (1): http://livingreviews.org/lreg-2009-1.

Laffan, Brigid (2003a) 'Ireland: Modernisation via Europeanisation', in Wolfgang Wessels, Andreas Maurer and Jürgen Mittag (eds), *Fifteen into One?: The European Union and its Member States* (Manchester: Manchester University Press), 248–270.

Laffan, Brigid (2003b) 'Managing Europe from Home: Impact of the EU on Executive Government – A Comparative Analysis', OEUE Phase 1, Occasional paper 0.1-09.03, Dublin Europe Institute, University College Dublin, www.oeue.net/papers/acomparativeanalysis-theimpact.pdf.

Laffan, Brigid (2008) 'Core Executives', in Paolo Graziano and Maarten P. Vink (eds), *Europeanization: New Research Agendas* (Basingstoke: Palgrave Macmillan), 128–140.

Leiber, Simone (2007) 'Transposition of EU Social Policy in Poland: Are there Different "Worlds of Compliance" in East and West?', *Journal of European Social Policy*, 17 (4): 349–360.

Lenschow, Andrea (2005) 'Environmental Policy', in Helen Wallace, William Wallace and Mark A. Pollack (eds), *Policy-Making in the European Union*, 5th edition (Oxford: Oxford University Press), 305–327.

Lewis, Jeffrey (2007) 'The Council of the European Union', in Michelle Cini (ed) *European Union Politics*, 2nd edition (Oxford: Oxford University Press), 154–173.

Lewis, Paul G. (2006) 'Party Systems in Post-Communist Central Europe: Patterns of Stability and Consolidation', *Democratization*, 13 (4): 562–583.

Lippert, Barbara, Gaby Umbach and Wolfgang Wessels (2001) 'Europeanization of CEE Executives: EU Membership Negotiations as a Shaping Power', *Journal of European Public Policy*, 8 (6): 980–1012.

Mailand, Mikkel (2008) 'The Uneven Impact of the European Employment Strategy on Member States' Employment Policies: A Comparative Analysis', *Journal of European Social Policy*, 18 (4): 353–365.

Mair, Peter (2000) 'The Limited Impact of Europe on National Party Systems', *West European Politics*, 23 (4): 27–51.

Mair, Peter (2007) 'Political Opposition and the European Union', *Government and Opposition*, 42 (1): 1–17.

Mair, Peter (2008) 'Political Parties and Party Systems', in Paolo Graziano and Maarten P. Vink (eds), *Europeanization: New Research Agendas* (Basingstoke: Palgrave Macmillan), 154–166.

Manners, Ian and Richard G. Whitman (2000) *The Foreign Policies of European Union Member States* (Manchester: Manchester University Press).

March, James G. and Johan P. Olsen (1998) 'The Institutional Dynamics of International Political Orders', *International Organization*, 52 (4): 943–969.

Marks, Gary, Liesbet Hooghe, and Kermit Blank (1996) 'European Integration from the 1980s', *Journal of Common Market Studies*, 34 (3): 341–378.

Marsh, Michael (2007) 'European Parliament Elections and Losses by Governing Parties', in Wouter van der Brug and Cees van der Eijk (eds), *European Elections & Domestic Politics: Lessons from the Past and Scenarios for the Future* (Notre Dame, IN: University of Notre Dame Press), 51–72.

Marshall, Adam (2006) 'Local Governance', in Ian Bache and Andrew Jordan (eds), *The Europeanization of British Politics* (Basingstoke: Palgrave Macmillan), 98–115.

Mattli, Walter and Anne-Marie Slaughter (1998) 'The Role of National Courts in the Process of European Integration: Accounting for Judicial Preferences and Constraints', in Anne-Marie Slaughter, Alec Stone Sweet and J. H. H. Weiler (eds), *The European Court and National Courts – Doctrine and Jurisprudence: Legal Change in Its Social Context* (Oxford: Hart Publishing), 253–276.

Maurer, Andreas and Wolfgang Wessels (2001) *National Parliaments on their Ways to Europe: Losers or Latecomers?* (Baden-Baden: Nomos).

Maveety, Nancy and Anke Grosskopf (2004) ' "Constrained" Constitutional Courts as Conduits for Democratic Consolidation', *Law & Society Review*, 38 (3): 463–489.

Mazey, Sonia and Jeremy Richardson (2003) 'Interests Groups and the Brussels Bureaucracy', in Jack Hayward and Anand Menon (eds), *Governing Europe* (Oxford: Oxford University Press), 208–227.

McLaren, Lauren (2006) *Identity, Interests and Attitudes to European Integration* (Basingstoke: Palgrave Macmillan).

Mendez, Carlos, Fiona Wishlade, and Douglas Yuill (2008) 'Made to Measure? Europeanization, Goodness of Fit and Adaptation Pressures in EU Competition Policy and Regional Aid', *Journal of Comparative Policy Analysis*, 10 (3): 279–298.

Mény, Yves and Vincent Wright (eds) (1985) *Centre-Periphery Relations in Western Europe* (London: George Allen & Unwin).

Miskimmon, Alister and William E. Paterson (2003) 'Foreign and Security Policy: On the Cusp between Transformation and Accommodation', in Ken Dyson and Klaus Goetz (eds), *Germany, Europe and the Politics of Constraint* (Oxford: Oxford University Press/Proceedings of the British Academy), 325–345.

Moore, Carolyn (2006) ' "Schloss Neuwahnstein"? Why the Länder Continue to Strengthen their Representations in Brussels', *German Politics*, 15 (2): 192–205.

Moravcsik, Andrew (1994) 'Why the European Community Strengthens the State: Domestic Politics and International Cooperation', *Center for European Studies Working Paper Series* no. 52, Harvard University.

Mudde, Cas (2007) 'Civil Society', in Stephen White, Judy Batt and Paul G. Lewis (eds), *Developments in Central and East European Politics 4* (Basingstoke: Palgrave Macmillan), 213–228.

Norton, Philip (1996) 'Conclusion: Addressing the Democratic Deficit', in Philip Norton (ed.), *National Parliaments and the European Union* (London: Frank Cass), 177–193.

Nugent, Neill (2006) *The Government and Politics of the European Union*, 6th edition (Basingstoke: Palgrave Macmillan).

Nyikos, Stacy A. (2008) 'Courts' in Paolo Graziano and Maarten P. Vink (eds) *Europeanization: New Research Agendas* (Basingstoke: Palgrave Macmillan), 182–194.

O'Brennan, John and Tapio Raunio (2007a) 'Introduction: Deparliamentarization and European Integration', in John O'Brennan and Tapio Raunio (eds), *National Parliaments within the Enlarged European Union: From 'Victims' of Integration to Competitive Actors?* (Abingdon: Routledge), 1–26.

O'Brennan and Tapio Raunio (2007b) 'Conclusion: National Parliaments Gradually Learning to Play the European Game?', in John O'Brennan and Tapio Raunio (eds), *National Parliaments within the Enlarged European Union: From 'Victims' of Integration to Competitive Actors?* (Abingdon: Routledge), 272–286.

Olsen, Johan (2002) 'The Many Faces of Europeanization', *Journal of Common Market Studies*, 40 (5): 921–952.

Pedersen, Ove K. (2007) 'Interest Organizations and European Integration', in Ronald Holzhacker and Erik Albæk (eds), *Democratic Governance and European Integration: Linking Societal and State Processes of Democracy* (Cheltenham: Edward Elgar), 88–109.

Pennings, Paul (2006) 'An Empirical Analysis of the Europeanization of National Party Manifestos, 1960–2003', *European Union Politics*, 7 (2): 257–270.

Pérez-Solórzano Borragán, Nieves (2004) 'EU Accession and Interest Politics in Central and Eastern Europe', *Perspectives on European Politics and Society*, 5 (2): 243–272.

Poguntke, Thomas, Nicholas Aylott, Elisabeth Carter, Robert Ladrech and Kurt Richard Luther (eds) (2007) *The Europeanization of National Political Parties* (Abingdon: Routledge).

Pomorska, Karolina (2007) 'The Impact of Enlargement: Europeanization of Polish Foreign Policy? Tracking Adaptation and Change in the Polish Ministry of Foreign Affairs', *The Hague Journal of Diplomacy*, 2: 25–51.

Prechal, Sacha (2007) 'National Courts in EU Judicial Structures', *Yearbook of European Law*, 25: 429–450.

Prechal, Sacha, R.H. van Ooik, J.H. Jans and K.J.M. Mortelmans (2005) 'Europeanisation of the Law: Consequences for the Dutch Judiciary, Report for the Raad voor de Rechtspraak', *Raad voor de rechtspraak Research Memoranda*, 1 (2): 1–83.

Pridham, Geoffrey (1996) 'Transnational Party Links and Transition to Democracy: Eastern Europe in Comparative Perspective', in Paul G. Lewis (ed.), *Party Structure and Organisation in East-Central Europe* (Cheltenham: Edward Elgar), 187–219.

Pridham, Geoffrey (2005) *Designing Democracy: EU Enlargement and Regime Change in Post-Communist Europe* (Basingstoke: Palgrave Macmillan).

Princen, Sebastiaan and Bart Kerremans (2008) 'Opportunity Structures in the EU Multi-Level System', *West European Politics*, 31 (6):1129–1146.

Quaglia, Lucia, Mari Neuvonen, Machiko Miyakoshi and Michelle Cini (2007) 'Europeanization', in Michelle Cini (ed.), *European Union Politics*, 2nd edition (Oxford: Oxford University Press), 405–420.

Radaelli, Claudio M. (2000) 'Whither Europeanization? Concept Stretching and Substantive Change', *European Integration on-line Papers*, 4 (8): http://eiop.or.at/eiop/texte/2000-008a.htm.

Radaelli, Claudio M. (2003) 'The Europeanization of Public Policy', in Kevin Featherstone and Claudia M. Radaelli (eds), *The Politics of Europeanization* (Oxford: Oxford University Press), 27–56.

Raunio, Tapio (2002) 'Why European Integration Increases Leadership Autonomy within Political Parties', *Party Politics*, 8 (4): 405–422.

Raunio, Tapio (2007) 'National Legislatures in the EU Constitutional Treaty', in John O'Brennan and Tapio Raunio (eds), *National Parliaments within the Enlarged European Union: From 'Victims' of Integration to Competitive Actors?* (Abingdon: Routledge), 79–92.

Raunio, Tapio and Simon Hix (2000) 'Backbenchers Learn to Fight Back: European Integration and Parliamentary Government', *West European Politics*, 23 (4): 142–168.

Rhodes, Martin (2005) 'Employment Policy', in Helen Wallace, William Wallace and Mark A. Pollack (eds), *Policy-Making in the European Union* (Oxford: Oxford University Press), 279–304.

Risse, Thomas, Maria Green Cowles, and James Caporaso (2001) 'Europeanization and Domestic Change: Introduction', in Maria Green Cowles, James Caporaso and Thomas Risse (eds), *Transforming Europe: Europeanization and Domestic Change* (Ithaca: Cornell University Press), 1–20.

Sadurski, Wojciech (2008) ' "Solange, Chapter 3": Constitutional Courts in Central Europe – Democracy – European Union', *European Law Journal*, 14 (1): 1–35.

Sarkozy, Nicholas (2009) Conference 'France, European Defence and NATO in the Twenty-first Century', Closing Speech by Nicholas Sarkozy, President of the Republic, Paris, 11 March 2009, https://pastel.diplomatie.gouv.fr/editorial/actual/ael2/bulletin.gb.asp?liste=20090313.gb.html.

Saurugger, Sabine (2007) 'Review Article: Collective Action in the European Union: From Interest Group Influence to Participation in Democracy', *Comparative Politics*, 39 (4): 481–500.

Schimmelfennig, Frank and Ulrich Sedelmeier (2005) *The Europeanization of Central and Eastern Europe* (Ithaca: Cornell University Press).

Schimmelfennig, Frank and Ulrich Sedelmeier (2008) 'Candidate Countries and Conditionality', in Paolo Graziano and Maarten P. Vink (eds), *Europeanization: New Research Agendas* (Basingstoke: Palgrave), 88–101.

Schmidt, Vivien A. (2006) *Democracy in Europe: The EU and National Polities* (Oxford: Oxford University Press).

Scully, Roger (2005) *Becoming Europeans? Attitudes, Behaviour and Socialization in the European Parliament* (Oxford: Oxford University Press).

Scully, Roger and David M. Farrell (2003) 'MEPs as Representatives: Individual and Institutional Roles', *Journal of Common Market Studies*, 41 (2): 269–288.

Sedelmeier, Ulrich (2006) 'Europeanisation in new member and candidate states', *Living Reviews in European Governance*, 1 (3): www.livingreviews.org/lreg-2006-3.

Smith, James (2006) 'Government in Scotland', in Ian Bache and Andrew Jordan (eds), *The Europeanization of British Politics* (Basingstoke: Palgrave Macmillan), 67–81.

Smith, Michael E. (2000) 'Conforming to Europe: The Domestic Impact of EU Foreign Policy Co-operation', *Journal of European Public Policy*, 7 (4): 613–631.

Smith, Michael E. (2004a) 'Toward a Theory of EU Foreign Policy-Making: Multi-level Governance, Domestic Policies, and National Adaptation to Europe's Common Foreign and Security Policy', *Journal of European Public Policy*, 11 (4): 740–758.

Smith, Michael E. (2004b) *Europe's Foreign and Security Policy: The Institutionalization of Cooperation* (Cambridge: Cambridge University Press).

Smith, Mitchell P. (1998) 'Autonomy by the Rules: The European Commission and the Development of State Aid Policy', *Journal of Common Market Studies*, 36 (1): 55–78.

Smith, W. Rand (1998) *The Left's Dirty Job: The Politics of Industrial Restructuring in France and Spain* (Pittsburgh: University of Pittsburgh Press).

Spence, David (1999) 'Foreign Ministries in National and European Context', in Brian Hocking (ed.), *Foreign Ministries: Change and Adaptation* (Basingstoke: Palgrave Macmillan), 247–268.

Spence, David (2002) 'The Evolving Role of Foreign Ministries in the Conduct of European Union Affairs', in Brian Hocking and David Spence (eds), *Foreign Ministries in the European Union: Integrating Diplomats* (Basingstoke: Palgrave Macmillan), 18–36.

Steenbergen, Marco R. and David J. Scott (2004) 'Contesting Europe? The Salience of European Integration as a Party Issue', in Gary Marks and Marco R. Steenbergen (eds), *European Integration and Political Conflict* (Cambridge: Cambridge University Press), 165–192.

Stone, Alec (1992) *The Birth of Judicial Politics in France: the Constitutional Council in Comparative Perspective* (Oxford: Oxford University Press).

Stone Sweet, Alec (2000) *Governing with Judges: Constitutional Politics in Europe* (Oxford: Oxford University Press).

Stone Sweet, Alec (2003) 'European Integration and the Legal System', in Tanja A. Börzel and Rachel A. Cichowski (eds), *The State of the Union: Law, Politics, and Society, Volume 6* (Oxford: Oxford University Press), 18–47.

Strøm, Kaare and Wolfgang C. Müller (1999) 'Political Parties and Hard Choices', in Wolfgang C. Müller and Kaare Strøm (eds), *Policy, Office, or Votes?: How Political Parties in Western Europe Make Hard Decisions* (Cambridge: Cambridge University Press), 1–30.

Strøm, Kaare, Wolfgang C. Müller and Torbjörn Bergman (2006) 'Challenges to Parliamentary Democracy', in Kaare Strøm, Wolfgang C. Müller, and Torbjörn (eds), *Delegation and Accountability in Parliamentary Democracies* (Oxford: Oxford University Press), 707–750.

Szukala, Andrea (2003) 'France: The European Transformation of the French Model', in Wolfgang Wessels, Andreas Maurer and Jürgen Mittag (eds), *Fifteen into One?: The European Union and its Member States* (Manchester: Manchester University Press), 216–247.

Thatcher, Mark (2006) 'European Regulation', in Jeremy Richardson (ed.), *European Union: Power and Policy-Making* (Abingdon: Routledge), 312–327.

Thatcher, Mark (2007) 'Reforming National Regulatory Institutions: the EU and Cross-National Variety in European Network Industries', in Bob Hancké, Martin Rhodes, and Mark Thatcher (eds), *Beyond Varieties of Capitalism: Conflict, Contradictions, and Complementarities in the European Economy* (Oxford: Oxford University Press), 147–172.

Tonra, Ben (2000) 'Denmark and Ireland', in Ian Manners and Richard G. Whitman (eds), *The Foreign Policies of European Union Member States* (Manchester: Manchester University Press), 224–242.

Tonra, Ben (2001) *The Europeanisation of National Foreign Policy: Dutch, Danish and Irish Foreign Policy in the European Union* (Aldershot: Ashgate).

Tonra, Ben (2002) 'Ireland', in Brian Hocking and David Spence (eds), *Foreign Ministries in the European Union: Integrating Diplomats* (Basingstoke: Palgrave Macmillan), 146–162.

Vachudová, Milada A. (2005) *Europe Undivided: Democracy, Leverage and Integration after Communism* (Oxford: Oxford University Press).

Vachudová, Milada A. (2008) 'Tempered by the EU? Political Parties and Party Systems before and after Accession', *Journal of European Public Policy*, 15 (6): 861–879.

Van Biezen, Ingrid (2003) *Political Parties in New Democracies: Party Organization in Southern and East-Central Europe* (Basingstoke: Palgrave).

Van der Eijk, Cees and Mark N. Franklin (2004) 'Potential for Contestation on European Matters at National Elections in Europe', in Gary Marks and Marco R. Steenbergen (eds), *European Integration and Political Conflict* (Cambridge: Cambridge University Press), 32–50.

Van der Eijk, Cees and Mark N. Franklin (2007) 'The Sleeping Giant: Potential for Political Mobilization of Disaffection with European Integration', in Wouter van der Brug and Cees van der Eijk (eds), *European Elections & Domestic Politics: Lessons from the Past and Scenarios for the Future* (Notre Dame, IN: University of Notre Dame Press), 189–208.

Vink, Maarten P. and Paolo Graziano (2008) 'Challenges of a New Research Agenda', in Paolo Graziano and Maarten P. Vink (eds), *Europeanization: New Research Agendas* (Basingstoke: Palgrave Macmillan), 3–20.

Walecki, Marcin (2007) 'The Europeanization of Political Parties: Influencing the Regulations on Political Finance', *EUI Working Papers*, MWP 2007/29.

Wallace, Helen (2005) 'An Institutional Anatomy and Five Policy Modes', in Helen Wallace, William Wallace, and Mark A. Pollack (eds), *Policy-Making in the European Union*, 5th edition (Oxford: Oxford University Press), 49–90.

Weiler, Joseph (1993) 'Journey to an Unknown Destination: A Retrospective and Prospective of the European Court of Justice in the Arena of Political Integration', *Journal of Common Market Studies*, 31 (4), 417–446.

Wessels, Bernhard (2004) 'Contestation Potential of Interest Groups in the EU: Emergence, Structure, and Political Alliances', in Gary Marks and Marco R. Steenbergen (eds), *European Integration and Political Conflict* (Cambridge: Cambridge University Press), 195–215.

Wessels, Wolfgang and Dietrich Rometsch (1996) 'German Administrative Interaction and European Union: The Fusion of Public Policies', in Yves Mény, Pierre Muller and Jean-Louis Quermonne (eds), *Adjusting to Europe: The Impact of the European Union on National Institutions and Policies* (London: Routledge), 73–109.

Wilks, Stephen (2005) 'Competition Policy: Challenge and Reform', in Helen Wallace, William Wallace and Mark A. Pollack (eds), *Policy-Making in the European Union*, 5th edition (Oxford: Oxford University Press), 113–139.

Wong, Reuben (2005) 'The Europeanization of Foreign Policy', in Christopher Hill and Michael Smith (eds), *International Relations and the European Union* (Oxford: Oxford University Press), 134–153.

Wong, Reuben (2008) 'Foreign Policy', in Paolo Graziano and Maarten P. Vink (eds), *Europeanization: New Research Agendas* (Basingstoke: Palgrave Macmillan), 321–334.

Zahn, Rebecca (2008) 'The *Viking and Laval* Cases in the Context of European Enlargement', *Web Journal of Current Legal Issues*, 3: 1–15.

Zeitlin, Jonathon (2005) 'Conclusion: The Open Method of Coordination in Action: Theoretical Promise, Empirical Realities, Reform Strategy', in Jonathon Zeitlin, with Philippe Pochet and Lars Magnusson (eds), *The Open Method of Coordination in Action: The European Employment and Social Inclusion Strategies* (Brussels: Peter Lang), 441–498.

Index